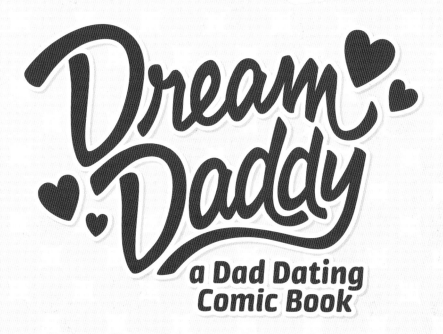

Dream Daddy

a Dad Dating Comic Book

GAME GRUMPS

ONI PRESS

AN ONI PRESS PUBLICATION

Dream Daddy

a Dad Dating Comic Book

AN ONI PRESS PUBLICATION

Dream Daddy
a Dad Dating Comic Book

PUBLISHED BY ONI PRESS, INC.

JOE NOZEMACK
founder & chief financial officer

JAMES LUCAS JONES
publisher

CHARLIE CHU
v.p. of creative & business development

BRAD ROOKS
director of operations

MELISSA MESZAROS
director of publicity

MARGOT WOOD
director of sales

SANDY TANAKA
marketing design manager

AMBER O'NEILL
special projects manager

TROY LOOK
director of design & production

KATE Z. STONE
senior graphic designer

SONJA SYNAK
graphic designer

ANGIE KNOWLES
digital prepress lead

ARI YARWOOD
executive editor

SARAH GAYDOS
editorial director of licensed publishing

ROBIN HERRERA
senior editor

DESIREE WILSON
associate editor

MICHELLE NGUYEN
executive assistant

JUNG LEE
logistics coordinator

SCOTT SHARKEY
warehouse assistant

designed by **Kate Z. Stone**
edited by **Ari Yarwood**
cover by **Kris Anka**
endpaper illustrations by **Drew Green**

1319 SE Martin Luther King, Jr. Blvd.
Suite 240
Portland, OR 97214

onipress.com
facebook.com/onipress
twitter.com/onipress
instagram.com/onipress

dreamdaddy.biz
twitter.com/dreamdaddygame

Dream Daddy™ created by Leighton Gray
& Vernon Shaw.

Special thanks to Vernon Shaw, Leighton Gray, Brent Lilley, & Game Grumps.

First Edition: May 2019
Retail ISBN: 978-1-62010-631-0
Oni Press Exclusive ISBN: 978-1-62010-632-7
eISBN: 978-1-62010-633-4

10 9 8 7 6 5 4 3 2 1

Library of Congress Control Number: 2018912661

Printed in China.

INTRODUCTION

WHAT'S UP, DADS! You've just opened up *Dream Daddy: A Dad Dating Comic Book.* Chances are you've either played our nice game and came here looking for more Dad content, or you have no idea what we're talking about and you might be a bit frightened and confused. Let us first address the confused.

Hello! It's Vernon Shaw and Leighton Gray, Forbes 30 Under 30 gaming recipients for some reason. We usually like writing things as a collective unit over Google Docs while Leighton's tiny dog tries to drop chew toys on our laptops, so that's what's happening here. We co-created and co-wrote a video game called *Dream Daddy: A Dad Dating Simulator.* It's a game where you play as a hot Dad and your goal is to meet and romance other hot Dads while also raising your teenage daughter who's about to leave for college. It's goofy and fun and a little steamy but mostly heartwarming in like a Trojan Horse kind of way where you don't expect to feel fuzzy but surprise! The Emotions Express just pulled into Your Heart Station and something something Leighton please finish this joke when you have the chance.

Leighton here. I made him delete a joke that got a little too Lynchian for an accessible comic intro. This is how the entire game was written. Anyway.

We know you might be asking: why do all of these Dads live in the same cul-de-sac? Why are they all attractive and single? Did you run a poll asking as many people as you could if the word "cul-de-sac" was well known enough to cross cultural boundaries? These are questions for sure.

The thing is, it turns out that people really like hot Dads. We wanted to make a piece of queer media that was about more than just the experience of being queer—we wanted the Dads to be interesting, complex characters who also happen to be gay or bi or pan, because there's so little content out there for the community that is simply goofy and fun. We had an amazing opportunity to create a positive queer game (and this comic) that ended up being really important to people, and bits aside, that's the most meaningful thing we've ever gotten to do in our lives.

So why did Oni Press approach us to make our game into a comic book in the first place? Again, also questions. But what we do know is that after we finished writing the game, there were definitely more stories we wanted to tell. What would a Dad-run D&D game look like? How did Robert, Damien, and Mary become the cutest trio in the world? Can we really convince Oni Press to let us do a cover that's just the *Reanimator* (1985) key art?

And let us assure you, getting the opportunity to let amazing writers, illustrators, colorists, letterers and more create stories within the world that had literally come from our brains is a *dissociative trip.* We got to work with so many people who we both look up to and fear, and the canonical, expanded Dream-Dadiverse is all the more better for it. All the good folks at Oni Press are consummate gems of human beings and extremely patient when we didn't respond to emails for weeks at a time. We're so excited and proud that we got to further explore the lives of all the residents of Maple Bay, and we got to do it because of all of you wonderful fans. So from the bottom of our hearts, thank you.

Now, without any further ado: let's date some Dads.

VERNON & LEIGHTON

"Much Abird About Nothing"

Written by Wendy Xu
Illustrated and colored by Ryan Maniulit
Lettered by Hassan Otsmane-Elhaou
Cover by Kris Anka

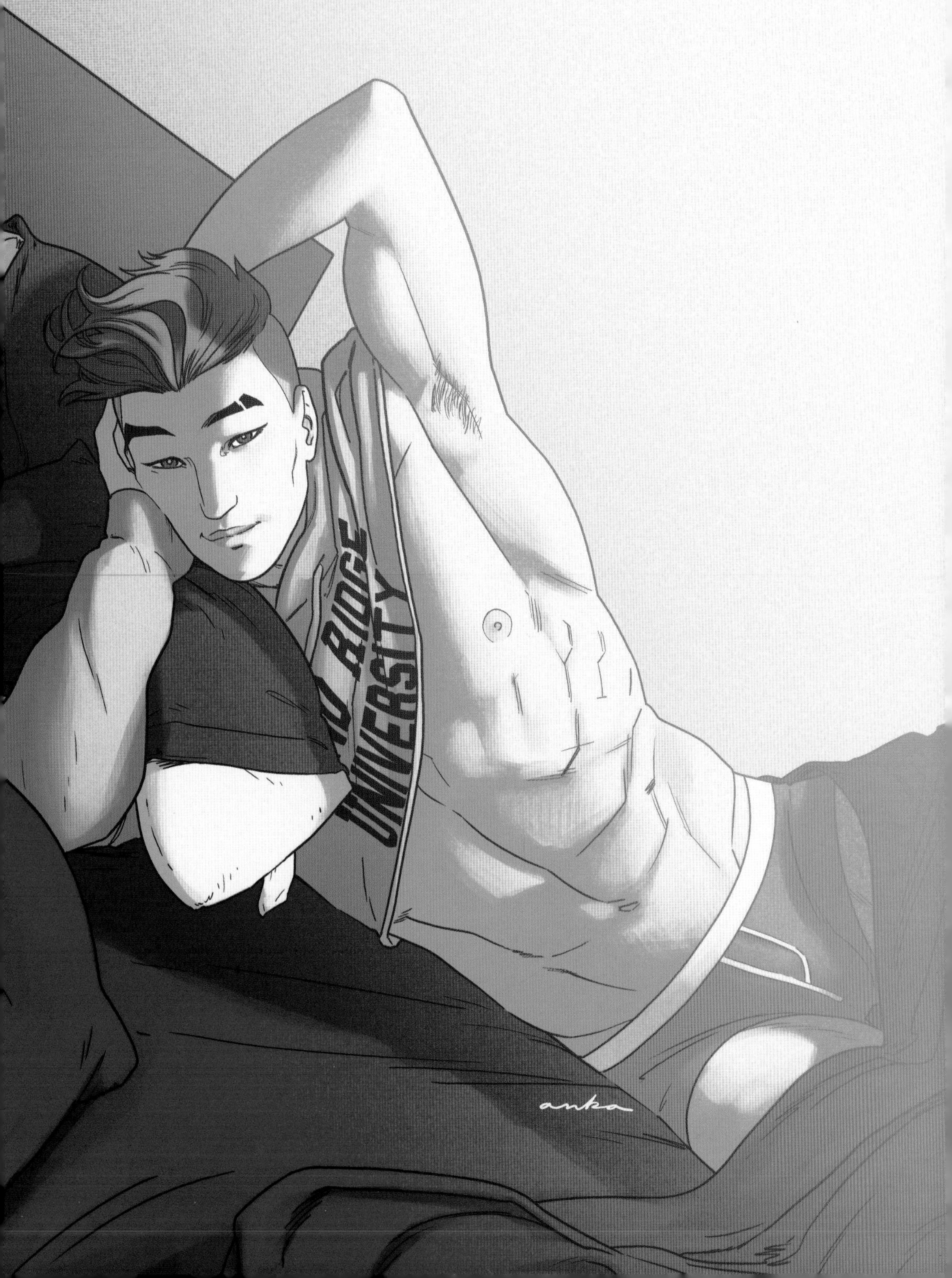
RIDGE
UNIVERSITY
anka

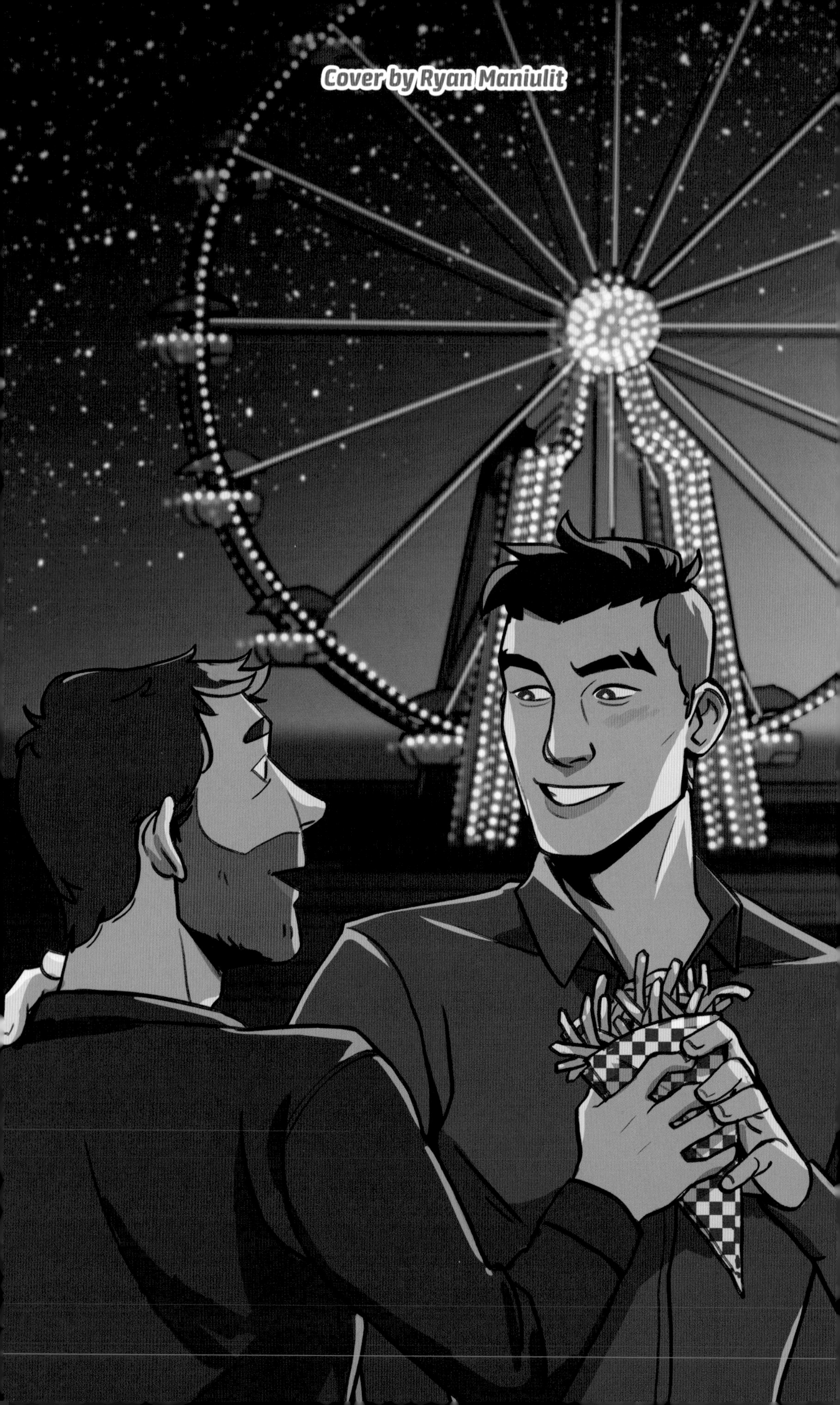
Cover by Ryan Maniulit

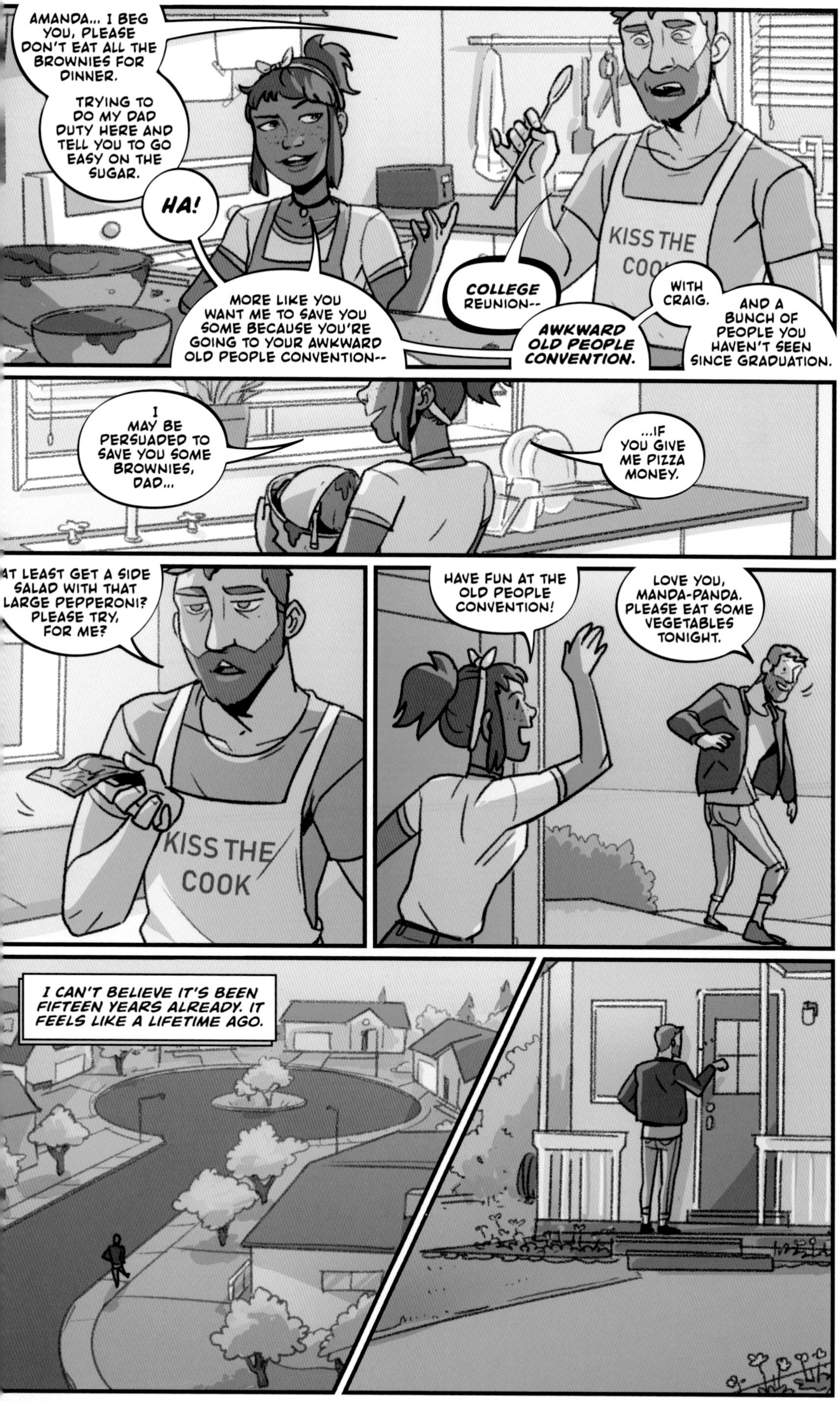
AMANDA... I BEG YOU, PLEASE DON'T EAT ALL THE BROWNIES FOR DINNER.
TRYING TO DO MY DAD DUTY HERE AND TELL YOU TO GO EASY ON THE SUGAR.
HA!
MORE LIKE YOU WANT ME TO SAVE YOU SOME BECAUSE YOU'RE GOING TO YOUR AWKWARD OLD PEOPLE CONVENTION--
COLLEGE REUNION--
AWKWARD OLD PEOPLE CONVENTION.
WITH CRAIG.
AND A BUNCH OF PEOPLE YOU HAVEN'T SEEN SINCE GRADUATION.
KISS THE COOK
I MAY BE PERSUADED TO SAVE YOU SOME BROWNIES, DAD...
...IF YOU GIVE ME PIZZA MONEY.
AT LEAST GET A SIDE SALAD WITH THAT LARGE PEPPERONI? PLEASE TRY, FOR ME?
KISS THE COOK
HAVE FUN AT THE OLD PEOPLE CONVENTION!
LOVE YOU, MANDA-PANDA. PLEASE EAT SOME VEGETABLES TONIGHT.
I CAN'T BELIEVE IT'S BEEN FIFTEEN YEARS ALREADY. IT FEELS LIKE A LIFETIME AGO.

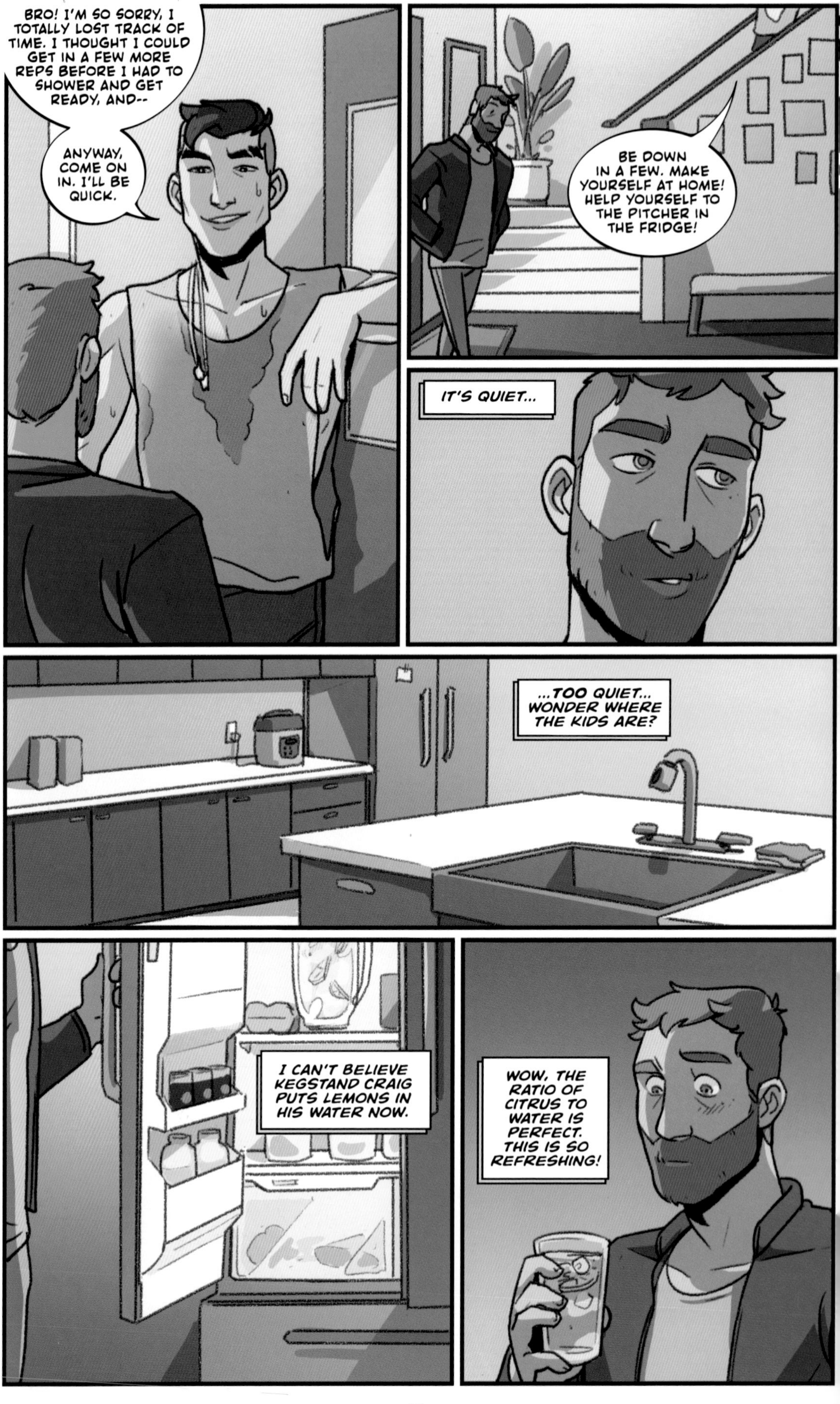
BRO! I'M SO SORRY, I TOTALLY LOST TRACK OF TIME. I THOUGHT I COULD GET IN A FEW MORE REPS BEFORE I HAD TO SHOWER AND GET READY, AND--
ANYWAY, COME ON IN. I'LL BE QUICK.
BE DOWN IN A FEW. MAKE YOURSELF AT HOME! HELP YOURSELF TO THE PITCHER IN THE FRIDGE!
IT'S QUIET...
...TOO QUIET... WONDER WHERE THE KIDS ARE?
I CAN'T BELIEVE KEGSTAND CRAIG PUTS LEMONS IN HIS WATER NOW.
WOW, THE RATIO OF CITRUS TO WATER IS PERFECT. THIS IS SO REFRESHING!

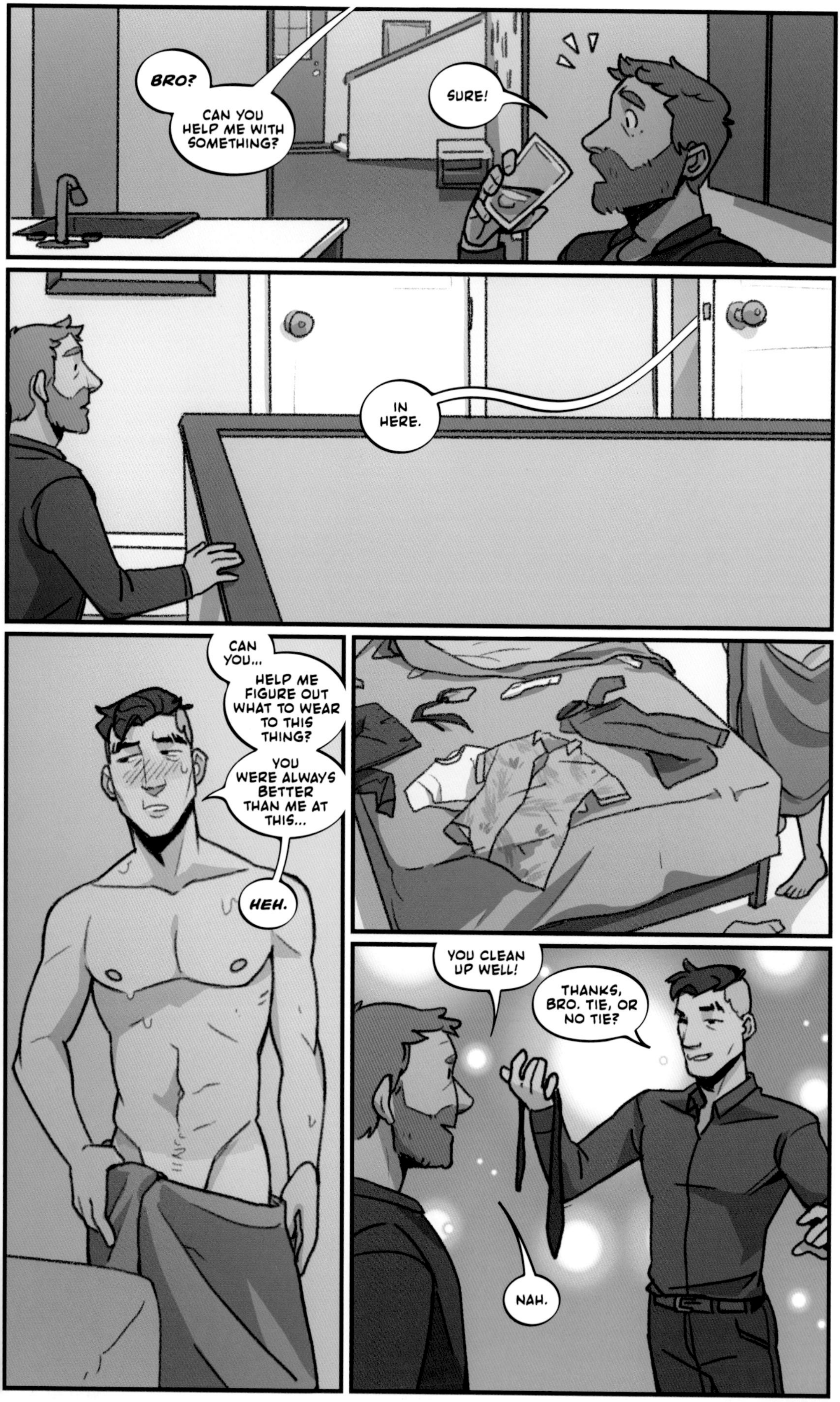
BRO?
CAN YOU HELP ME WITH SOMETHING?
SURE!
IN HERE.
CAN YOU...
HELP ME FIGURE OUT WHAT TO WEAR TO THIS THING?
YOU WERE ALWAYS BETTER THAN ME AT THIS...
HEH.
YOU CLEAN UP WELL!
THANKS, BRO. TIE, OR NO TIE?
NAH.

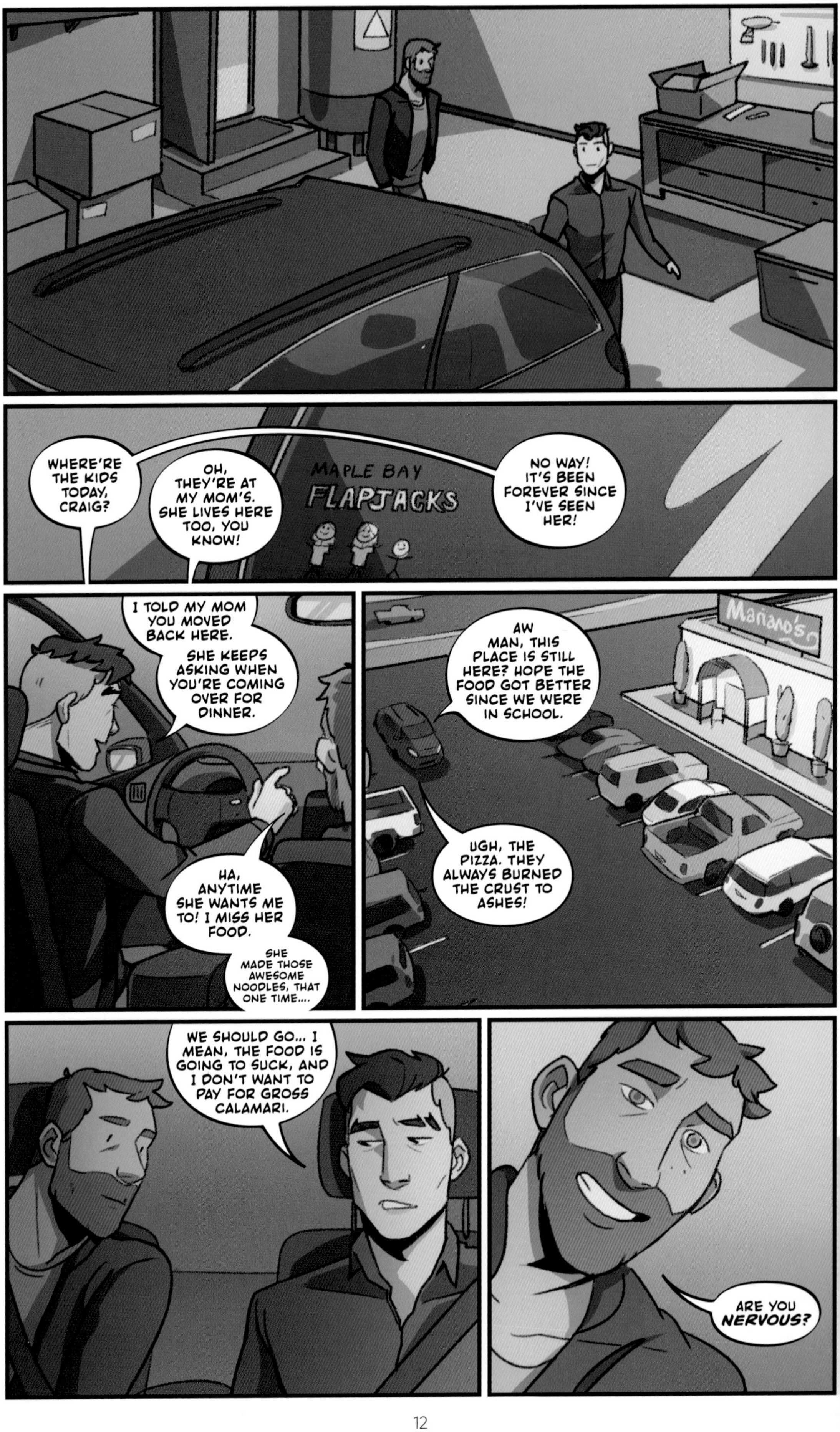

WHERE'RE THE KIDS TODAY, CRAIG?
OH, THEY'RE AT MY MOM'S. SHE LIVES HERE TOO, YOU KNOW!
MAPLE BAY
FLAPJACKS
NO WAY! IT'S BEEN FOREVER SINCE I'VE SEEN HER!
I TOLD MY MOM YOU MOVED BACK HERE.
SHE KEEPS ASKING WHEN YOU'RE COMING OVER FOR DINNER.
HA, ANYTIME SHE WANTS ME TO! I MISS HER FOOD.
SHE MADE THOSE AWESOME NOODLES, THAT ONE TIME....
Mariano's
AW MAN, THIS PLACE IS STILL HERE? HOPE THE FOOD GOT BETTER SINCE WE WERE IN SCHOOL.
UGH, THE PIZZA. THEY ALWAYS BURNED THE CRUST TO ASHES!
WE SHOULD GO... I MEAN, THE FOOD IS GOING TO SUCK, AND I DON'T WANT TO PAY FOR GROSS CALAMARI.
ARE YOU **NERVOUS?**

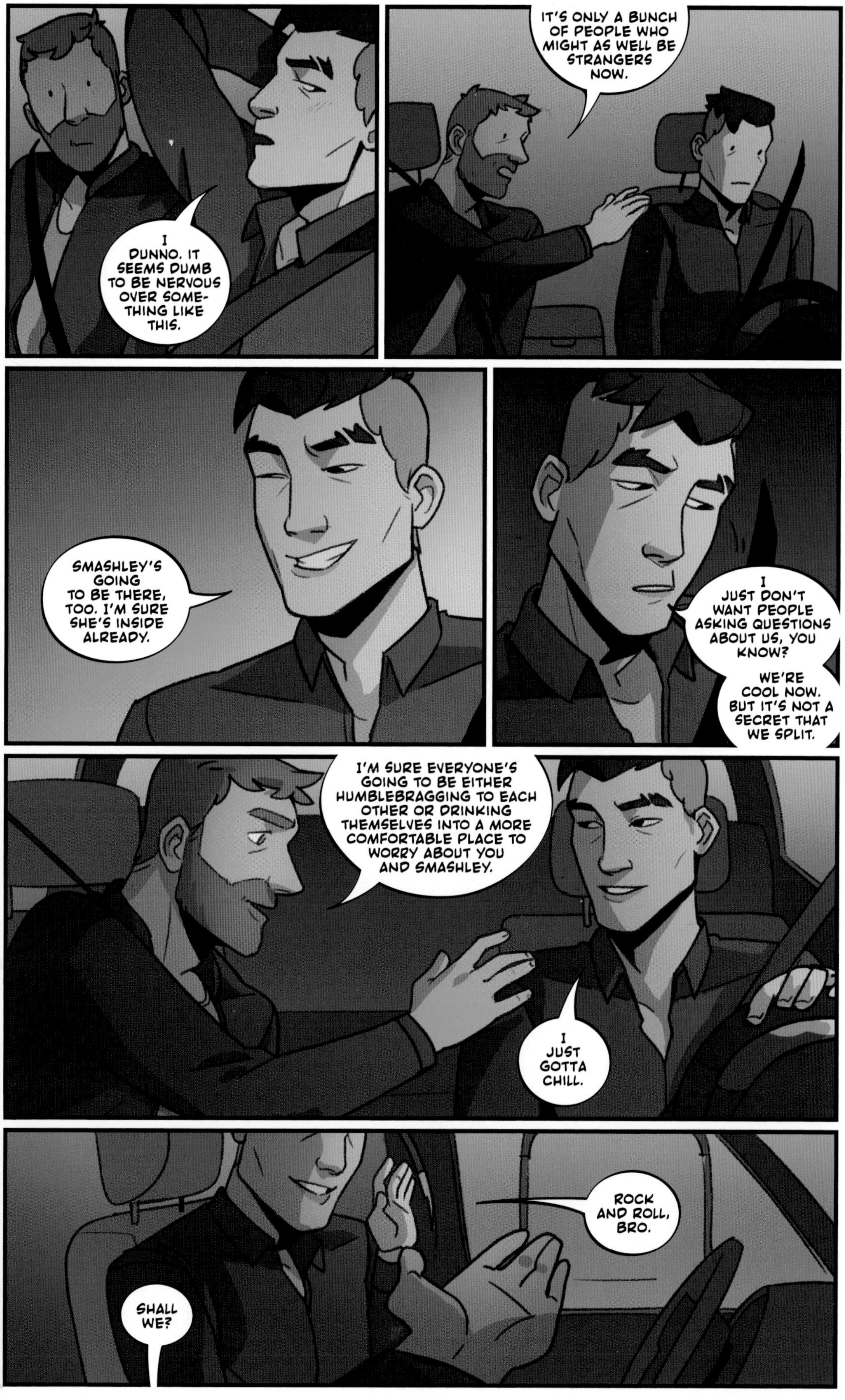
I DUNNO. IT SEEMS DUMB TO BE NERVOUS OVER SOME-THING LIKE THIS.
IT'S ONLY A BUNCH OF PEOPLE WHO MIGHT AS WELL BE STRANGERS NOW.
SMASHLEY'S GOING TO BE THERE, TOO. I'M SURE SHE'S INSIDE ALREADY.
I JUST DON'T WANT PEOPLE ASKING QUESTIONS ABOUT US, YOU KNOW?
WE'RE COOL NOW. BUT IT'S NOT A SECRET THAT WE SPLIT.
I'M SURE EVERYONE'S GOING TO BE EITHER HUMBLEBRAGGING TO EACH OTHER OR DRINKING THEMSELVES INTO A MORE COMFORTABLE PLACE TO WORRY ABOUT YOU AND SMASHLEY.
I JUST GOTTA CHILL.
SHALL WE?
ROCK AND ROLL, BRO.

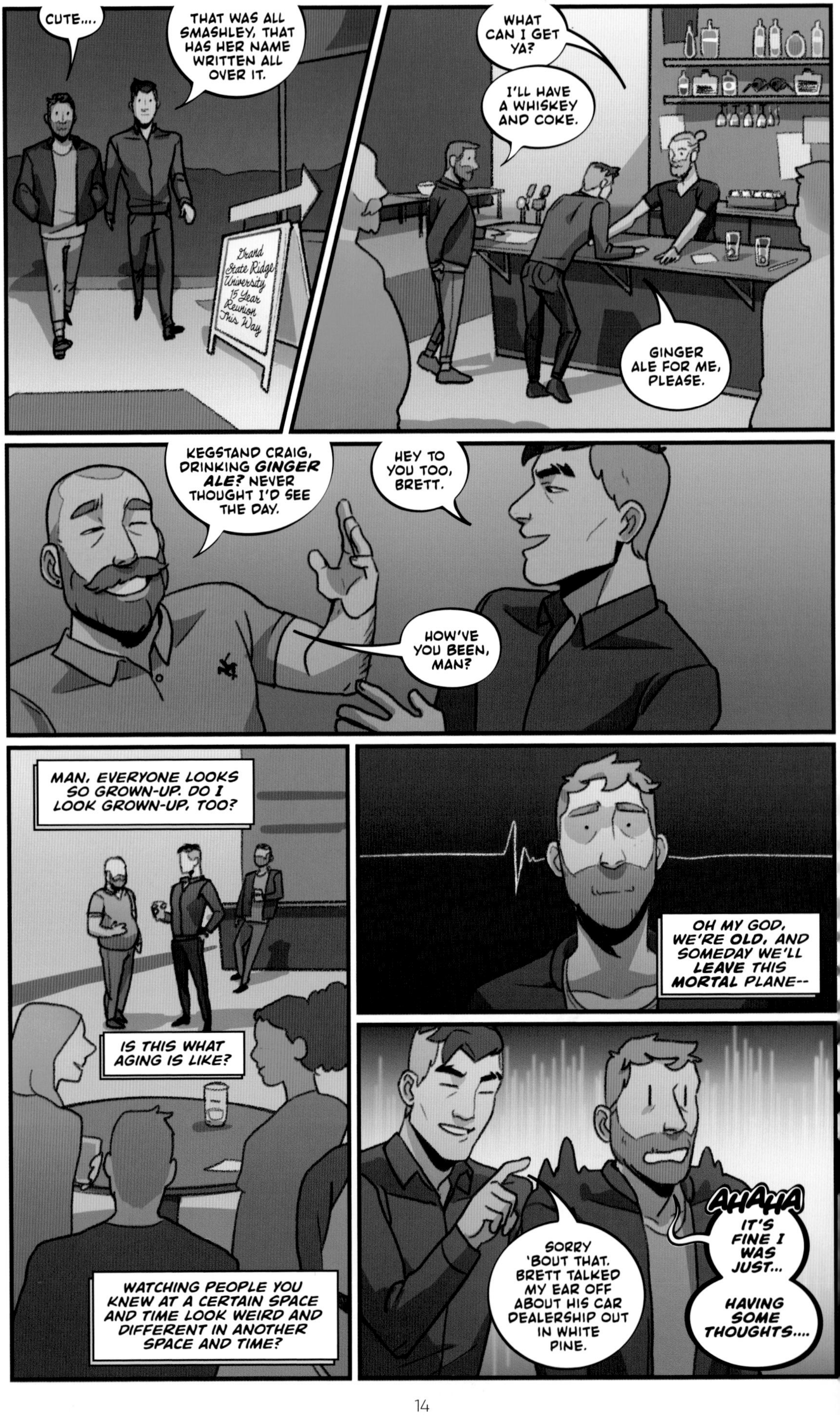
CUTE....
THAT WAS ALL SMASHLEY, THAT HAS HER NAME WRITTEN ALL OVER IT.
Grand State Ridge University 15 Year Reunion This Way
WHAT CAN I GET YA?
I'LL HAVE A WHISKEY AND COKE.
GINGER ALE FOR ME, PLEASE.
KEGSTAND CRAIG, DRINKING GINGER ALE? NEVER THOUGHT I'D SEE THE DAY.
HEY TO YOU TOO, BRETT.
HOW'VE YOU BEEN, MAN?
MAN, EVERYONE LOOKS SO GROWN-UP. DO I LOOK GROWN-UP, TOO?
IS THIS WHAT AGING IS LIKE?
WATCHING PEOPLE YOU KNEW AT A CERTAIN SPACE AND TIME LOOK WEIRD AND DIFFERENT IN ANOTHER SPACE AND TIME?
OH MY GOD, WE'RE OLD, AND SOMEDAY WE'LL LEAVE THIS MORTAL PLANE--
SORRY 'BOUT THAT. BRETT TALKED MY EAR OFF ABOUT HIS CAR DEALERSHIP OUT IN WHITE PINE.
AHAHA
IT'S FINE I WAS JUST...
HAVING SOME THOUGHTS....

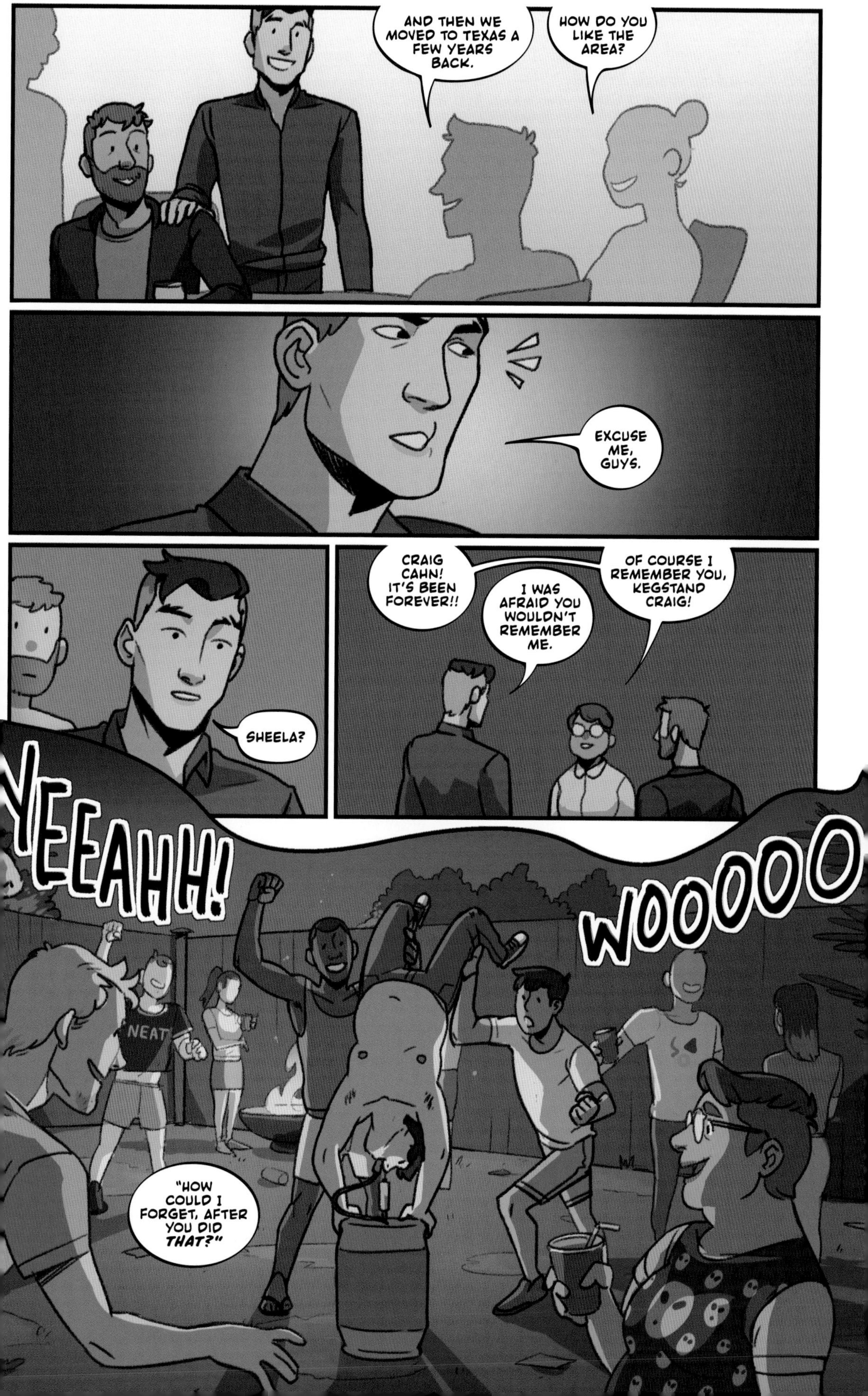
AND THEN WE MOVED TO TEXAS A FEW YEARS BACK.
HOW DO YOU LIKE THE AREA?
EXCUSE ME, GUYS.
SHEELA?
CRAIG CAHN! IT'S BEEN FOREVER!!
I WAS AFRAID YOU WOULDN'T REMEMBER ME.
OF COURSE I REMEMBER YOU, KEGSTAND CRAIG!
YEEAHH!
WOOOOO
NEAT
"HOW COULD I FORGET, AFTER YOU DID *THAT?*"

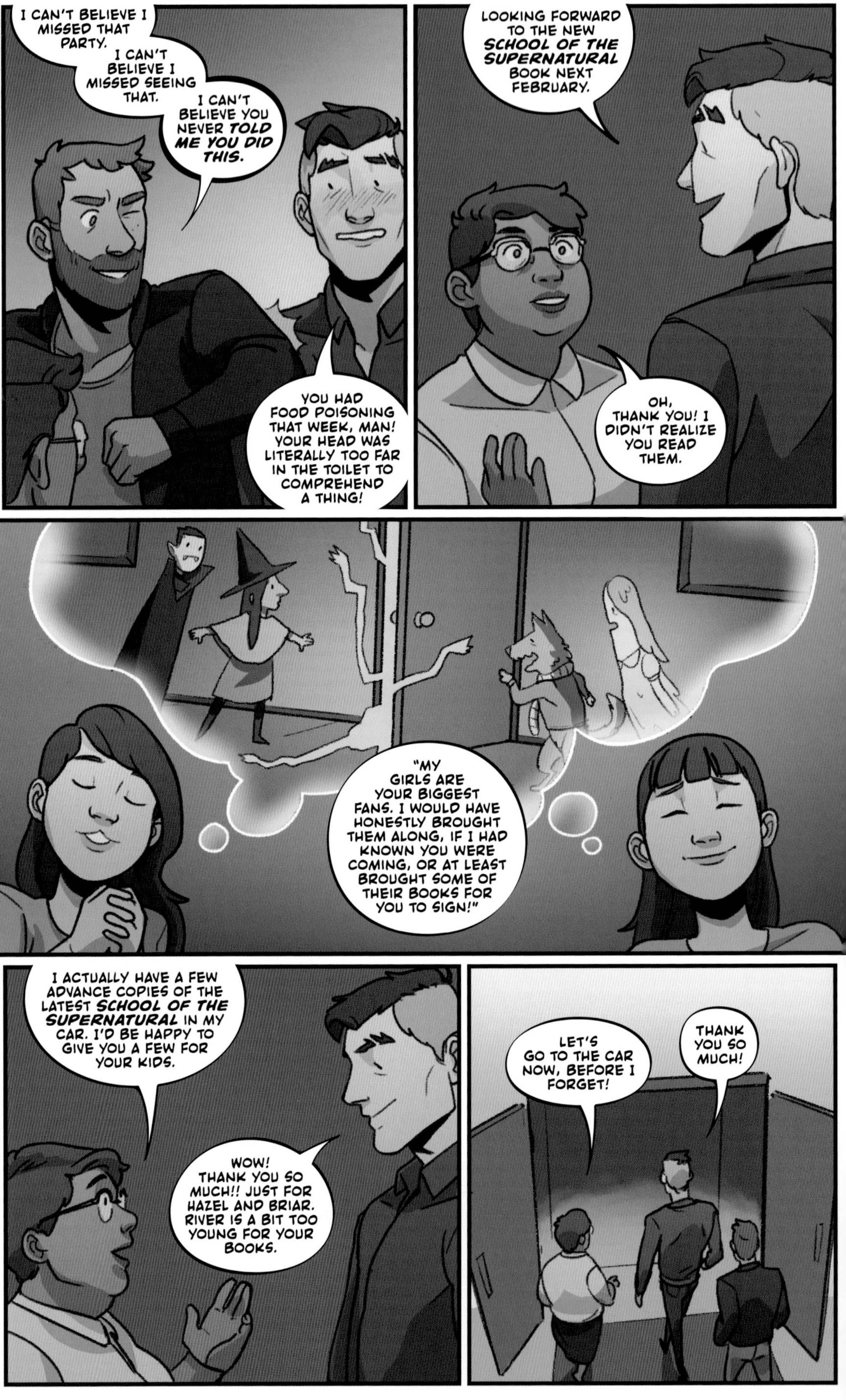
I CAN'T BELIEVE I MISSED THAT PARTY.
I CAN'T BELIEVE I MISSED SEEING THAT.
I CAN'T BELIEVE YOU NEVER ***TOLD ME YOU DID THIS.***
YOU HAD FOOD POISONING THAT WEEK, MAN! YOUR HEAD WAS LITERALLY TOO FAR IN THE TOILET TO COMPREHEND A THING!
LOOKING FORWARD TO THE NEW ***SCHOOL OF THE SUPERNATURAL*** BOOK NEXT FEBRUARY.
OH, THANK YOU! I DIDN'T REALIZE YOU READ THEM.
"MY GIRLS ARE YOUR BIGGEST FANS. I WOULD HAVE HONESTLY BROUGHT THEM ALONG, IF I HAD KNOWN YOU WERE COMING, OR AT LEAST BROUGHT SOME OF THEIR BOOKS FOR YOU TO SIGN!"
I ACTUALLY HAVE A FEW ADVANCE COPIES OF THE LATEST ***SCHOOL OF THE SUPERNATURAL*** IN MY CAR. I'D BE HAPPY TO GIVE YOU A FEW FOR YOUR KIDS.
WOW! THANK YOU SO MUCH!! JUST FOR HAZEL AND BRIAR. RIVER IS A BIT TOO YOUNG FOR YOUR BOOKS.
LET'S GO TO THE CAR NOW, BEFORE I FORGET!
THANK YOU SO MUCH!

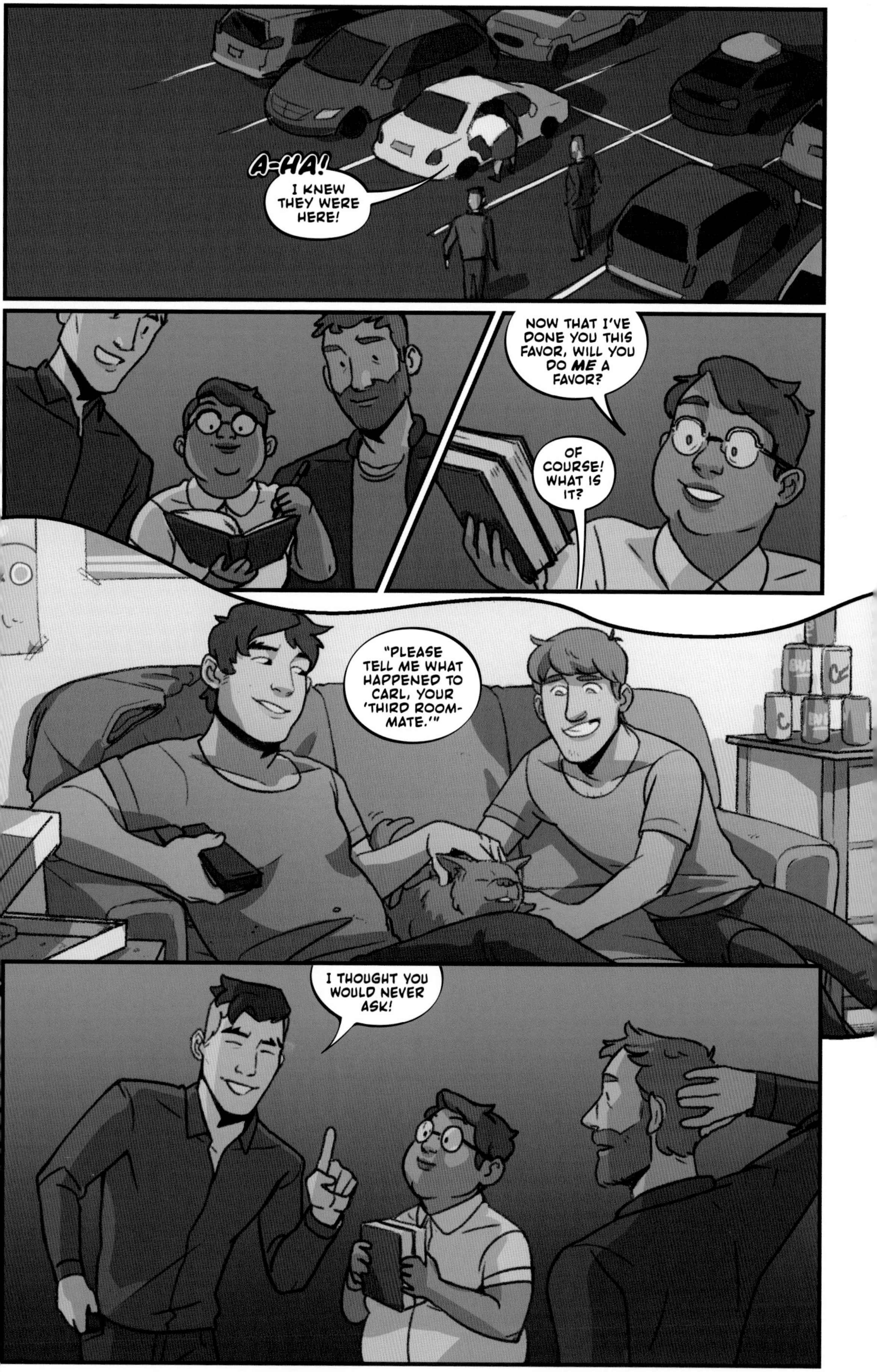
A-HA!
I KNEW THEY WERE HERE!
NOW THAT I'VE DONE YOU THIS FAVOR, WILL YOU DO *ME* A FAVOR?
OF COURSE! WHAT IS IT?
"PLEASE TELL ME WHAT HAPPENED TO CARL, YOUR 'THIRD ROOM-MATE.'"
I THOUGHT YOU WOULD NEVER ASK!

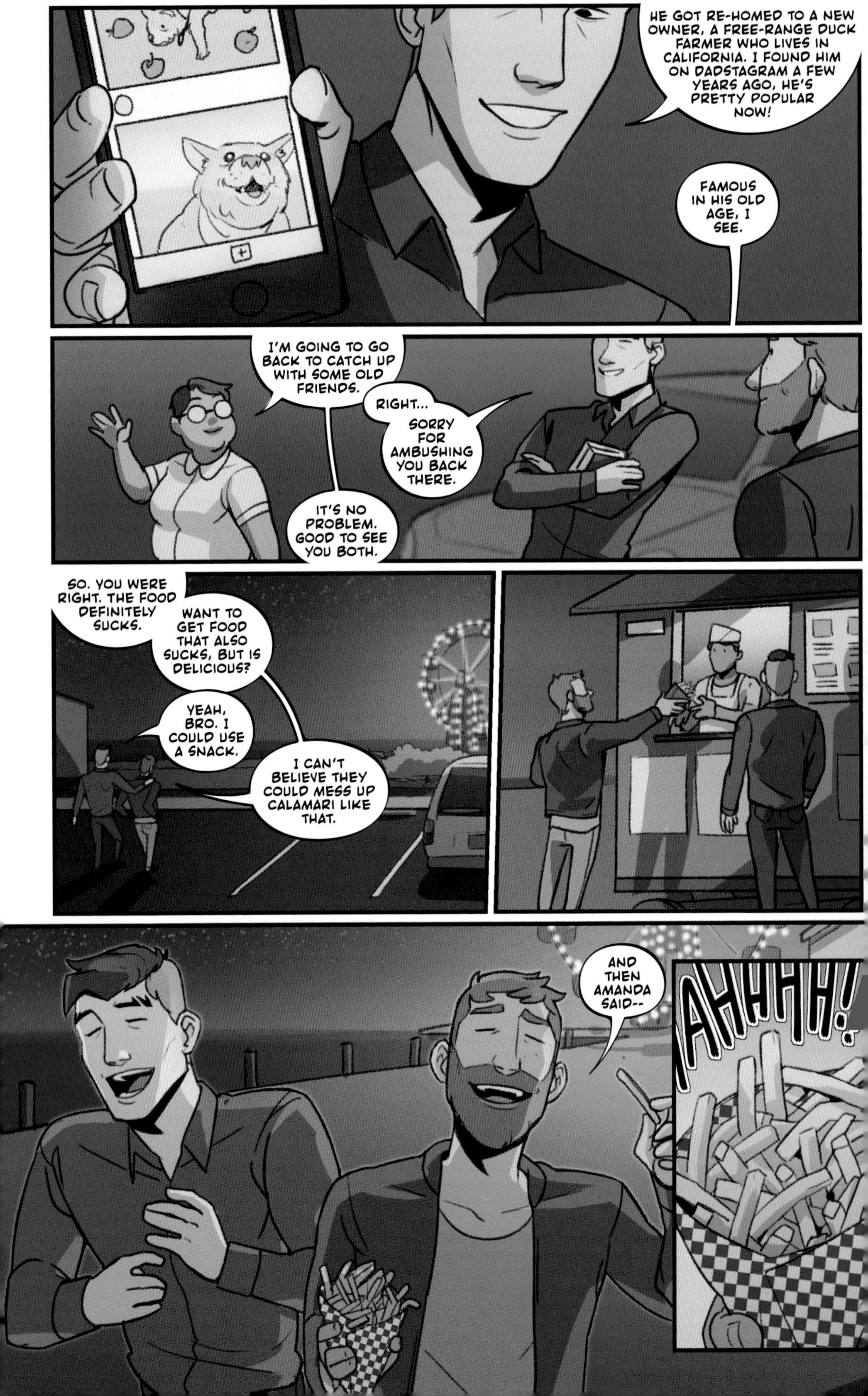
HE GOT RE-HOMED TO A NEW OWNER, A FREE-RANGE DUCK FARMER WHO LIVES IN CALIFORNIA. I FOUND HIM ON DADSTAGRAM A FEW YEARS AGO, HE'S PRETTY POPULAR NOW!
FAMOUS IN HIS OLD AGE, I SEE.
I'M GOING TO GO BACK TO CATCH UP WITH SOME OLD FRIENDS.
RIGHT...
SORRY FOR AMBUSHING YOU BACK THERE.
IT'S NO PROBLEM. GOOD TO SEE YOU BOTH.
SO. YOU WERE RIGHT. THE FOOD DEFINITELY SUCKS.
WANT TO GET FOOD THAT ALSO SUCKS, BUT IS DELICIOUS?
YEAH, BRO. I COULD USE A SNACK.
I CAN'T BELIEVE THEY COULD MESS UP CALAMARI LIKE THAT.
AND THEN AMANDA SAID--
AHHHH!

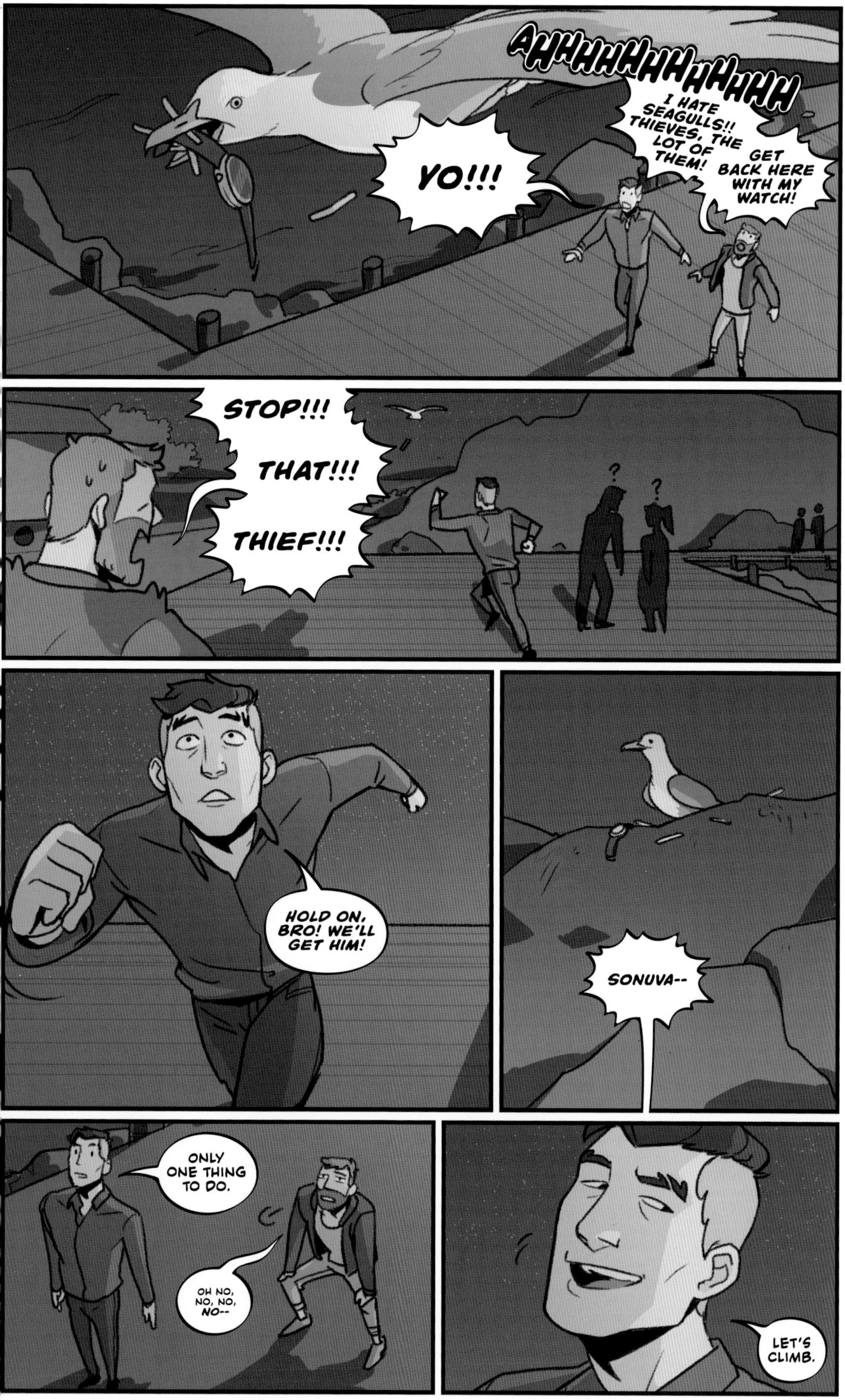
AHHHHHHHHHHHHH
I HATE SEAGULLS!! THIEVES, THE LOT OF THEM!
YO!!!
GET BACK HERE WITH MY WATCH!
STOP!!!
THAT!!!
THIEF!!!
?
?
HOLD ON, BRO! WE'LL GET HIM!
SONUVA--
ONLY ONE THING TO DO.
OH NO, NO, NO, NO--
LET'S CLIMB.

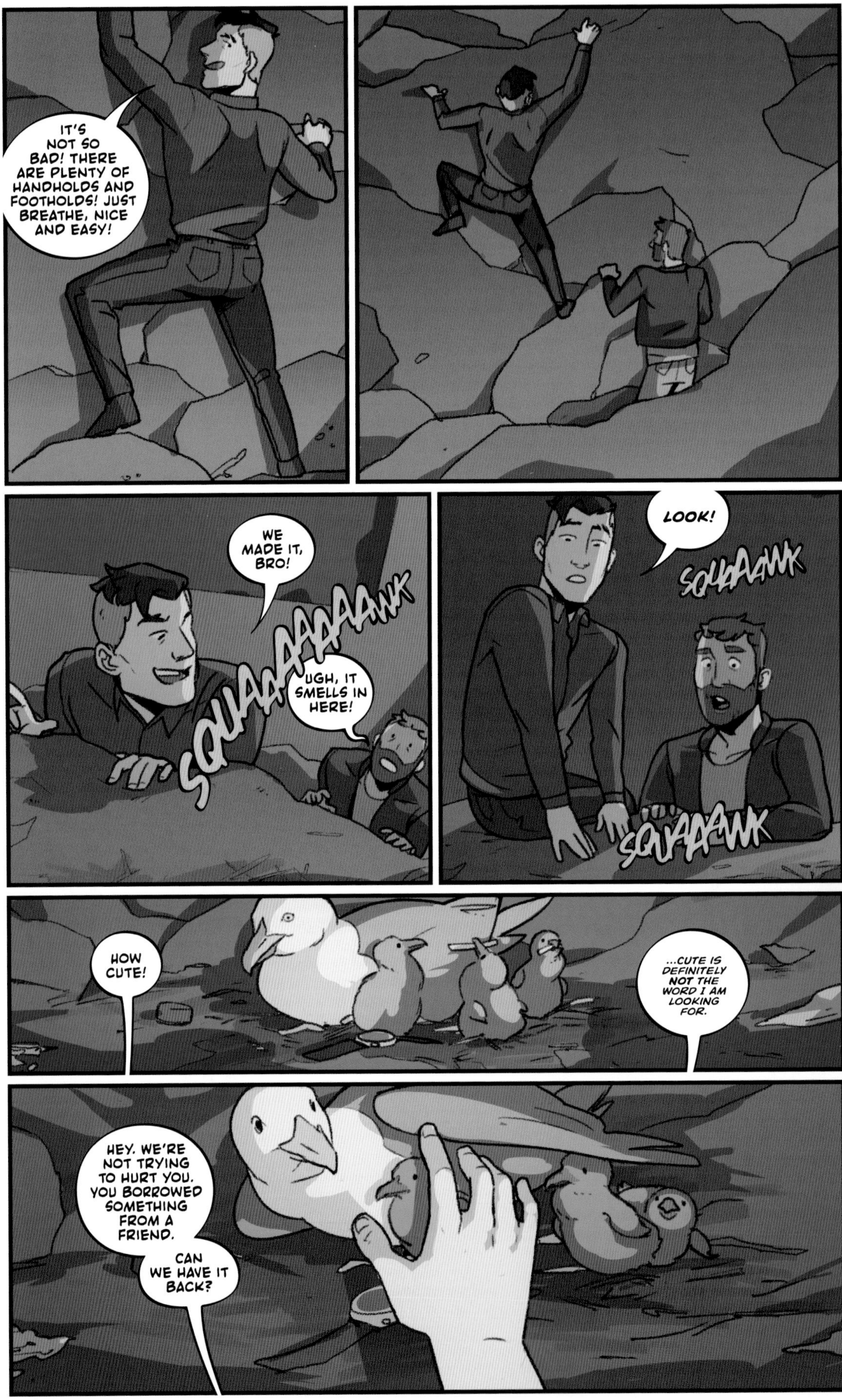
IT'S NOT SO BAD! THERE ARE PLENTY OF HANDHOLDS AND FOOTHOLDS! JUST BREATHE, NICE AND EASY!
WE MADE IT, BRO!
SQUAAAAAAAAWK
UGH, IT SMELLS IN HERE!
LOOK!
SQUAAAWK
SQUAAAWK
HOW CUTE!
...CUTE IS DEFINITELY NOT THE WORD I AM LOOKING FOR.
HEY. WE'RE NOT TRYING TO HURT YOU. YOU BORROWED SOMETHING FROM A FRIEND.
CAN WE HAVE IT BACK?

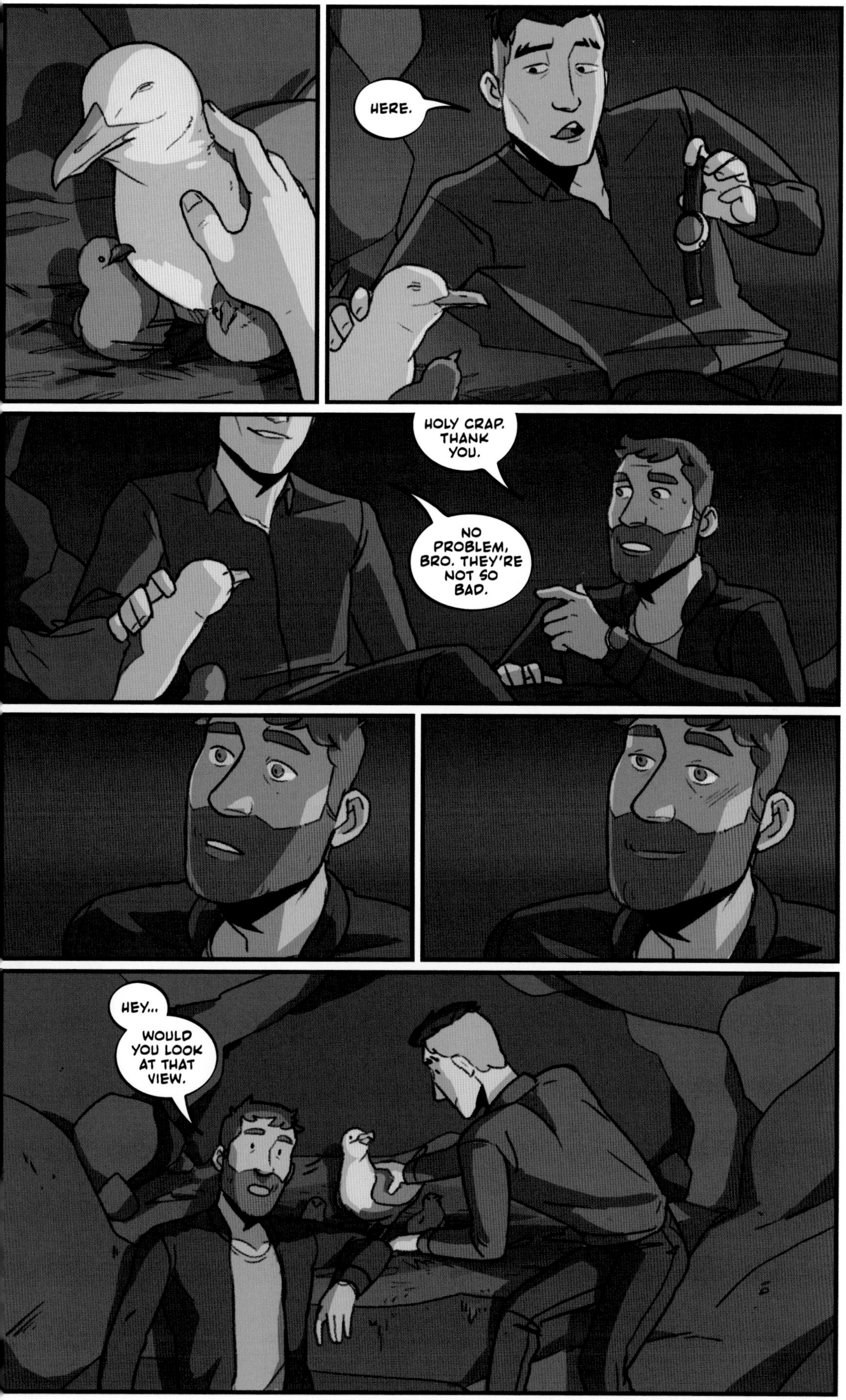
HERE.
HOLY CRAP. THANK YOU.
NO PROBLEM, BRO. THEY'RE NOT SO BAD.
HEY...
WOULD YOU LOOK AT THAT VIEW.

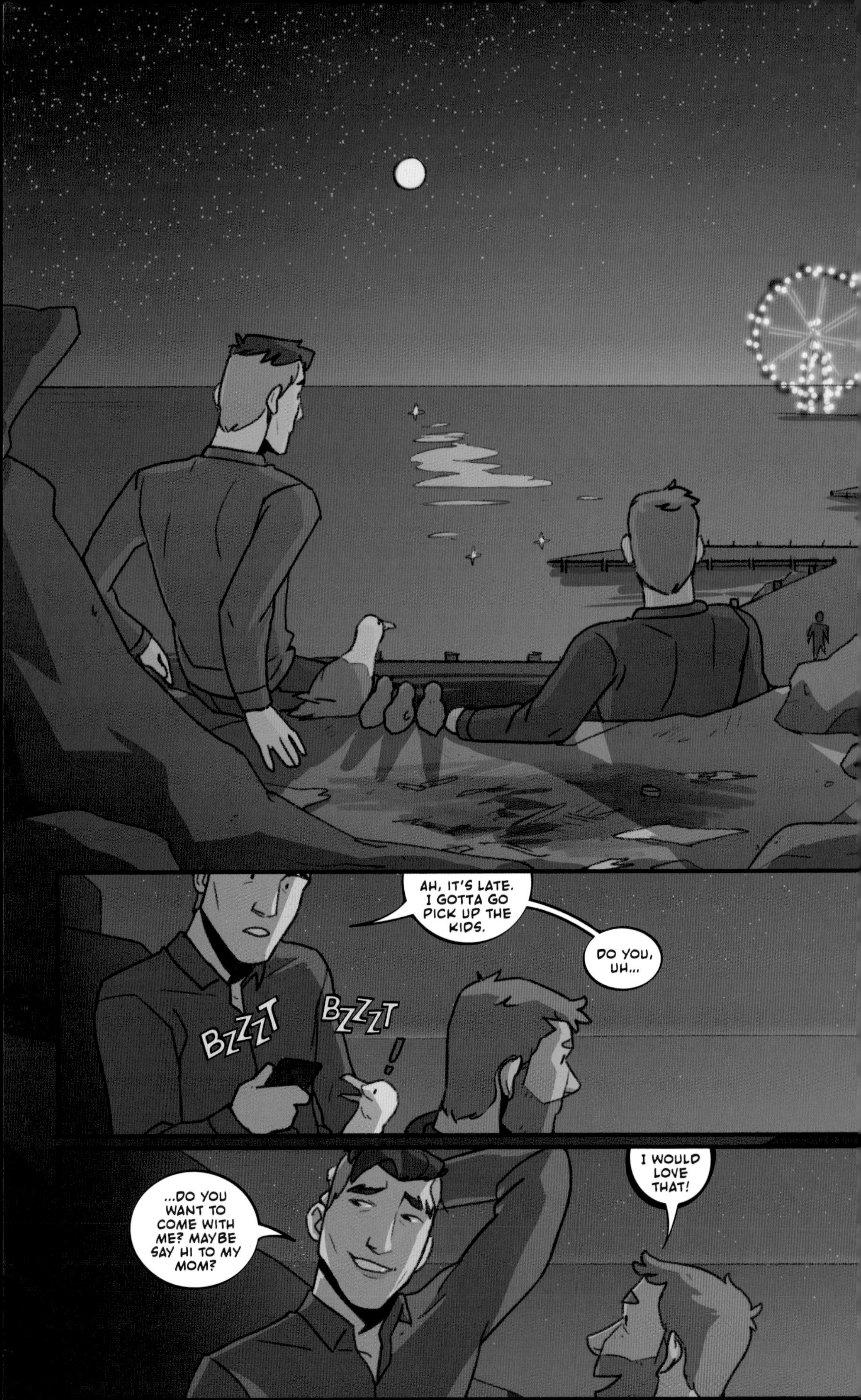
AH, IT'S LATE. I GOTTA GO PICK UP THE KIDS.
DO YOU, UH...
BZZZT
BZZZT
!
...DO YOU WANT TO COME WITH ME? MAYBE SAY HI TO MY MOM?
I WOULD LOVE THAT!

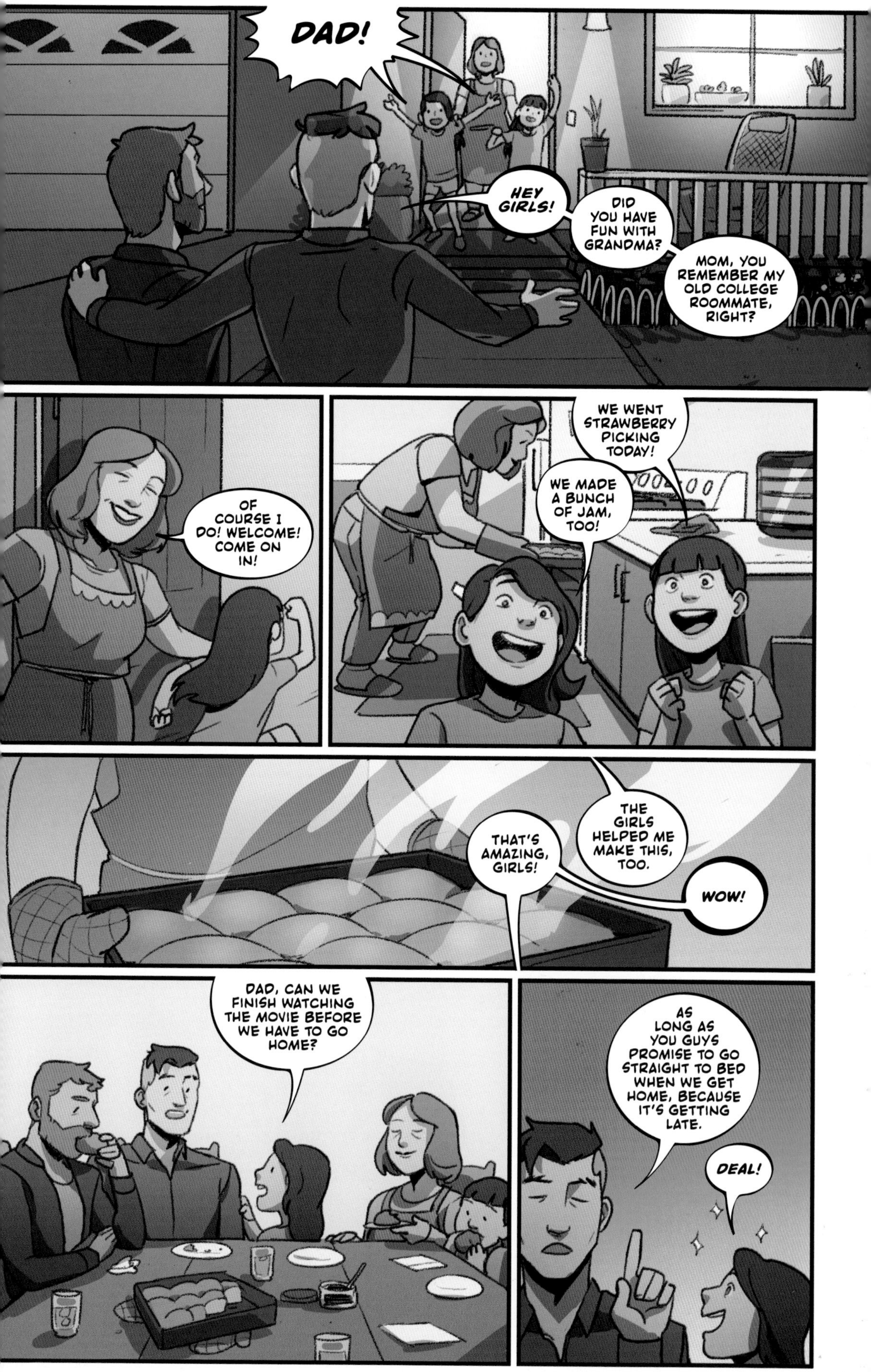
DAD!
HEY GIRLS!
DID YOU HAVE FUN WITH GRANDMA?
MOM, YOU REMEMBER MY OLD COLLEGE ROOMMATE, RIGHT?
OF COURSE I DO! WELCOME! COME ON IN!
WE WENT STRAWBERRY PICKING TODAY!
WE MADE A BUNCH OF JAM, TOO!
THAT'S AMAZING, GIRLS!
THE GIRLS HELPED ME MAKE THIS, TOO.
WOW!
DAD, CAN WE FINISH WATCHING THE MOVIE BEFORE WE HAVE TO GO HOME?
AS LONG AS YOU GUYS PROMISE TO GO STRAIGHT TO BED WHEN WE GET HOME, BECAUSE IT'S GETTING LATE.
DEAL!

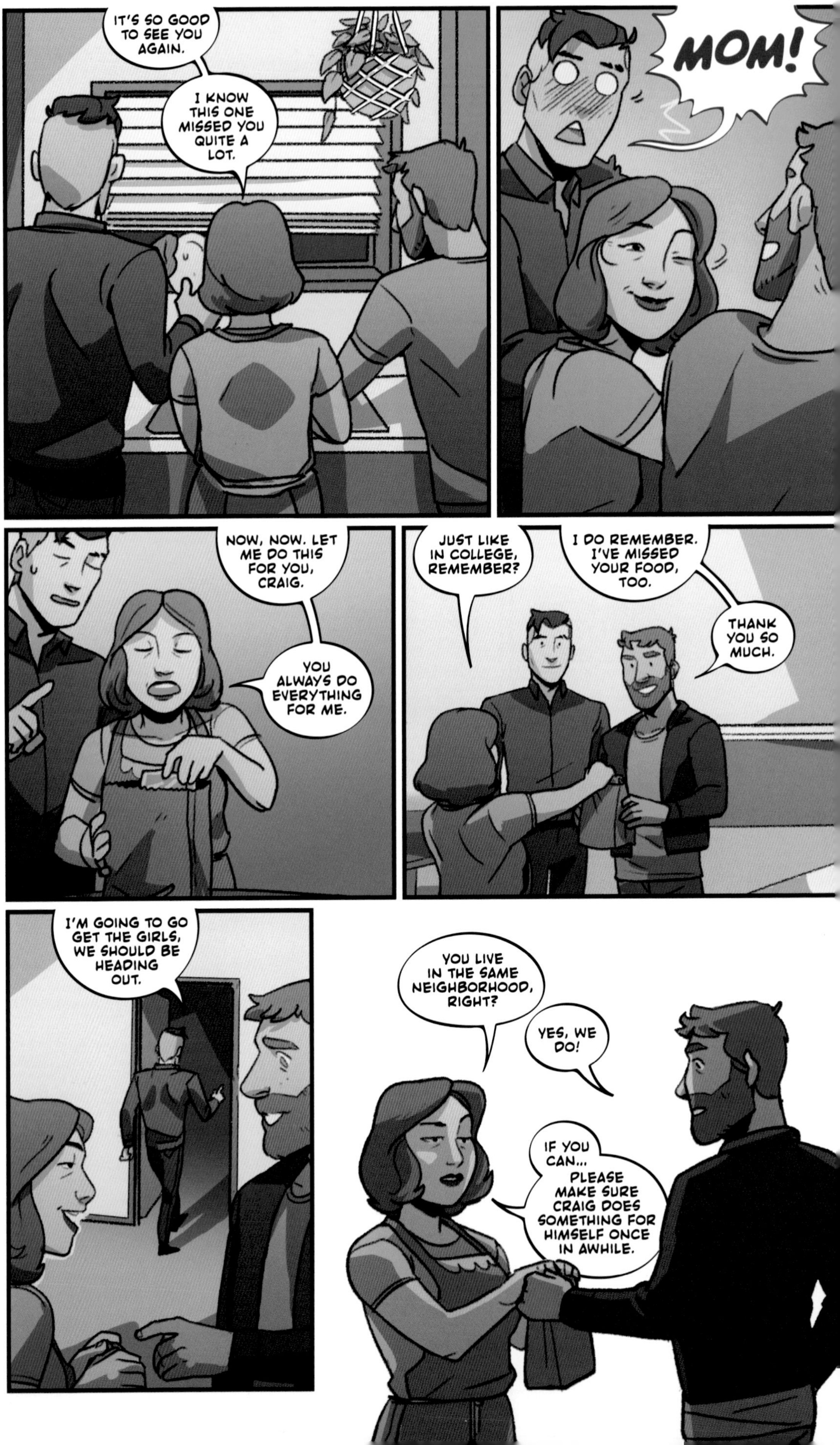
IT'S SO GOOD TO SEE YOU AGAIN.
I KNOW THIS ONE MISSED YOU QUITE A LOT.
MOM!
NOW, NOW. LET ME DO THIS FOR YOU, CRAIG.
YOU ALWAYS DO EVERYTHING FOR ME.
JUST LIKE IN COLLEGE, REMEMBER?
I DO REMEMBER. I'VE MISSED YOUR FOOD, TOO.
THANK YOU SO MUCH.
I'M GOING TO GO GET THE GIRLS, WE SHOULD BE HEADING OUT.
YOU LIVE IN THE SAME NEIGHBORHOOD, RIGHT?
YES, WE DO!
IF YOU CAN... PLEASE MAKE SURE CRAIG DOES SOMETHING FOR HIMSELF ONCE IN AWHILE.

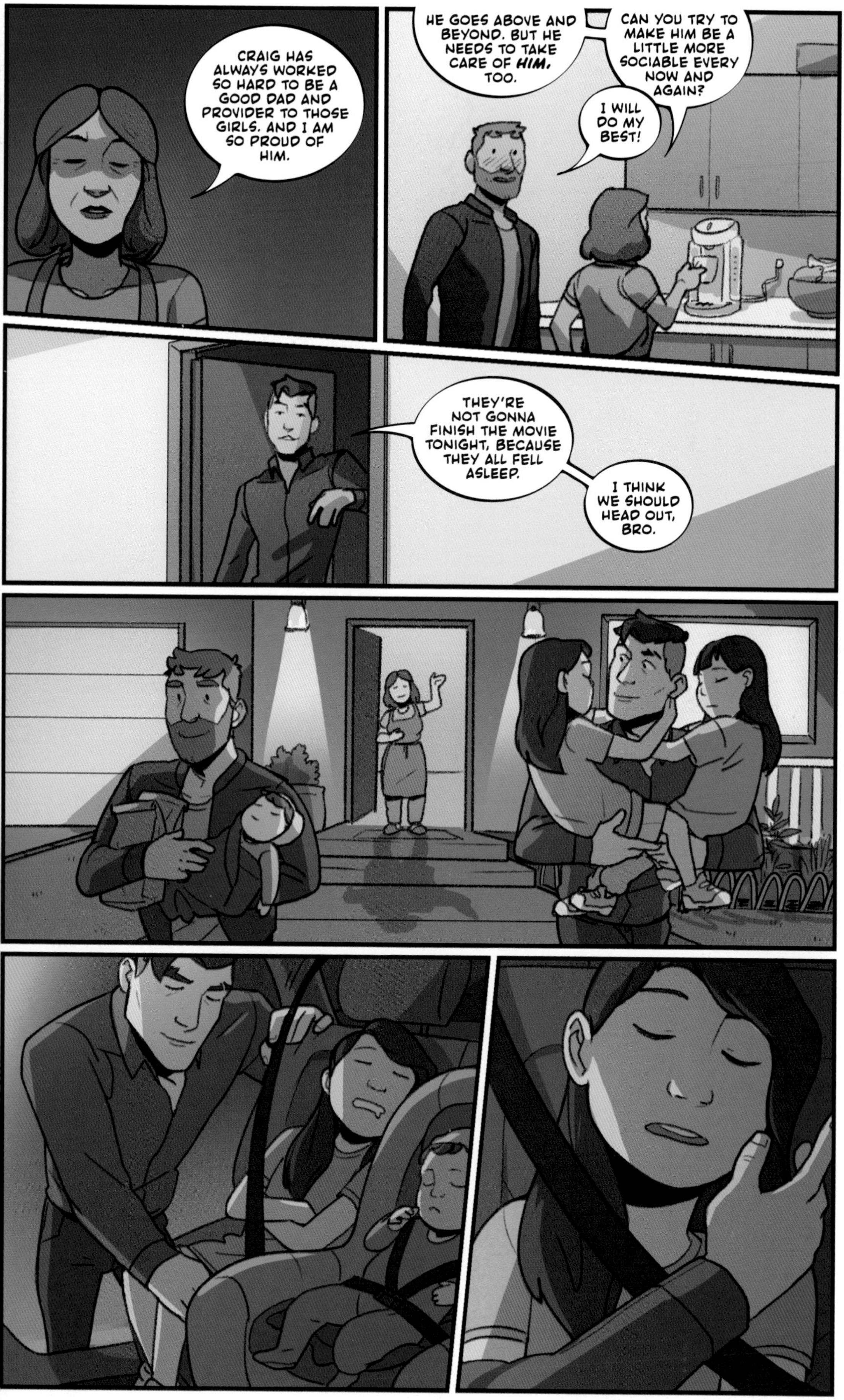
CRAIG HAS ALWAYS WORKED SO HARD TO BE A GOOD DAD AND PROVIDER TO THOSE GIRLS. AND I AM SO PROUD OF HIM.
HE GOES ABOVE AND BEYOND. BUT HE NEEDS TO TAKE CARE OF *HIM*, TOO.
CAN YOU TRY TO MAKE HIM BE A LITTLE MORE SOCIABLE EVERY NOW AND AGAIN?
I WILL DO MY BEST!
THEY'RE NOT GONNA FINISH THE MOVIE TONIGHT, BECAUSE THEY ALL FELL ASLEEP.
I THINK WE SHOULD HEAD OUT, BRO.

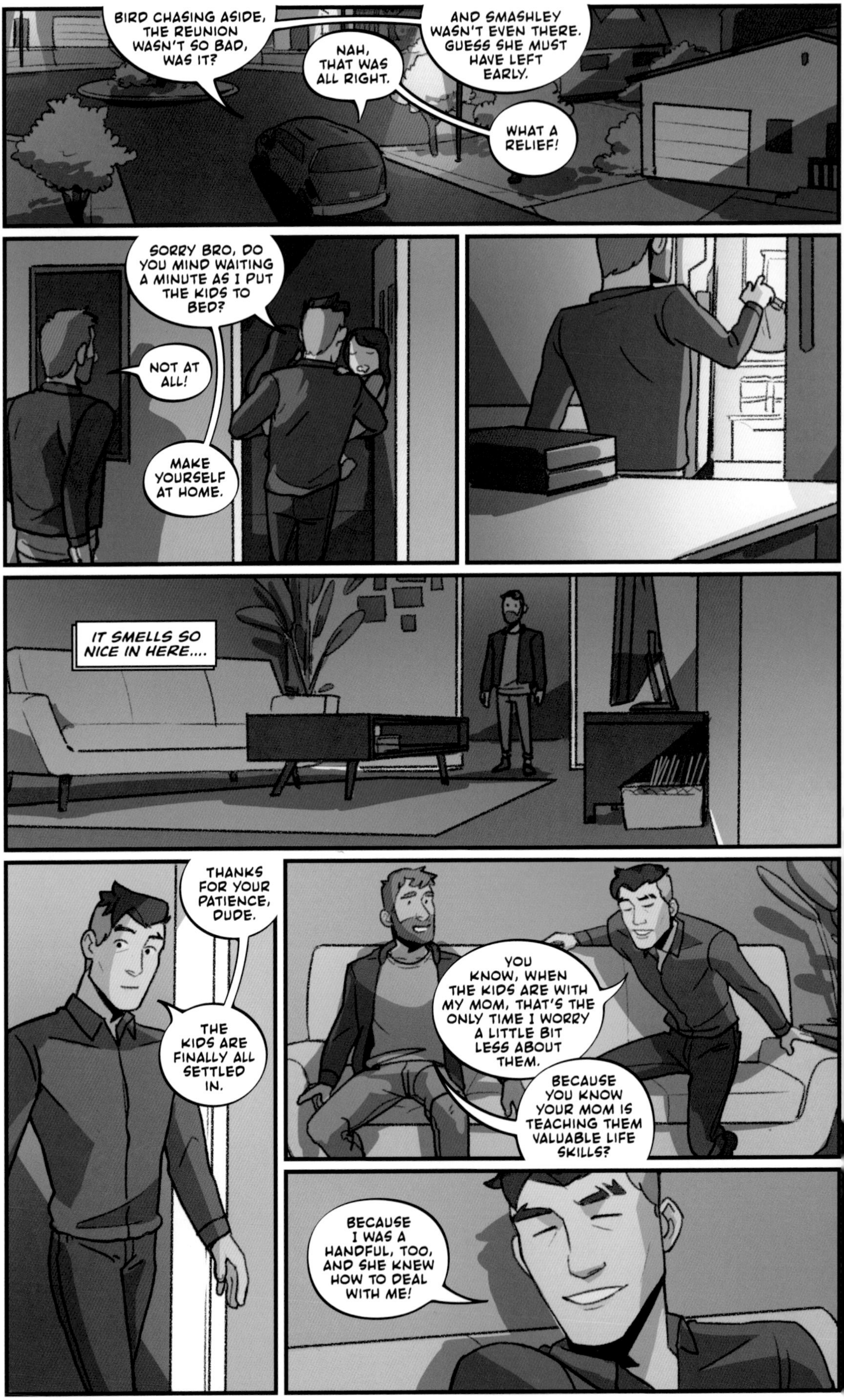
BIRD CHASING ASIDE, THE REUNION WASN'T SO BAD, WAS IT?
NAH, THAT WAS ALL RIGHT.
AND SMASHLEY WASN'T EVEN THERE. GUESS SHE MUST HAVE LEFT EARLY.
WHAT A RELIEF!
SORRY BRO, DO YOU MIND WAITING A MINUTE AS I PUT THE KIDS TO BED?
NOT AT ALL!
MAKE YOURSELF AT HOME.
IT SMELLS SO NICE IN HERE....
THANKS FOR YOUR PATIENCE, DUDE.
THE KIDS ARE FINALLY ALL SETTLED IN.
YOU KNOW, WHEN THE KIDS ARE WITH MY MOM, THAT'S THE ONLY TIME I WORRY A LITTLE BIT LESS ABOUT THEM.
BECAUSE YOU KNOW YOUR MOM IS TEACHING THEM VALUABLE LIFE SKILLS?
BECAUSE I WAS A HANDFUL, TOO, AND SHE KNEW HOW TO DEAL WITH ME!

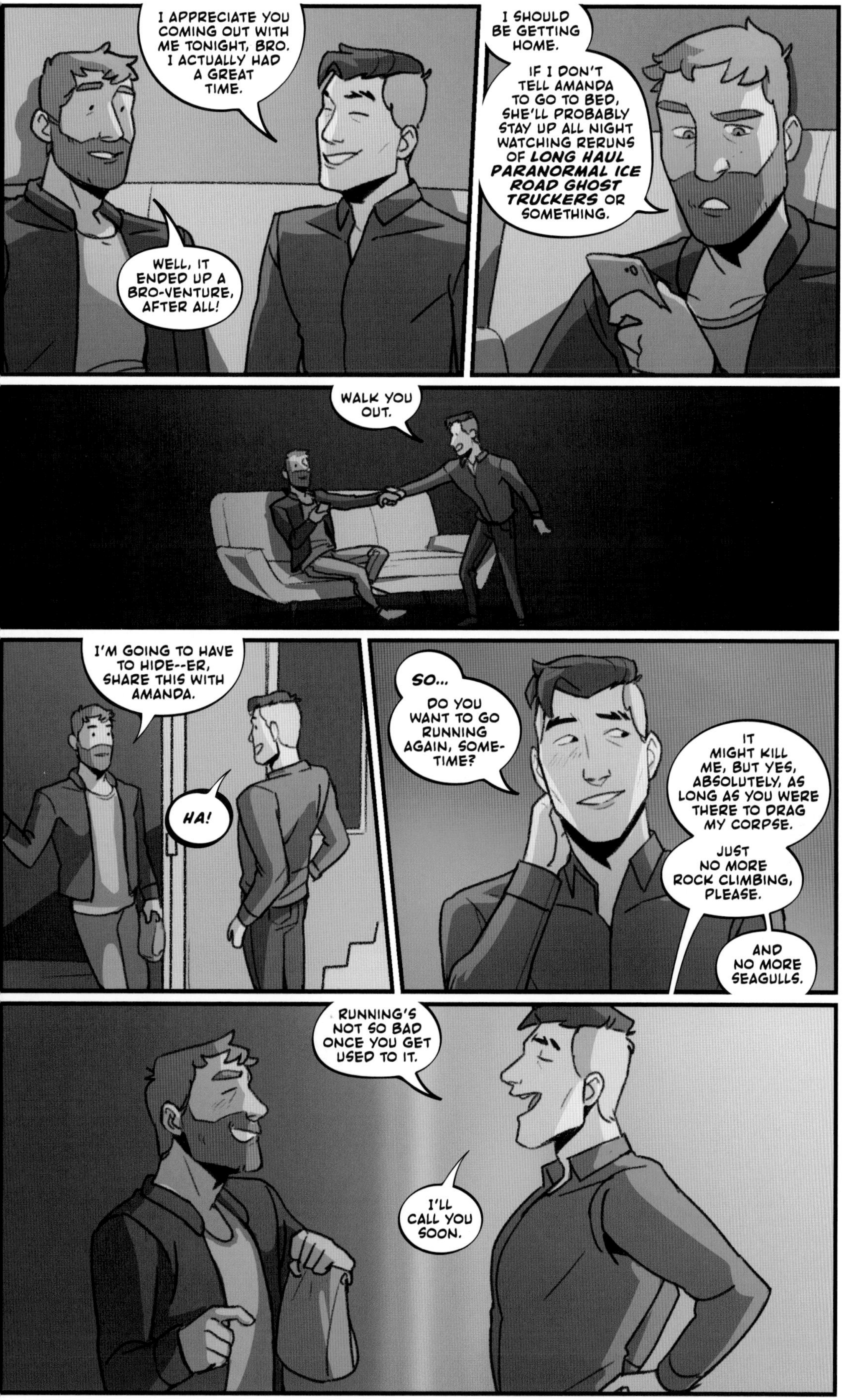
I APPRECIATE YOU COMING OUT WITH ME TONIGHT, BRO. I ACTUALLY HAD A GREAT TIME.
WELL, IT ENDED UP A BRO-VENTURE, AFTER ALL!
I SHOULD BE GETTING HOME.
IF I DON'T TELL AMANDA TO GO TO BED, SHE'LL PROBABLY STAY UP ALL NIGHT WATCHING RERUNS OF ***LONG HAUL PARANORMAL ICE ROAD GHOST TRUCKERS*** OR SOMETHING.
WALK YOU OUT.
I'M GOING TO HAVE TO HIDE--ER, SHARE THIS WITH AMANDA.
HA!
SO...
DO YOU WANT TO GO RUNNING AGAIN, SOME-TIME?
IT MIGHT KILL ME, BUT YES, ABSOLUTELY, AS LONG AS YOU WERE THERE TO DRAG MY CORPSE.
JUST NO MORE ROCK CLIMBING, PLEASE.
AND NO MORE SEAGULLS.
RUNNING'S NOT SO BAD ONCE YOU GET USED TO IT.
I'LL CALL YOU SOON.

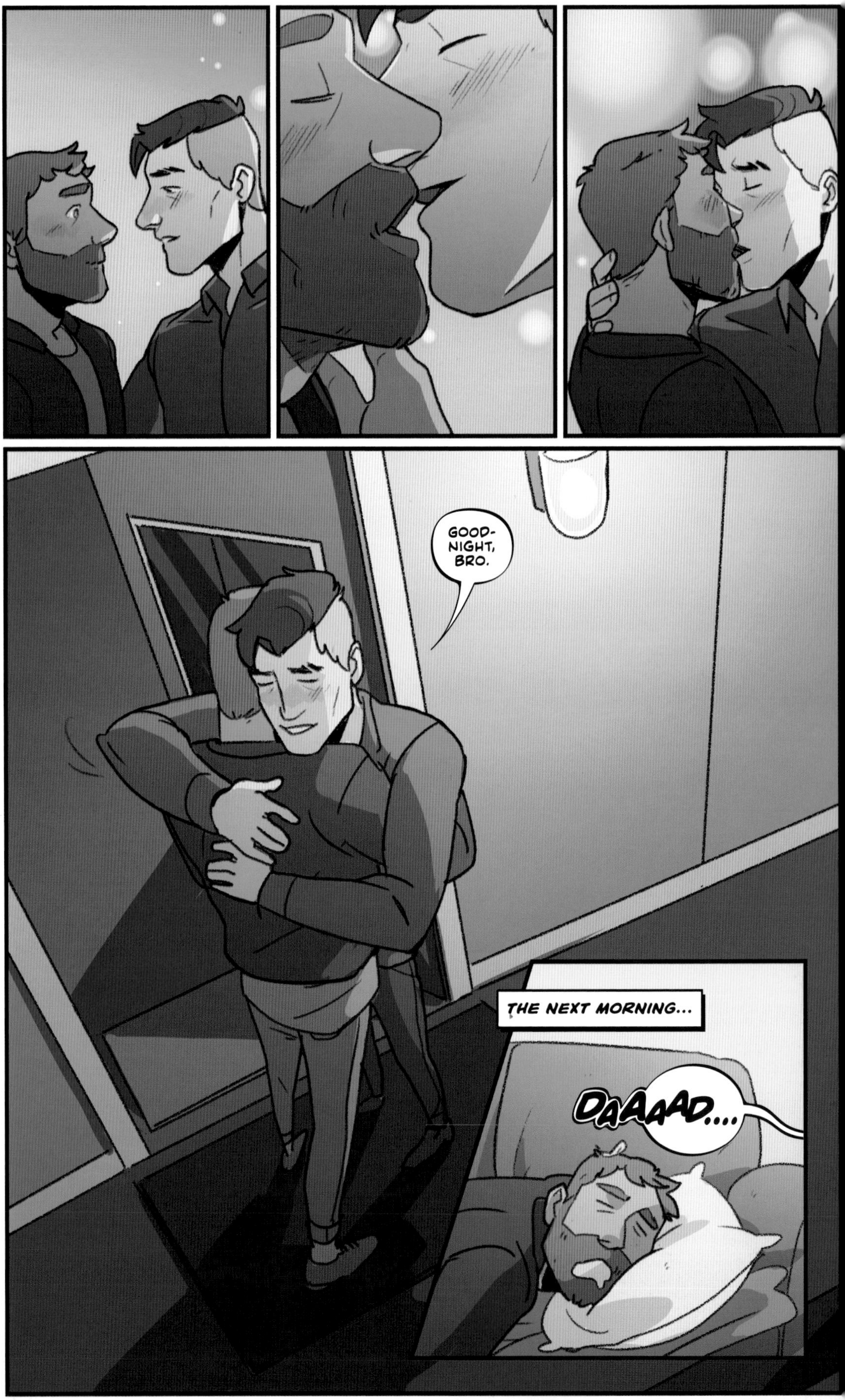
GOOD-NIGHT, BRO.
THE NEXT MORNING...
DAAAAD....

END!

"Let the Right Dad In"

Written by Lee C. A.
Illustrated and colored by Jack Gross
Lettered by Hassan Otsmane-Elhaou
Cover by Kris Anka

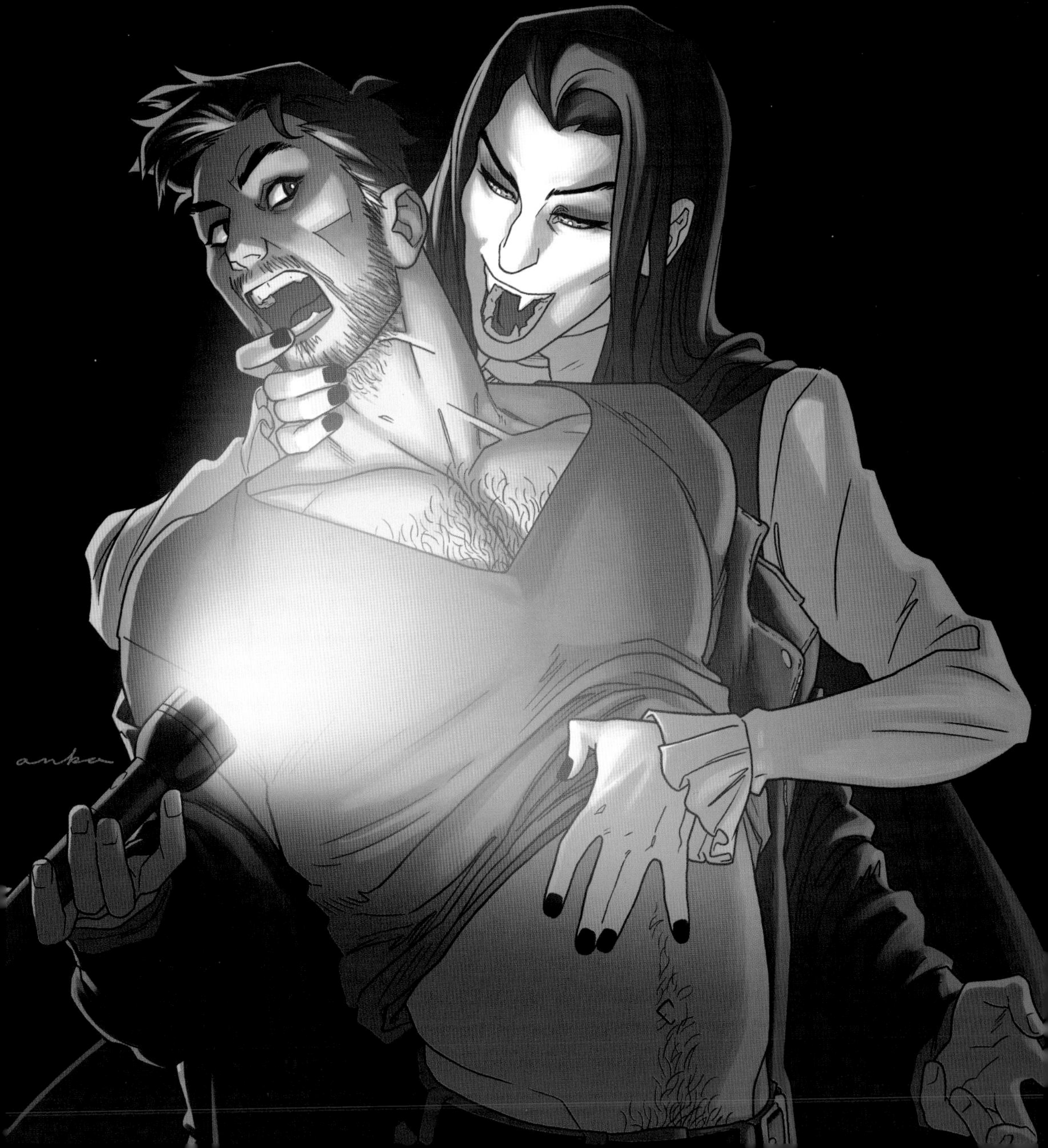
anka

Cover by Jack Gross

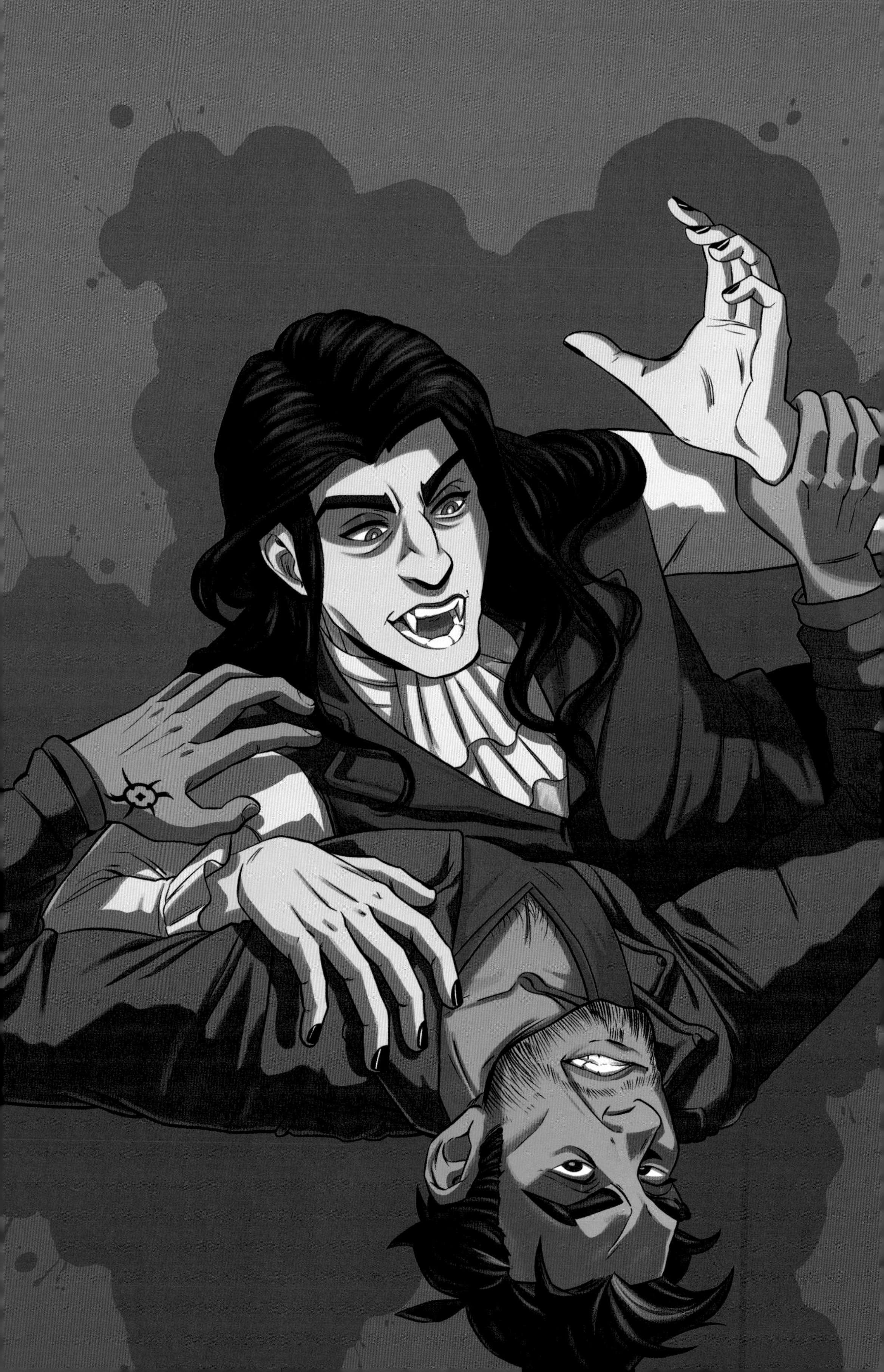

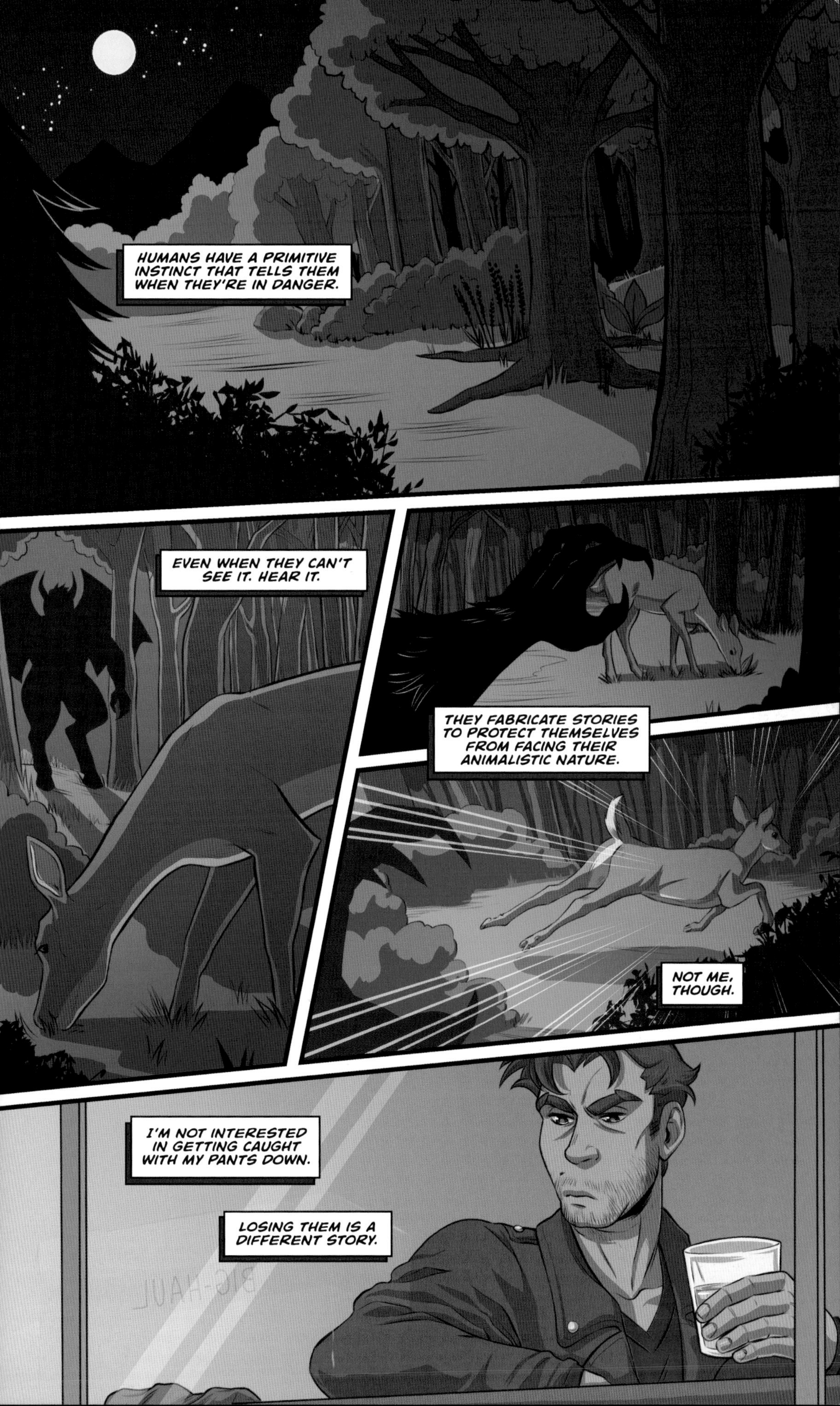
HUMANS HAVE A PRIMITIVE INSTINCT THAT TELLS THEM WHEN THEY'RE IN DANGER.
EVEN WHEN THEY CAN'T SEE IT. HEAR IT.
THEY FABRICATE STORIES TO PROTECT THEMSELVES FROM FACING THEIR ANIMALISTIC NATURE.
NOT ME, THOUGH.
I'M NOT INTERESTED IN GETTING CAUGHT WITH MY PANTS DOWN.
LOSING THEM IS A DIFFERENT STORY.

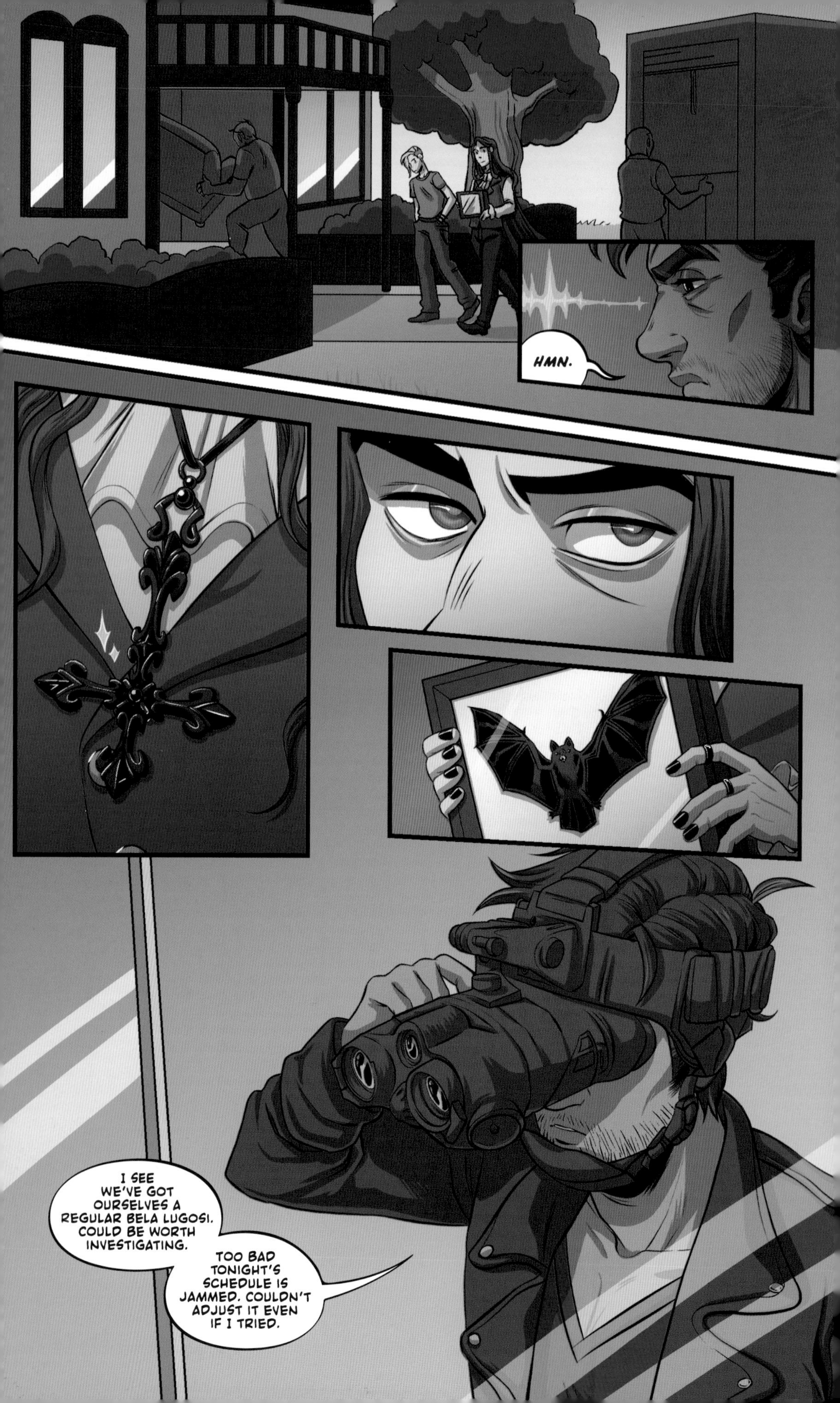
HMN.
I SEE WE'VE GOT OURSELVES A REGULAR BELA LUGOSI. COULD BE WORTH INVESTIGATING.
TOO BAD TONIGHT'S SCHEDULE IS JAMMED. COULDN'T ADJUST IT EVEN IF I TRIED.

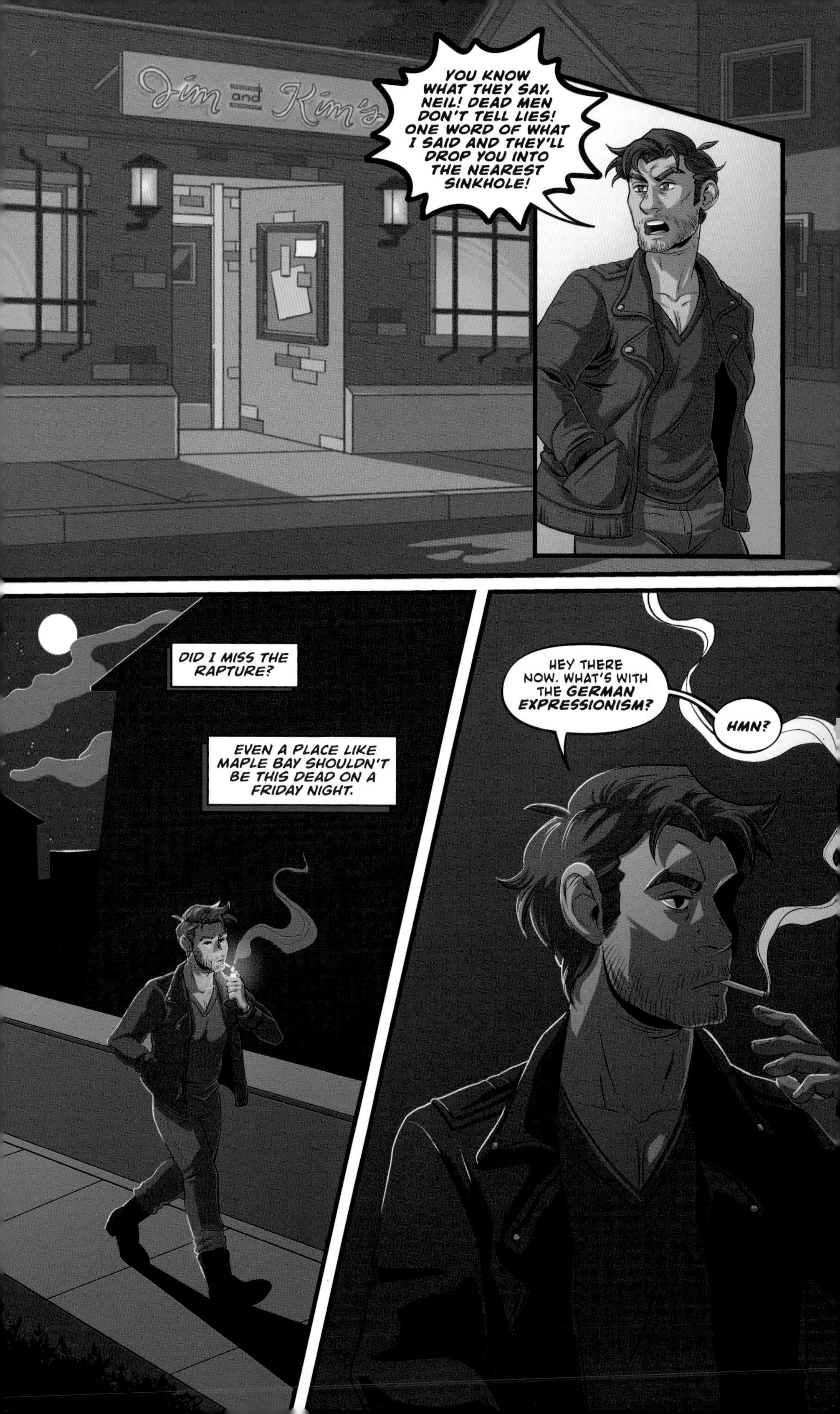
Jim and Kim's
YOU KNOW WHAT THEY SAY, NEIL! DEAD MEN DON'T TELL LIES! ONE WORD OF WHAT I SAID AND THEY'LL DROP YOU INTO THE NEAREST SINKHOLE!
DID I MISS THE RAPTURE?
EVEN A PLACE LIKE MAPLE BAY SHOULDN'T BE THIS DEAD ON A FRIDAY NIGHT.
HEY THERE NOW. WHAT'S WITH THE GERMAN EXPRESSIONISM?
HMN?

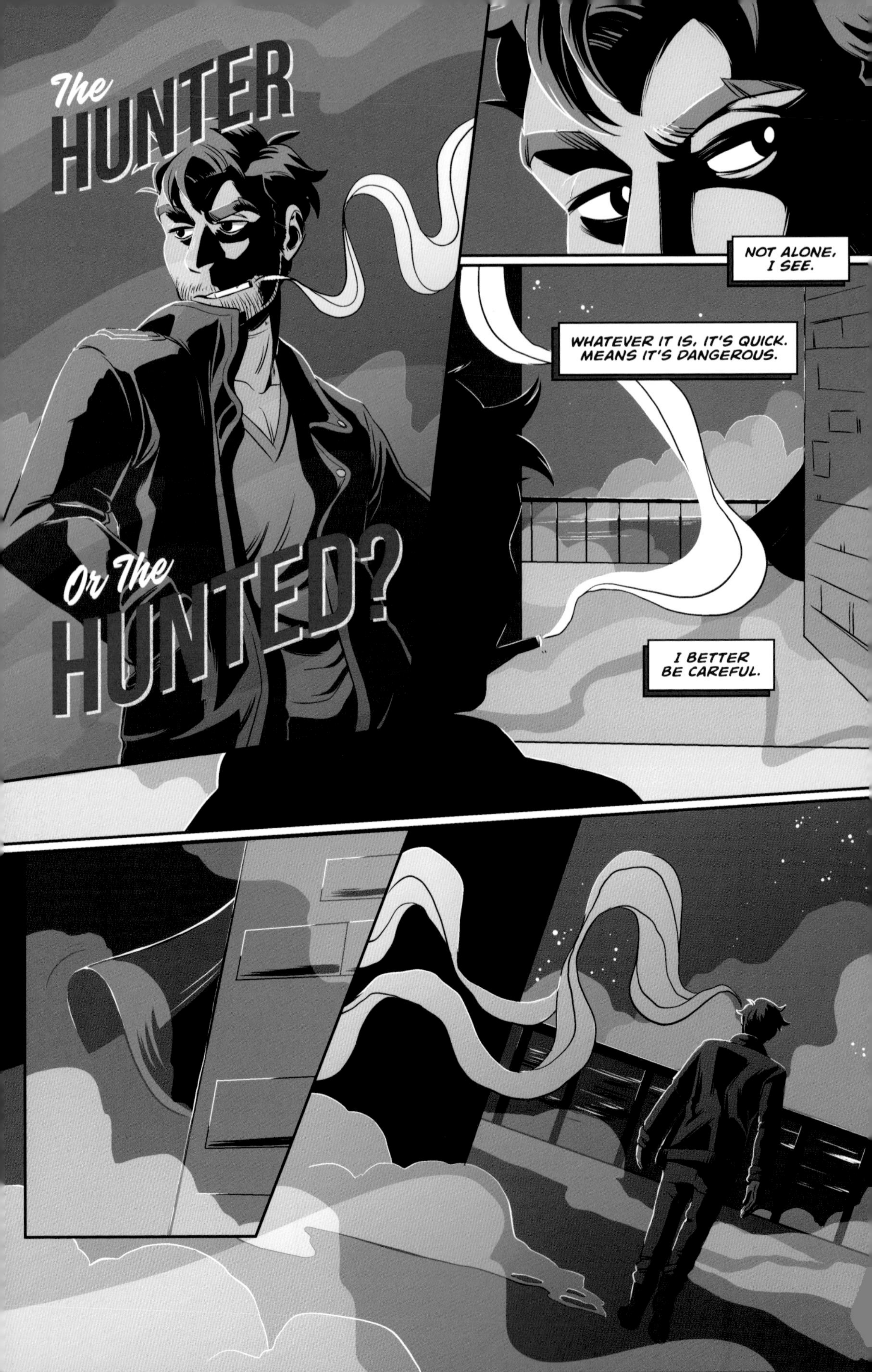

DIRECTOR • CINEMATOGRAPHER • WRITER
PRODUCER • COSTUME DESIGNER • CRAFT SERVICES | ROBERT SMALL

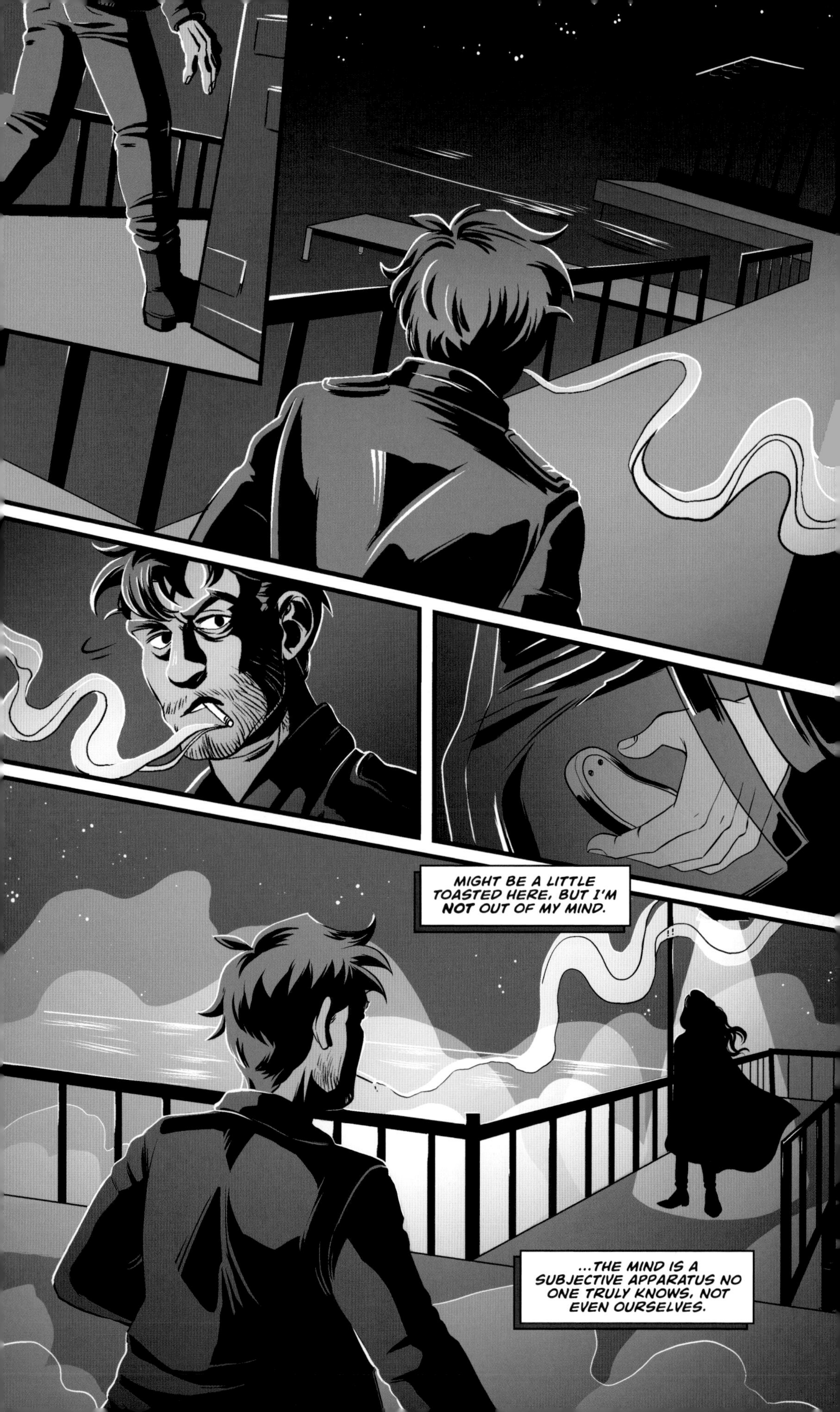
MIGHT BE A LITTLE TOASTED HERE, BUT I'M NOT OUT OF MY MIND.
...THE MIND IS A SUBJECTIVE APPARATUS NO ONE TRULY KNOWS, NOT EVEN OURSELVES.

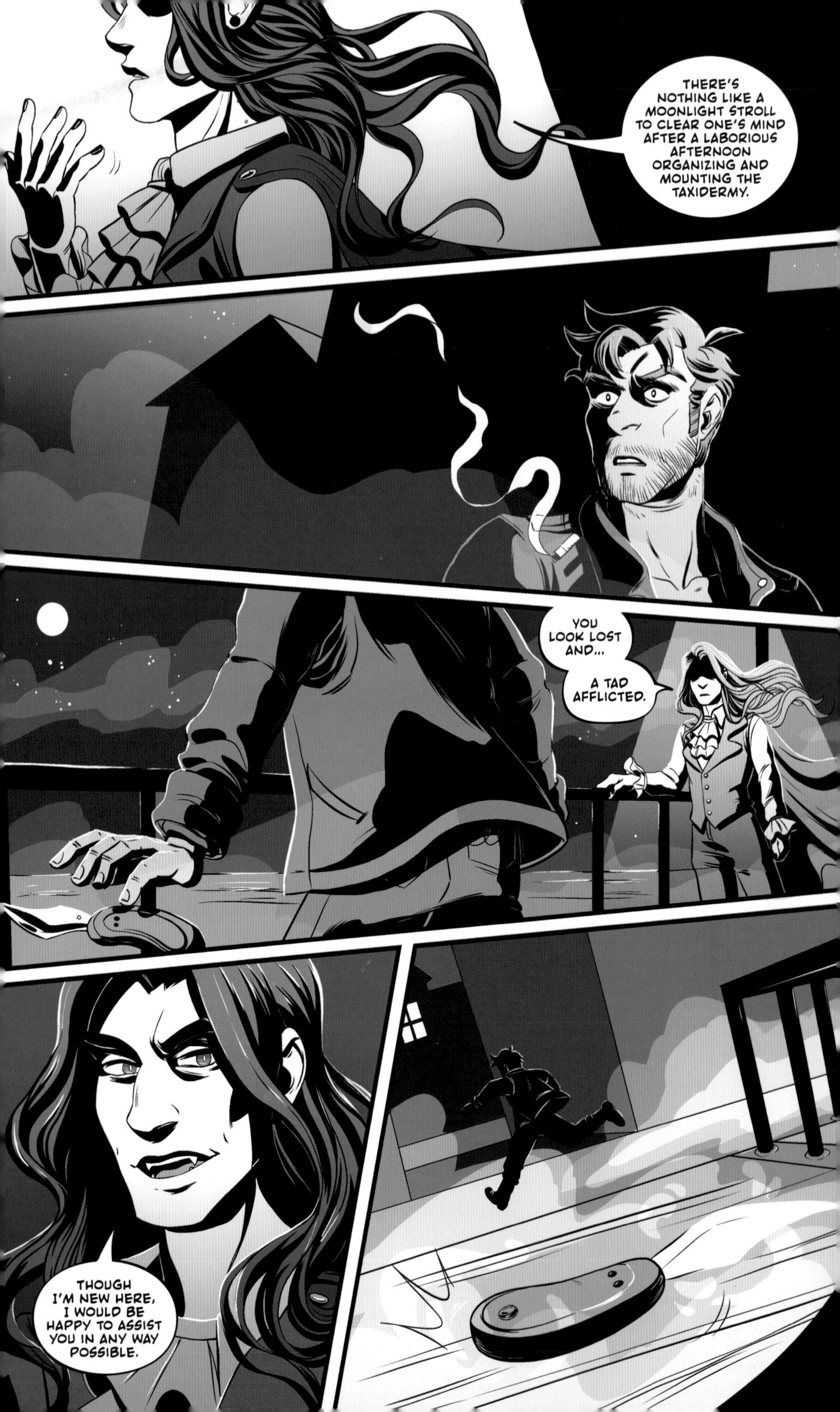
THERE'S NOTHING LIKE A MOONLIGHT STROLL TO CLEAR ONE'S MIND AFTER A LABORIOUS AFTERNOON ORGANIZING AND MOUNTING THE TAXIDERMY.
YOU LOOK LOST AND...
A TAD AFFLICTED.
THOUGH I'M NEW HERE, I WOULD BE HAPPY TO ASSIST YOU IN ANY WAY POSSIBLE.

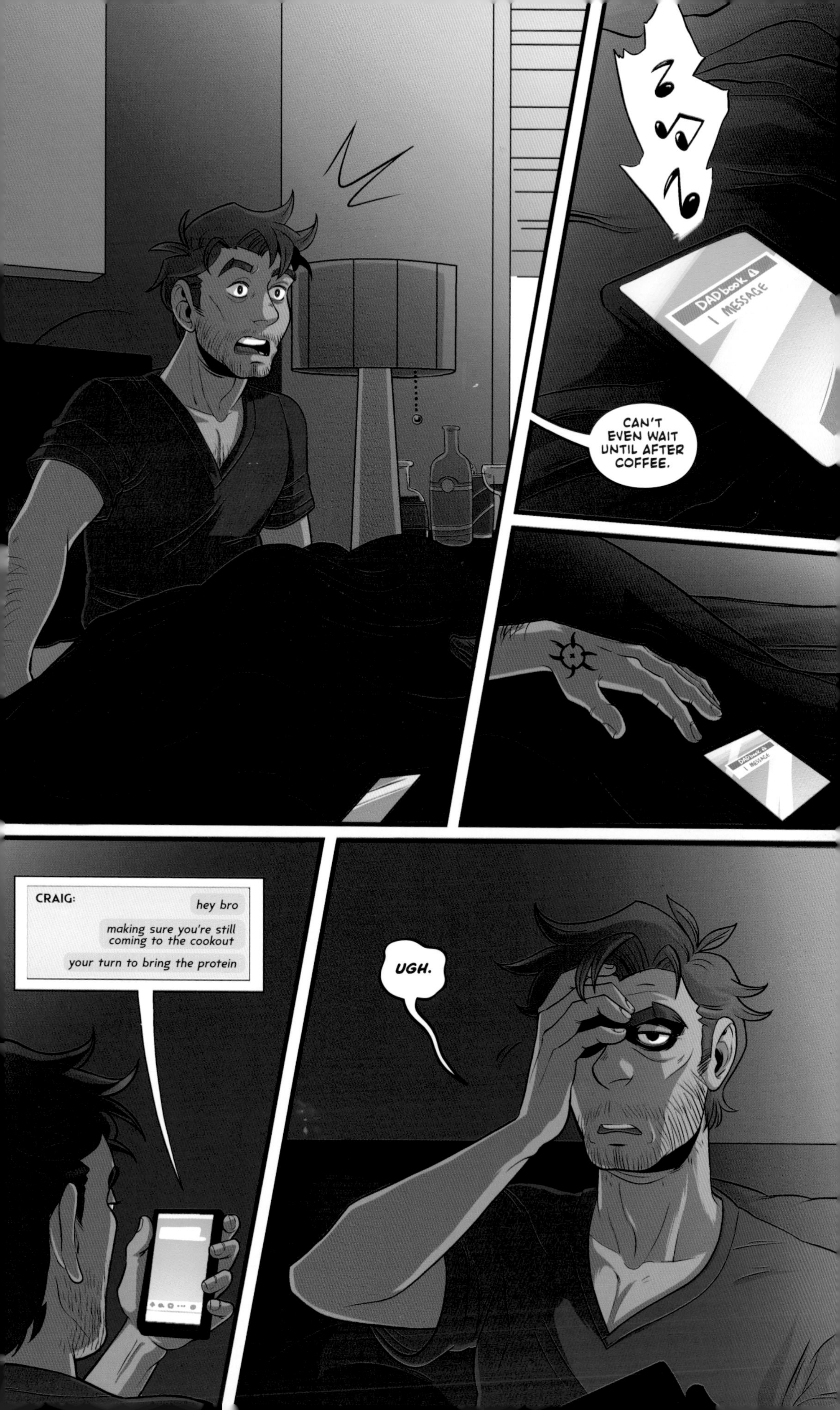
DADbook
1 MESSAGE
CAN'T EVEN WAIT UNTIL AFTER COFFEE.
CRAIG:
hey bro
making sure you're still coming to the cookout
your turn to bring the protein
UGH.

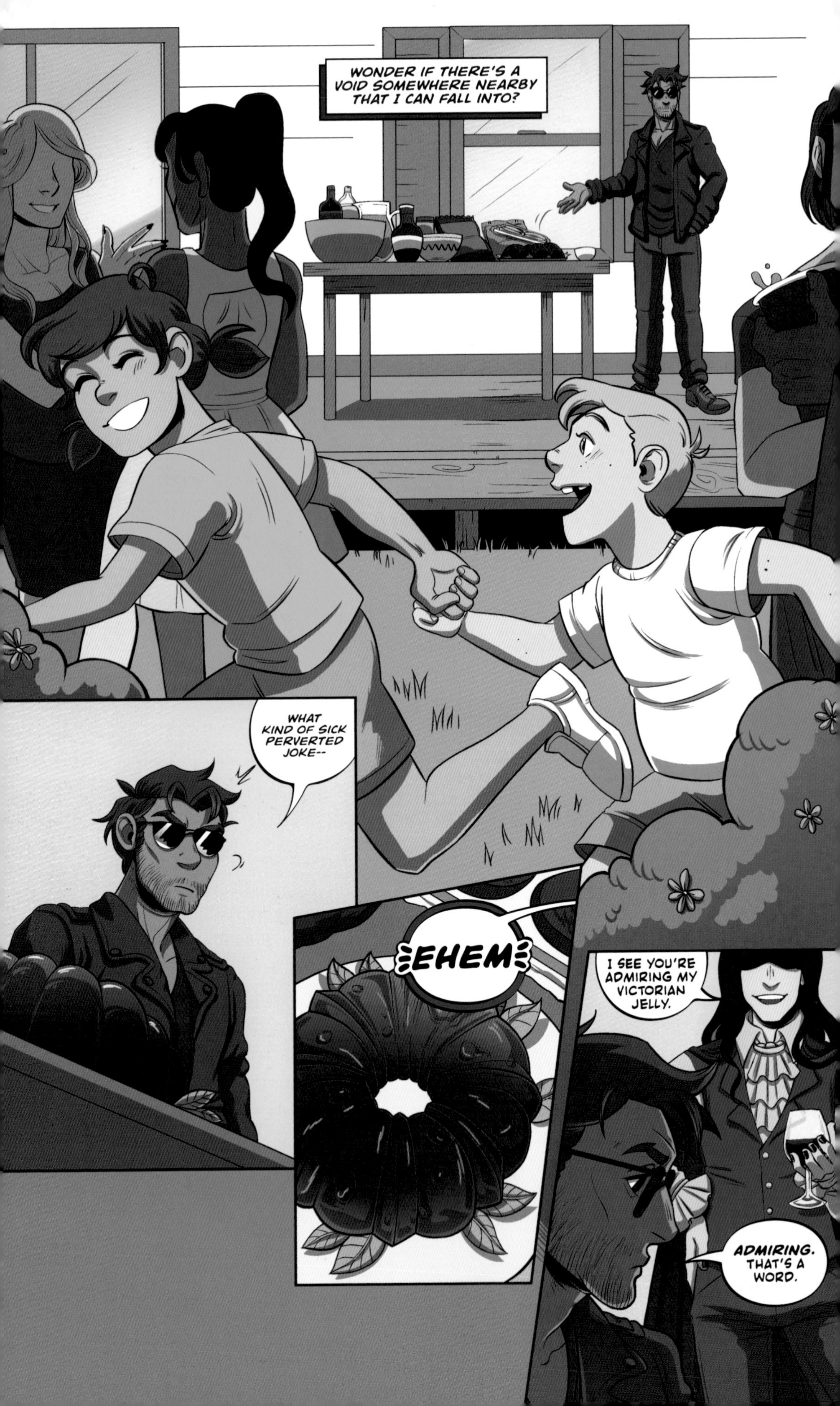
WONDER IF THERE'S A VOID SOMEWHERE NEARBY THAT I CAN FALL INTO?
WHAT KIND OF SICK PERVERTED JOKE--
EHEM
I SEE YOU'RE ADMIRING MY VICTORIAN JELLY.
ADMIRING. THAT'S A WORD.

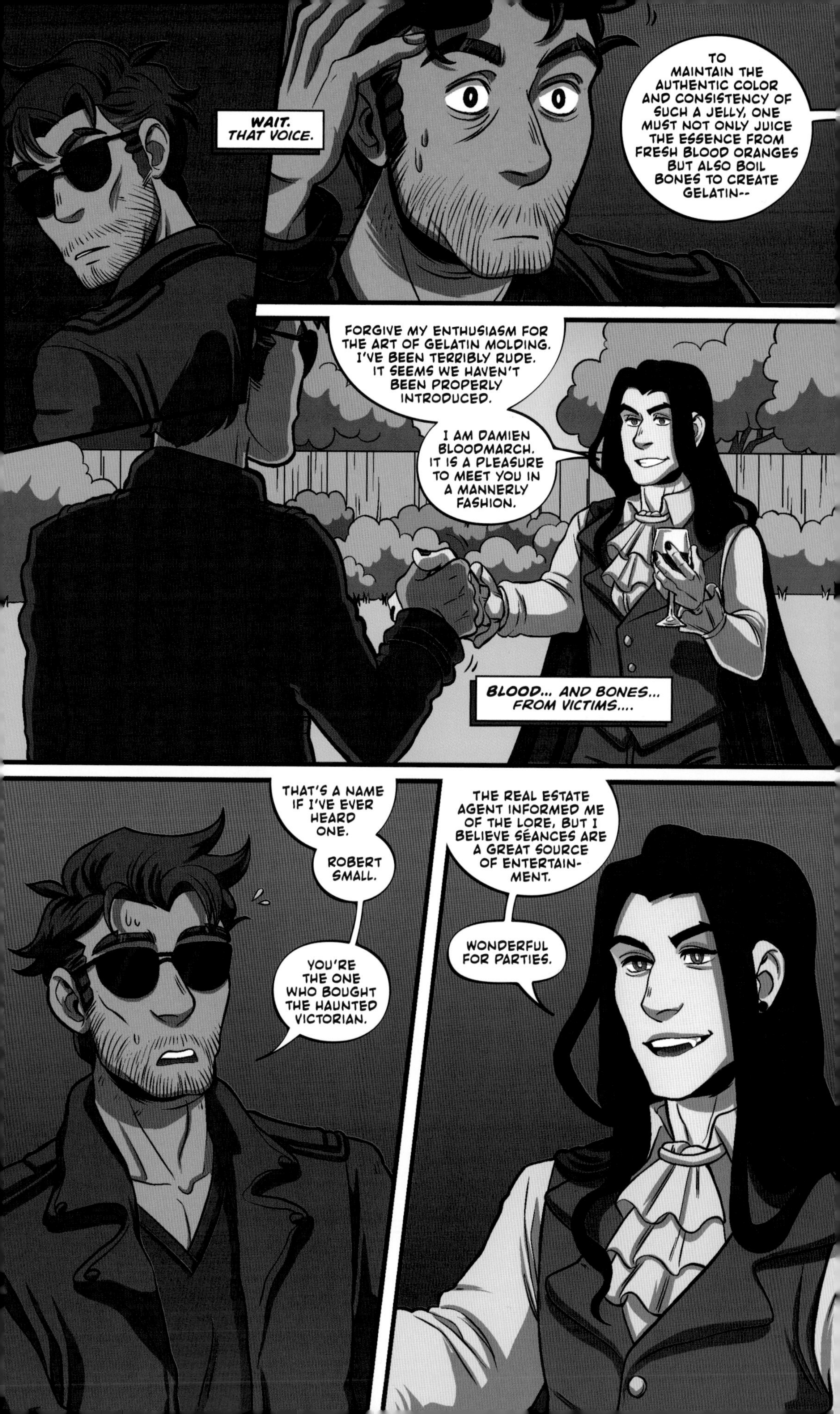
WAIT. THAT VOICE.
TO MAINTAIN THE AUTHENTIC COLOR AND CONSISTENCY OF SUCH A JELLY, ONE MUST NOT ONLY JUICE THE ESSENCE FROM FRESH BLOOD ORANGES BUT ALSO BOIL BONES TO CREATE GELATIN--
FORGIVE MY ENTHUSIASM FOR THE ART OF GELATIN MOLDING. I'VE BEEN TERRIBLY RUDE. IT SEEMS WE HAVEN'T BEEN PROPERLY INTRODUCED.
I AM DAMIEN BLOODMARCH. IT IS A PLEASURE TO MEET YOU IN A MANNERLY FASHION.
BLOOD... AND BONES... FROM VICTIMS....
THAT'S A NAME IF I'VE EVER HEARD ONE.
ROBERT SMALL.
YOU'RE THE ONE WHO BOUGHT THE HAUNTED VICTORIAN.
THE REAL ESTATE AGENT INFORMED ME OF THE LORE, BUT I BELIEVE SÉANCES ARE A GREAT SOURCE OF ENTERTAIN-MENT.
WONDERFUL FOR PARTIES.

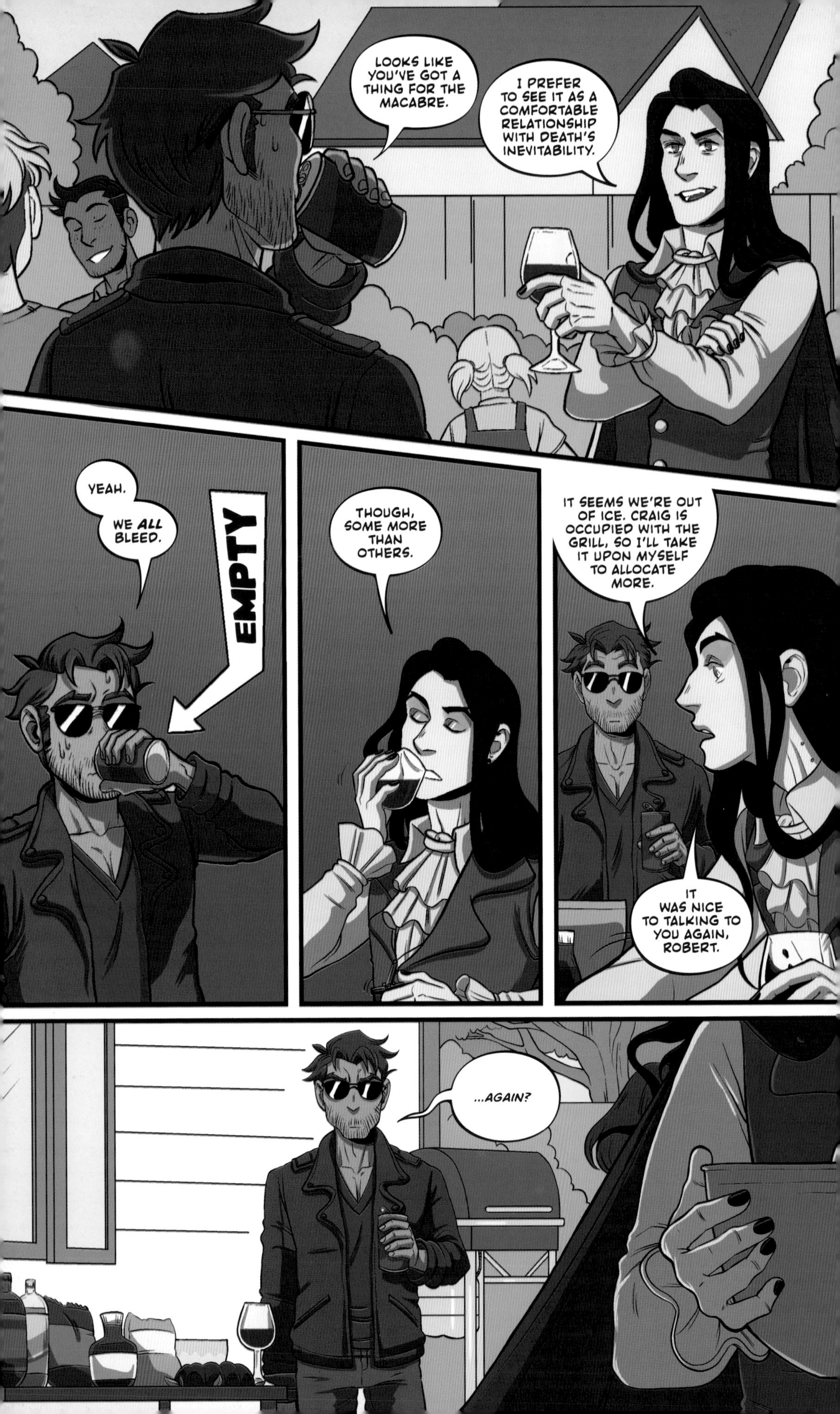
LOOKS LIKE YOU'VE GOT A THING FOR THE MACABRE.
I PREFER TO SEE IT AS A COMFORTABLE RELATIONSHIP WITH DEATH'S INEVITABILITY.
YEAH.
WE *ALL* BLEED.
EMPTY
THOUGH, SOME MORE THAN OTHERS.
IT SEEMS WE'RE OUT OF ICE. CRAIG IS OCCUPIED WITH THE GRILL, SO I'LL TAKE IT UPON MYSELF TO ALLOCATE MORE.
IT WAS NICE TO TALKING TO YOU AGAIN, ROBERT.
...AGAIN?

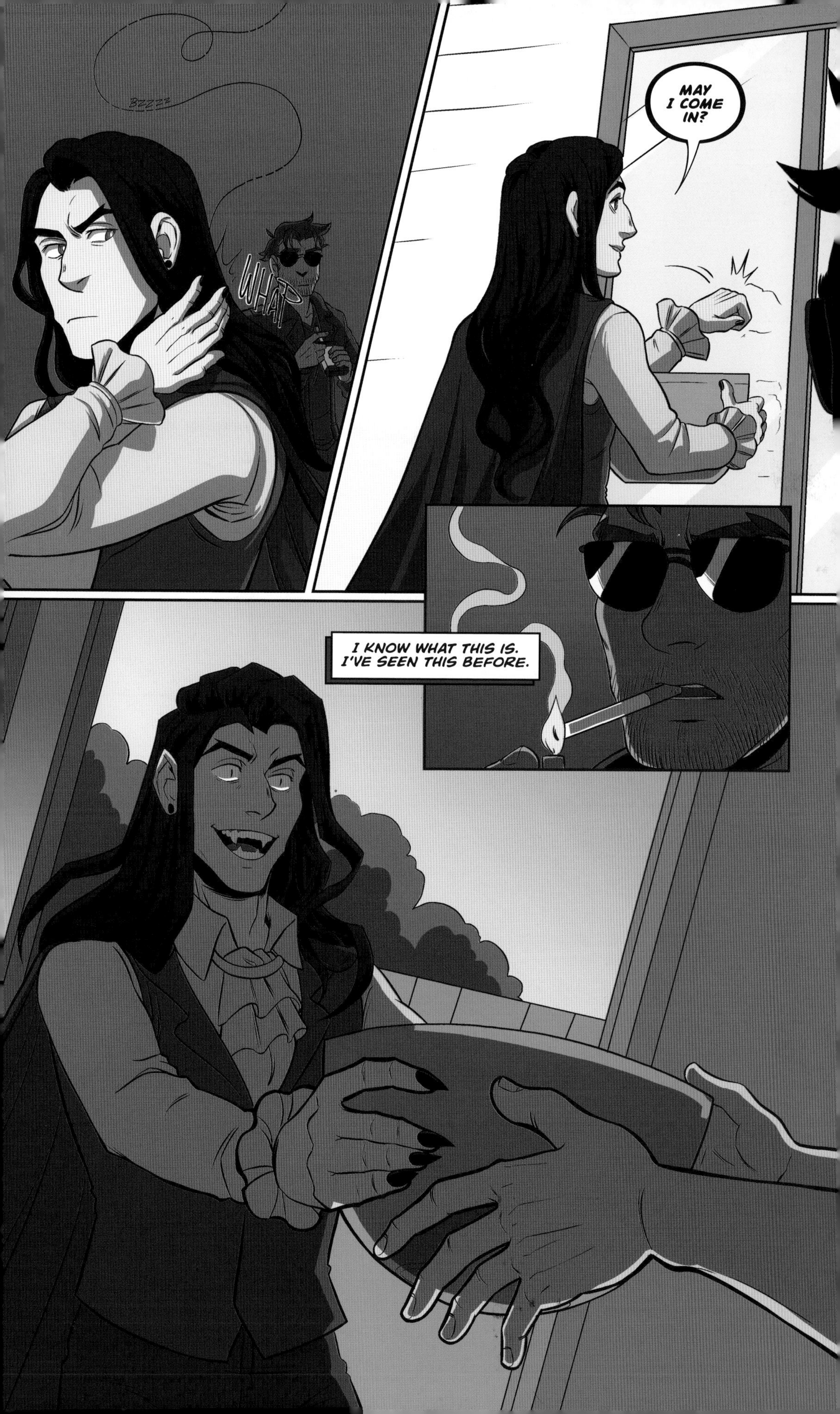
BZZZZ
WHAT
MAY I COME IN?
I KNOW WHAT THIS IS. I'VE SEEN THIS BEFORE.

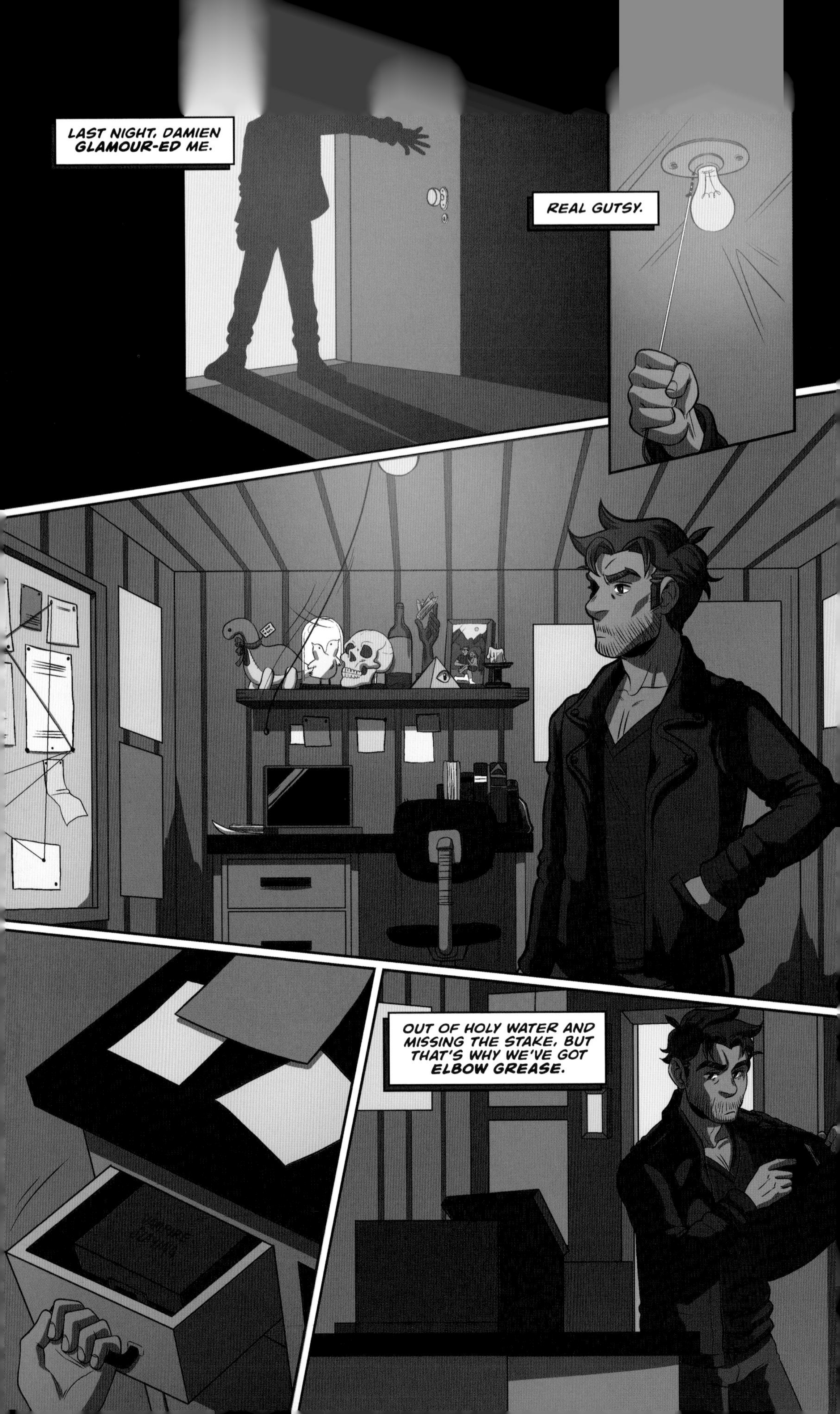
LAST NIGHT, DAMIEN GLAMOUR-ED ME.
REAL GUTSY.
OUT OF HOLY WATER AND MISSING THE STAKE, BUT THAT'S WHY WE'VE GOT ELBOW GREASE.

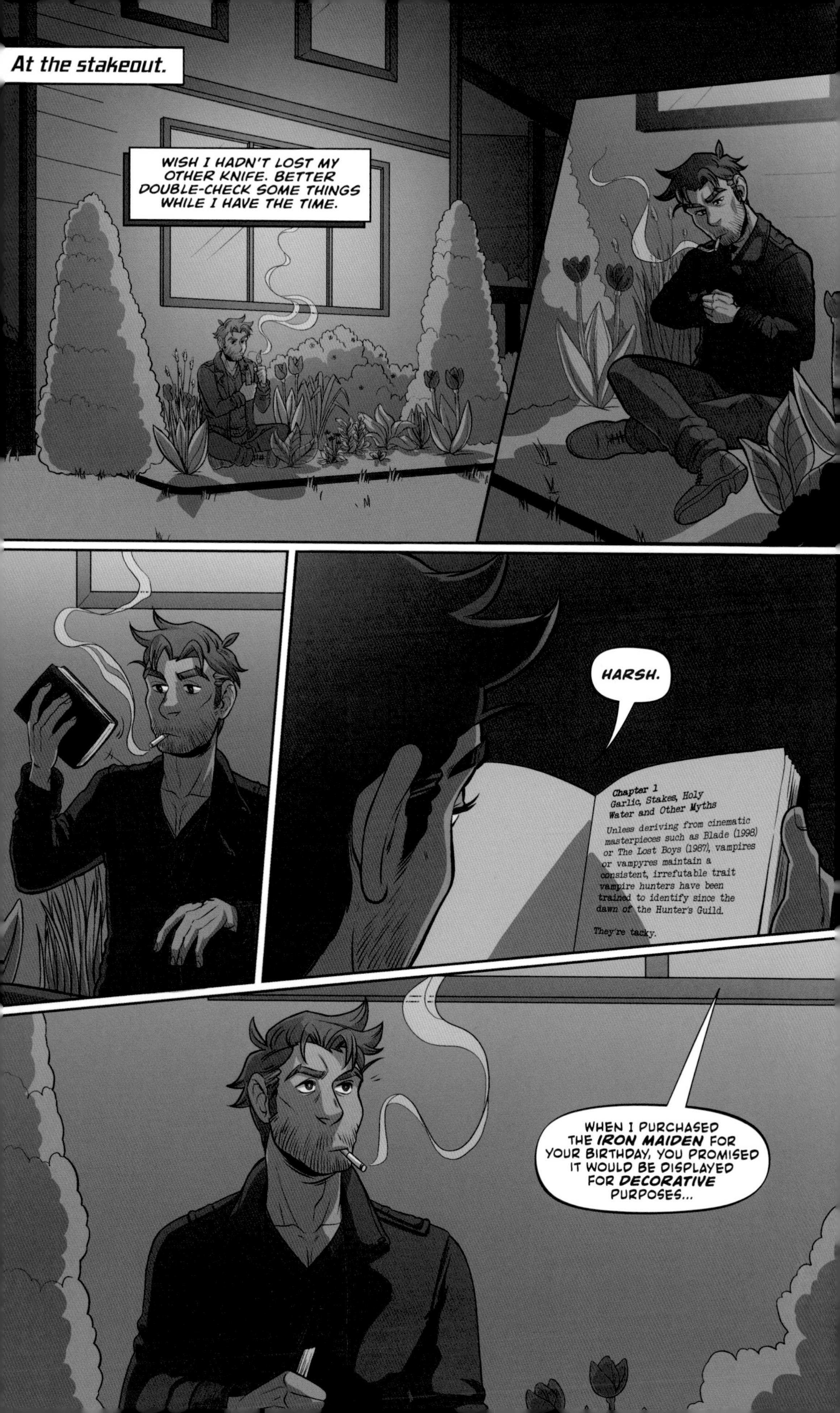
At the stakeout.
WISH I HADN'T LOST MY OTHER KNIFE. BETTER DOUBLE-CHECK SOME THINGS WHILE I HAVE THE TIME.
HARSH.
Chapter 1
Garlic, Stakes, Holy Water and Other Myths
Unless deriving from cinematic masterpieces such as Blade (1998) or The Lost Boys (1987), vampires or vampyres maintain a consistent, irrefutable trait vampire hunters have been trained to identify since the dawn of the Hunter's Guild.
They're tacky.
WHEN I PURCHASED THE ***IRON MAIDEN*** FOR YOUR BIRTHDAY, YOU PROMISED IT WOULD BE DISPLAYED FOR ***DECORATIVE*** PURPOSES...

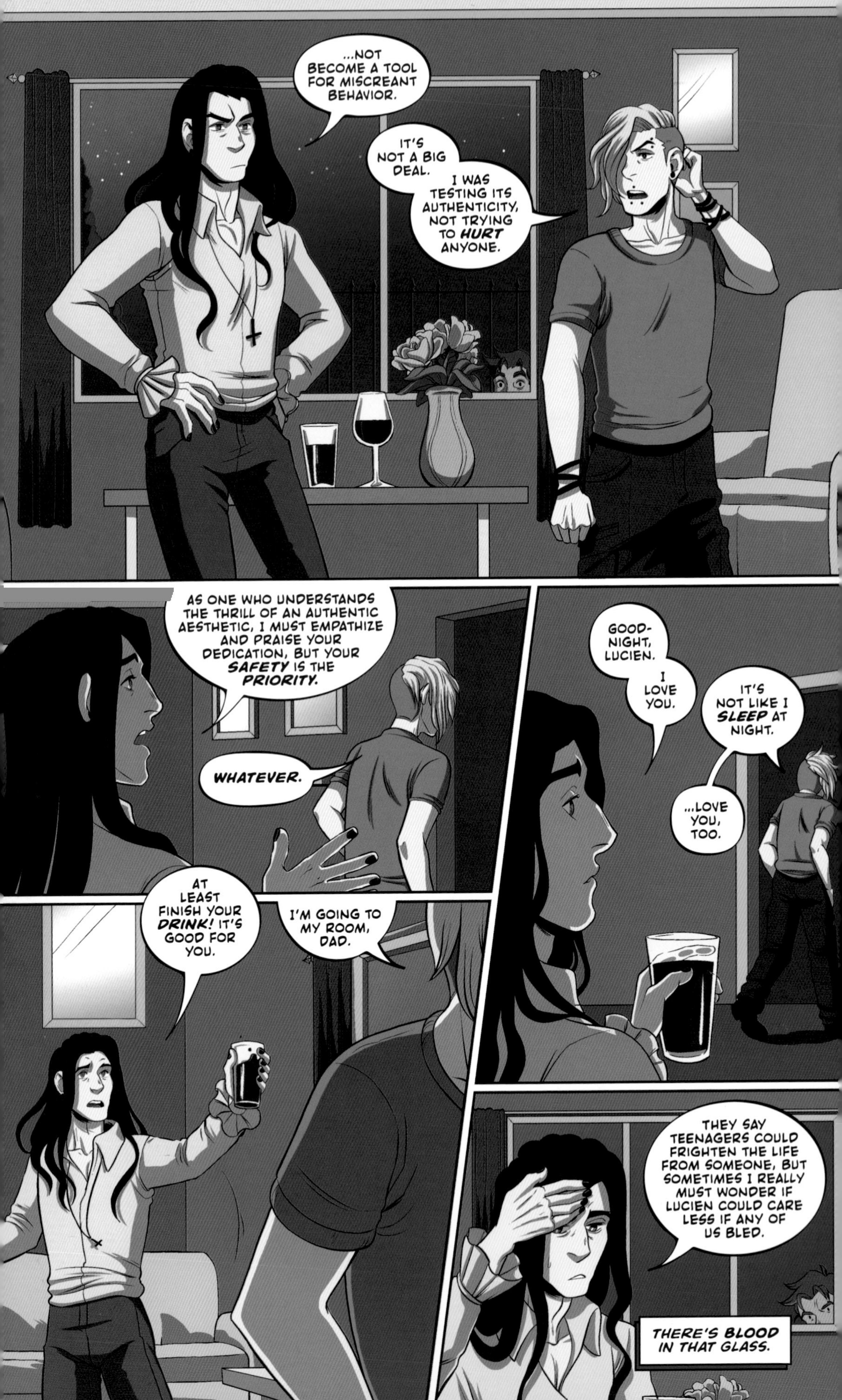
...NOT BECOME A TOOL FOR MISCREANT BEHAVIOR.
IT'S NOT A BIG DEAL.
I WAS TESTING ITS AUTHENTICITY, NOT TRYING TO ***HURT*** ANYONE.
AS ONE WHO UNDERSTANDS THE THRILL OF AN AUTHENTIC AESTHETIC, I MUST EMPATHIZE AND PRAISE YOUR DEDICATION, BUT YOUR ***SAFETY*** IS THE ***PRIORITY.***
WHATEVER.
AT LEAST FINISH YOUR ***DRINK!*** IT'S GOOD FOR YOU.
I'M GOING TO MY ROOM, DAD.
GOOD-NIGHT, LUCIEN.
I LOVE YOU.
IT'S NOT LIKE I ***SLEEP*** AT NIGHT.
...LOVE YOU, TOO.
THEY SAY TEENAGERS COULD FRIGHTEN THE LIFE FROM SOMEONE, BUT SOMETIMES I REALLY MUST WONDER IF LUCIEN COULD CARE LESS IF ANY OF US BLED.
*THERE'S **BLOOD** IN THAT GLASS.*

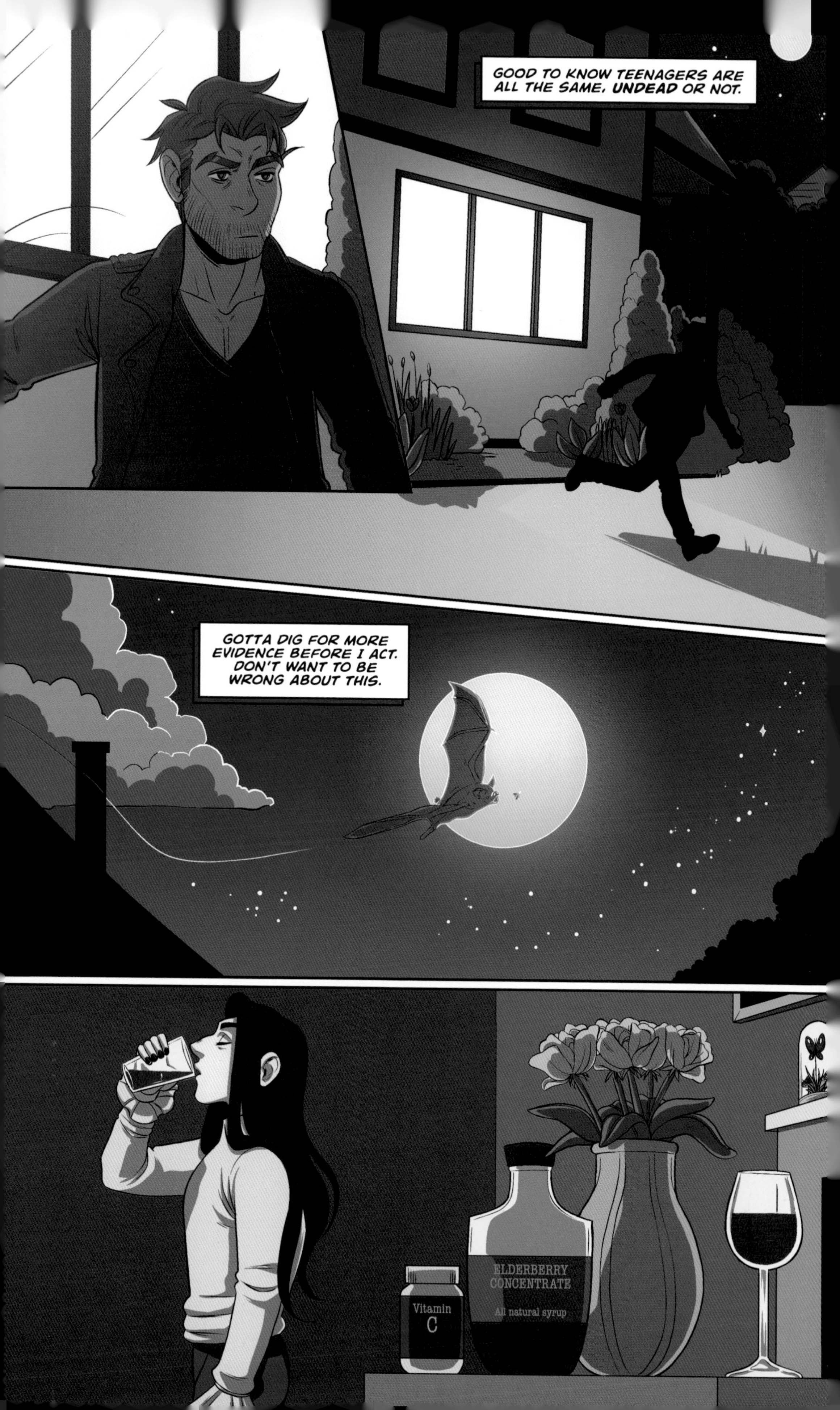
GOOD TO KNOW TEENAGERS ARE ALL THE SAME, UNDEAD OR NOT.
GOTTA DIG FOR MORE EVIDENCE BEFORE I ACT. DON'T WANT TO BE WRONG ABOUT THIS.
Vitamin C
ELDERBERRY CONCENTRATE
All natural syrup

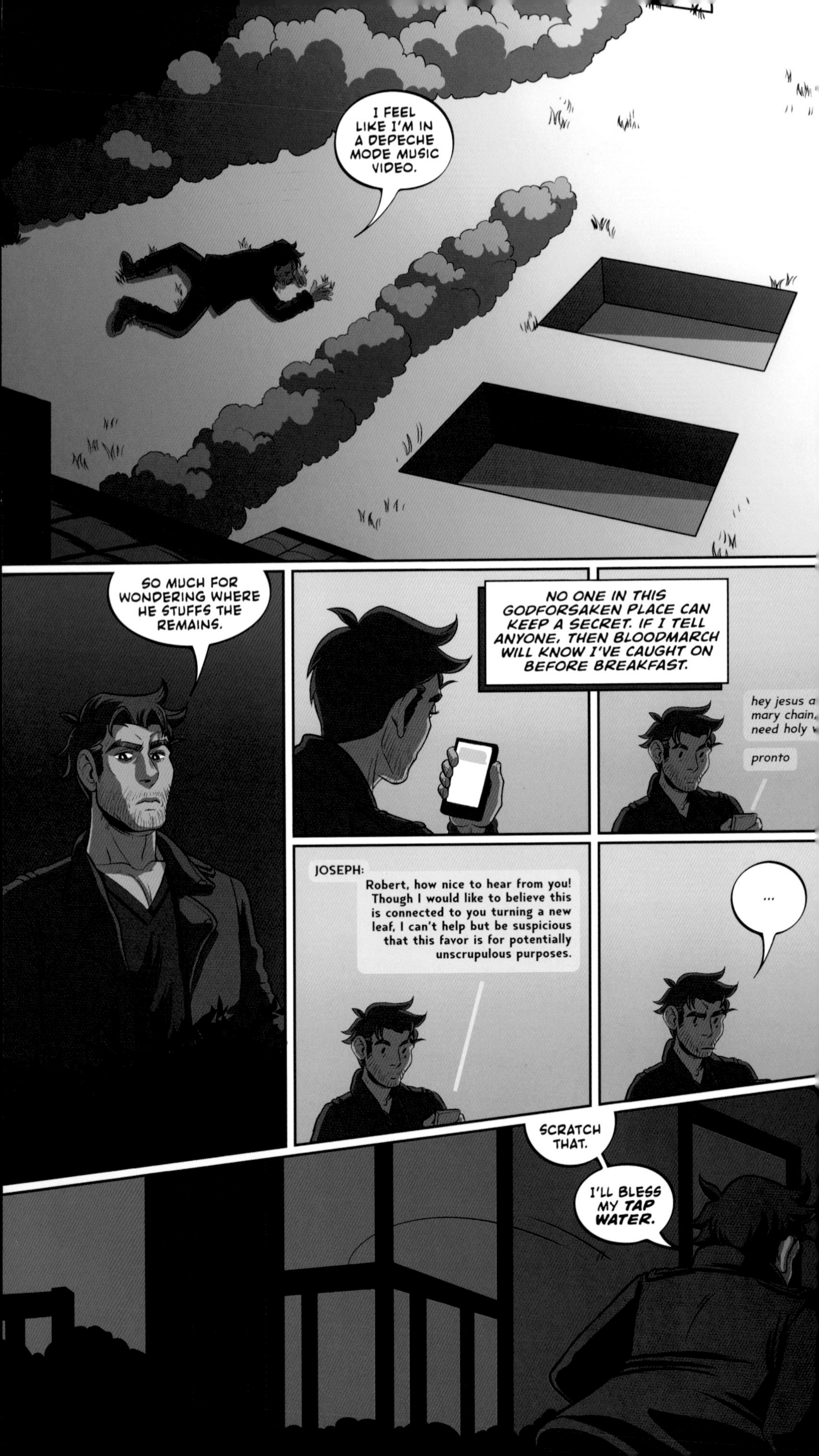

I FEEL LIKE I'M IN A DEPECHE MODE MUSIC VIDEO.
SO MUCH FOR WONDERING WHERE HE STUFFS THE REMAINS.
NO ONE IN THIS GODFORSAKEN PLACE CAN KEEP A SECRET. IF I TELL ANYONE, THEN BLOODMARCH WILL KNOW I'VE CAUGHT ON BEFORE BREAKFAST.
hey jesus a
mary chain,
need holy
pronto
JOSEPH:
Robert, how nice to hear from you! Though I would like to believe this is connected to you turning a new leaf, I can't help but be suspicious that this favor is for potentially unscrupulous purposes.
...
SCRATCH THAT.
I'LL BLESS MY TAP WATER.

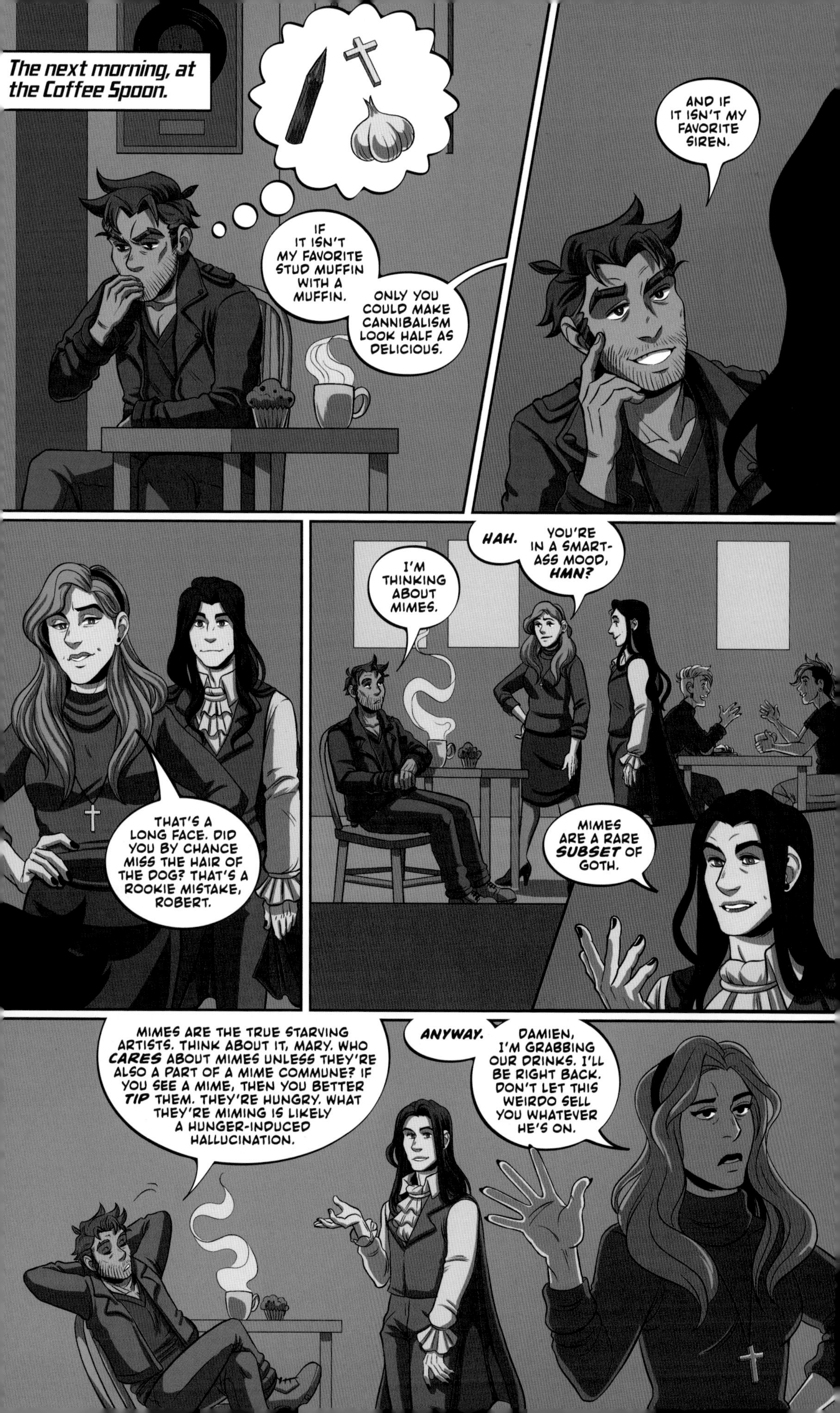
The next morning, at the Coffee Spoon.
IF IT ISN'T MY FAVORITE STUD MUFFIN WITH A MUFFIN.
ONLY YOU COULD MAKE CANNIBALISM LOOK HALF AS DELICIOUS.
AND IF IT ISN'T MY FAVORITE SIREN.
THAT'S A LONG FACE. DID YOU BY CHANCE MISS THE HAIR OF THE DOG? THAT'S A ROOKIE MISTAKE, ROBERT.
I'M THINKING ABOUT MIMES.
HAH.
YOU'RE IN A SMART-ASS MOOD, HMN?
MIMES ARE A RARE SUBSET OF GOTH.
MIMES ARE THE TRUE STARVING ARTISTS. THINK ABOUT IT, MARY. WHO CARES ABOUT MIMES UNLESS THEY'RE ALSO A PART OF A MIME COMMUNE? IF YOU SEE A MIME, THEN YOU BETTER TIP THEM. THEY'RE HUNGRY. WHAT THEY'RE MIMING IS LIKELY A HUNGER-INDUCED HALLUCINATION.
ANYWAY.
DAMIEN, I'M GRABBING OUR DRINKS. I'LL BE RIGHT BACK. DON'T LET THIS WEIRDO SELL YOU WHATEVER HE'S ON.

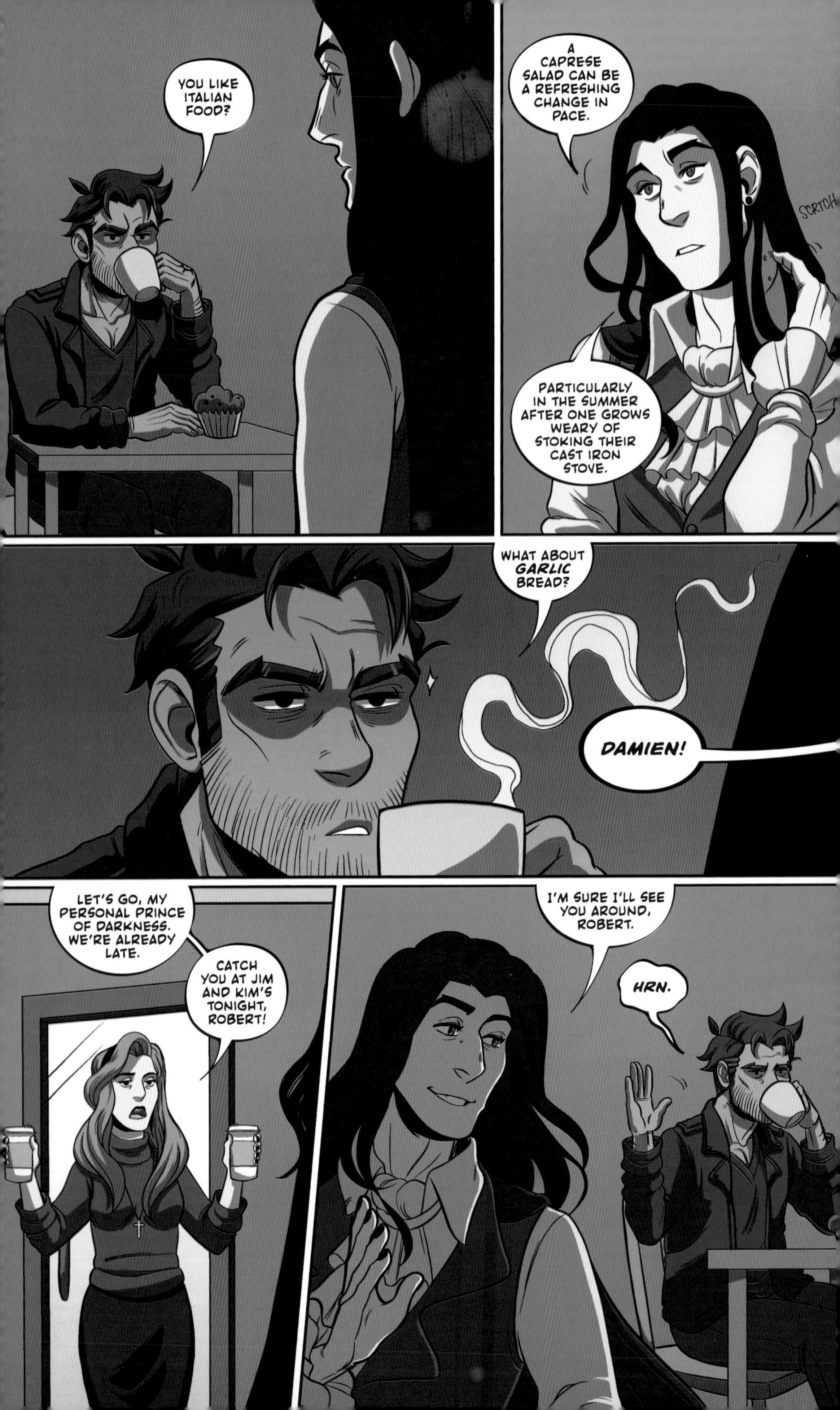

YOU LIKE ITALIAN FOOD?
A CAPRESE SALAD CAN BE A REFRESHING CHANGE IN PACE.
SCRTCH
PARTICULARLY IN THE SUMMER AFTER ONE GROWS WEARY OF STOKING THEIR CAST IRON STOVE.
WHAT ABOUT *GARLIC* BREAD?
DAMIEN!
LET'S GO, MY PERSONAL PRINCE OF DARKNESS. WE'RE ALREADY LATE.
CATCH YOU AT JIM AND KIM'S TONIGHT, ROBERT!
I'M SURE I'LL SEE YOU AROUND, ROBERT.
HRN.

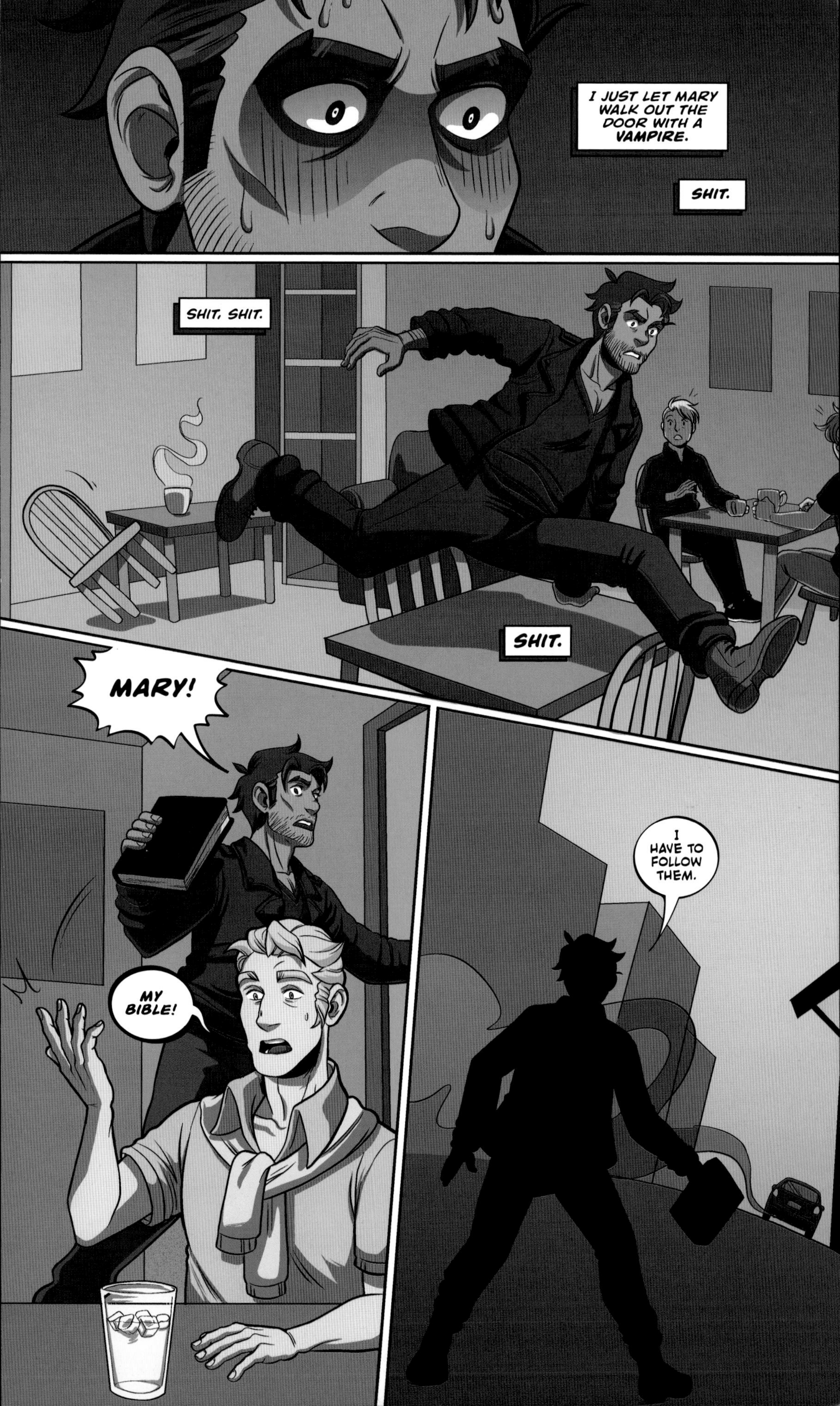
I JUST LET MARY WALK OUT THE DOOR WITH A VAMPIRE.
SHIT.
SHIT, SHIT.
SHIT.
MARY!
MY BIBLE!
I HAVE TO FOLLOW THEM.

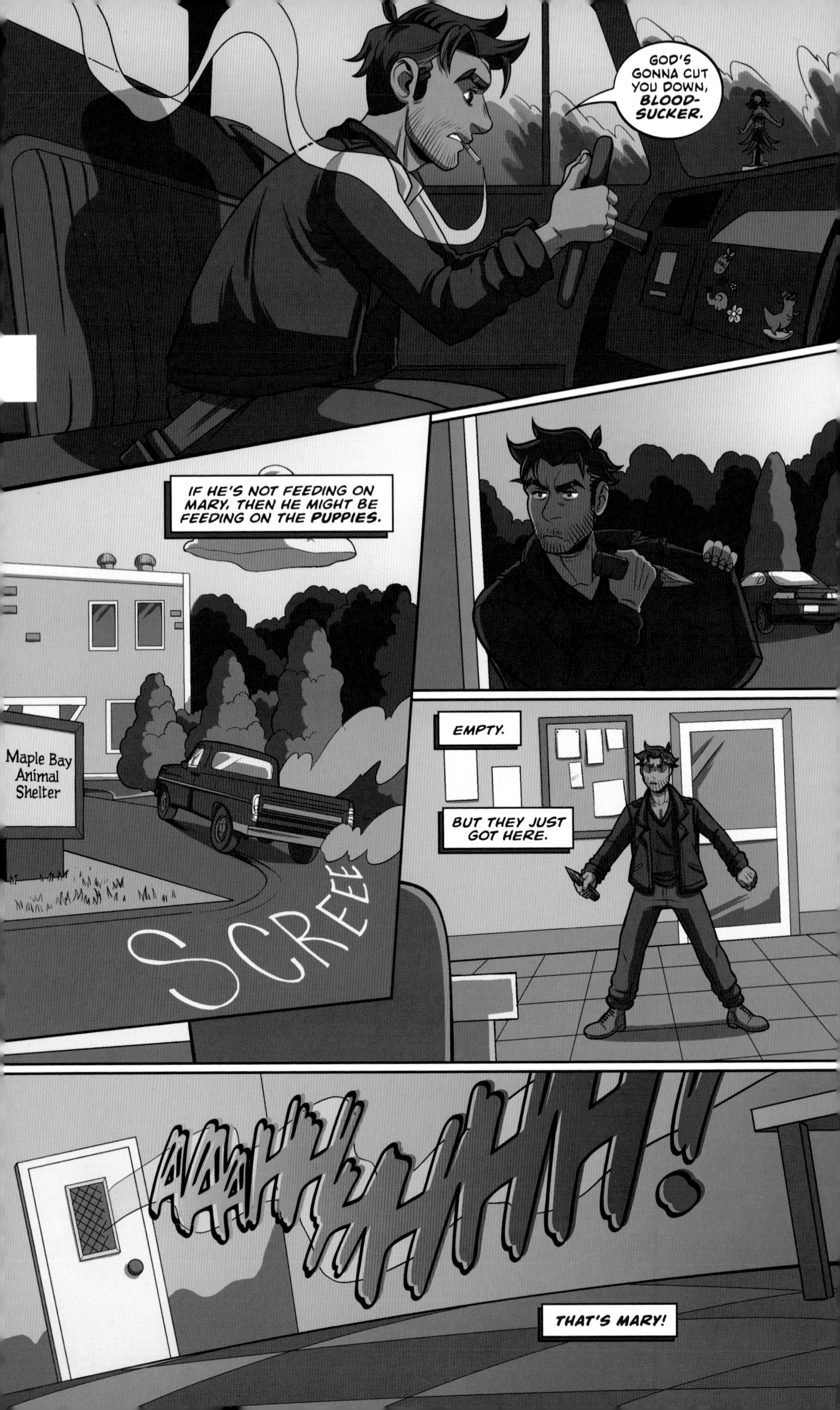
GOD'S GONNA CUT YOU DOWN, BLOOD-SUCKER.
IF HE'S NOT FEEDING ON MARY, THEN HE MIGHT BE FEEDING ON THE PUPPIES.
Maple Bay Animal Shelter
SCREEE
EMPTY.
BUT THEY JUST GOT HERE.
AAHHHHHH!
THAT'S MARY!

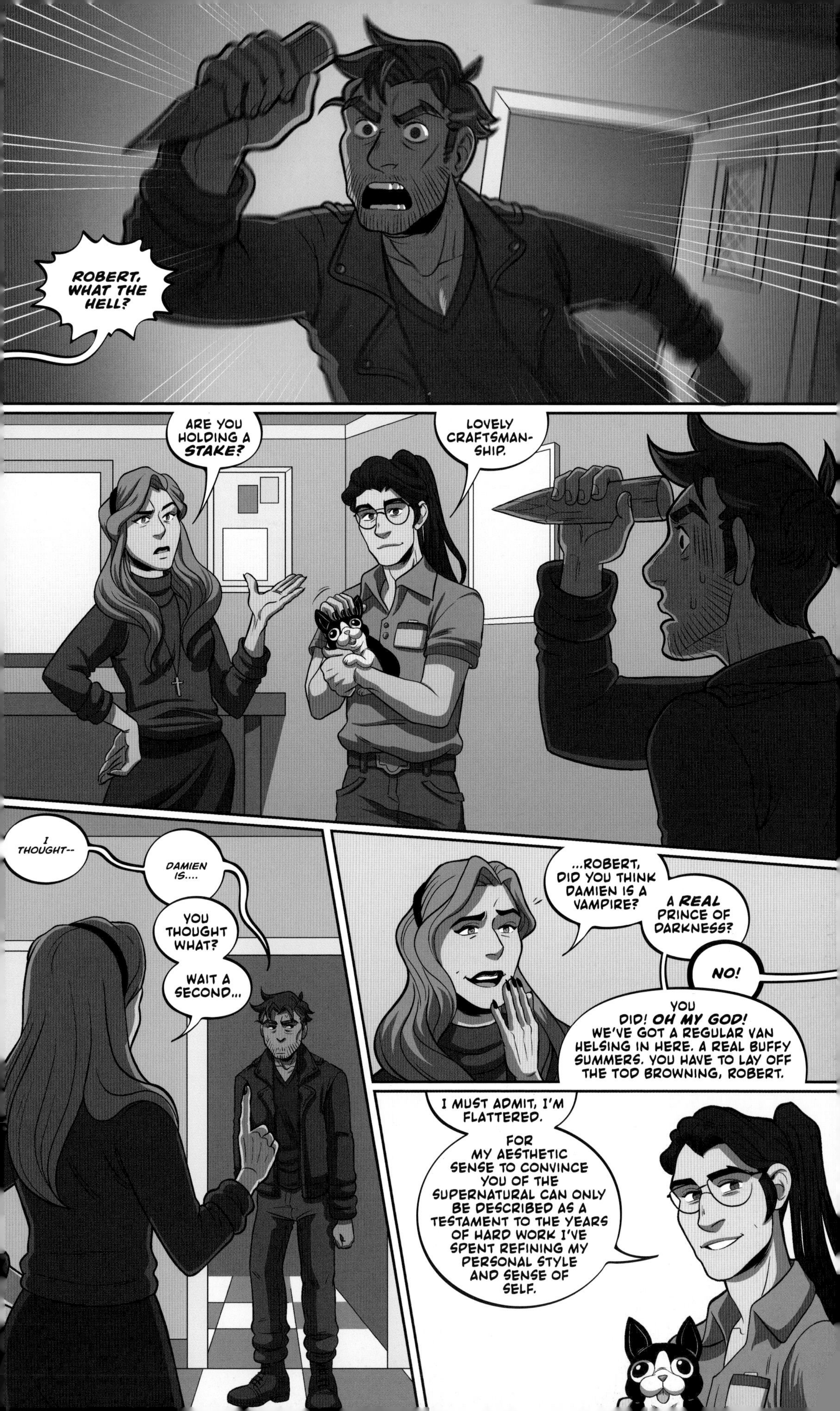

ROBERT, WHAT THE HELL?
ARE YOU HOLDING A *STAKE?*
LOVELY CRAFTSMAN-SHIP.
I THOUGHT--
DAMIEN IS....
YOU THOUGHT WHAT?
WAIT A SECOND...
...ROBERT, DID YOU THINK DAMIEN IS A VAMPIRE?
A *REAL* PRINCE OF DARKNESS?
NO!
YOU DID! ***OH MY GOD!*** WE'VE GOT A REGULAR VAN HELSING IN HERE. A REAL BUFFY SUMMERS. YOU HAVE TO LAY OFF THE TOD BROWNING, ROBERT.
I MUST ADMIT, I'M FLATTERED.
FOR MY AESTHETIC SENSE TO CONVINCE YOU OF THE SUPERNATURAL CAN ONLY BE DESCRIBED AS A TESTAMENT TO THE YEARS OF HARD WORK I'VE SPENT REFINING MY PERSONAL STYLE AND SENSE OF SELF.

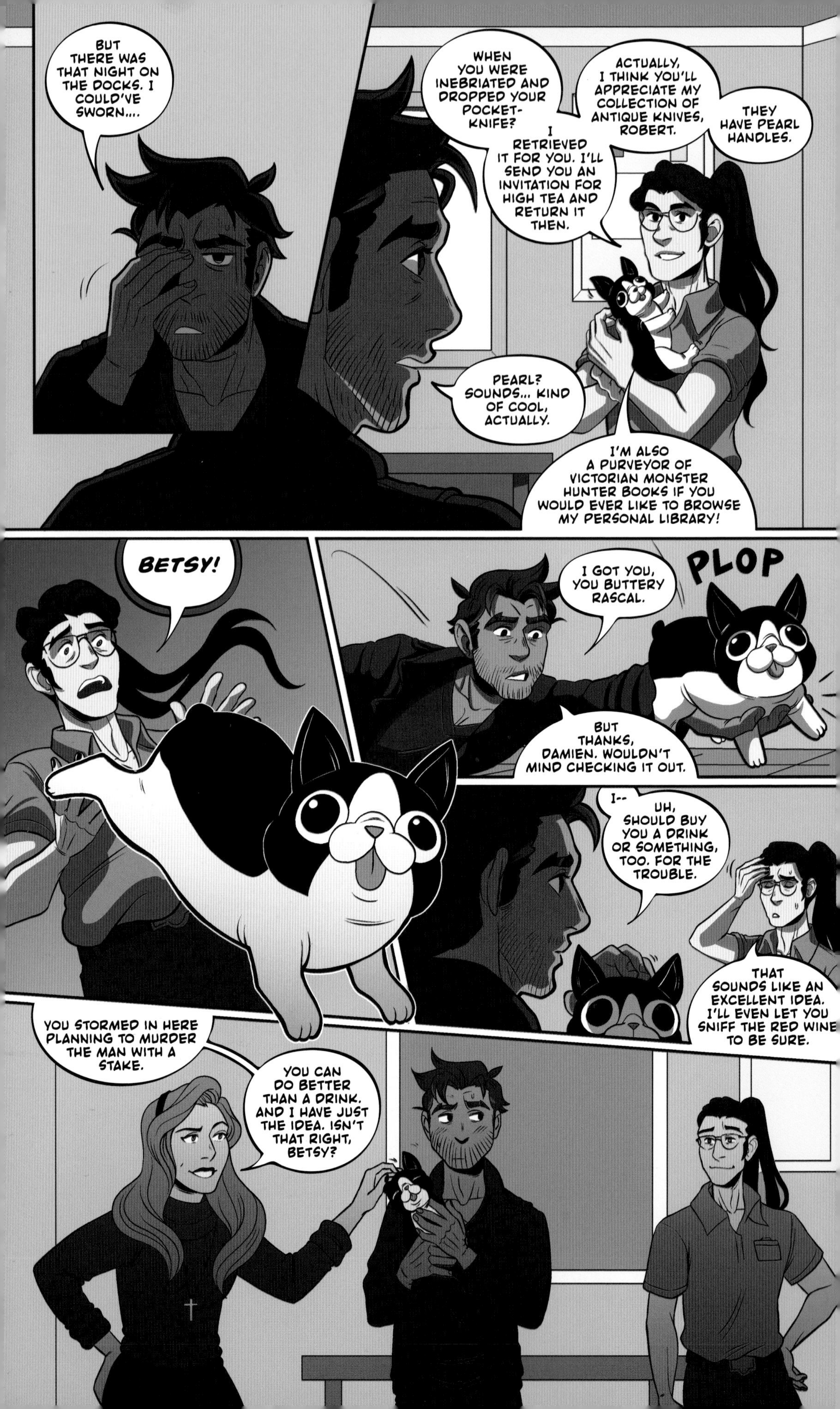
BUT THERE WAS THAT NIGHT ON THE DOCKS. I COULD'VE SWORN....
WHEN YOU WERE INEBRIATED AND DROPPED YOUR POCKET-KNIFE?
I RETRIEVED IT FOR YOU. I'LL SEND YOU AN INVITATION FOR HIGH TEA AND RETURN IT THEN.
ACTUALLY, I THINK YOU'LL APPRECIATE MY COLLECTION OF ANTIQUE KNIVES, ROBERT.
THEY HAVE PEARL HANDLES.
PEARL? SOUNDS... KIND OF COOL, ACTUALLY.
I'M ALSO A PURVEYOR OF VICTORIAN MONSTER HUNTER BOOKS IF YOU WOULD EVER LIKE TO BROWSE MY PERSONAL LIBRARY!
BETSY!
PLOP
I GOT YOU, YOU BUTTERY RASCAL.
BUT THANKS, DAMIEN. WOULDN'T MIND CHECKING IT OUT.
I--
UH, SHOULD BUY YOU A DRINK OR SOMETHING, TOO. FOR THE TROUBLE.
THAT SOUNDS LIKE AN EXCELLENT IDEA. I'LL EVEN LET YOU SNIFF THE RED WINE TO BE SURE.
YOU STORMED IN HERE PLANNING TO MURDER THE MAN WITH A STAKE.
YOU CAN DO BETTER THAN A DRINK. AND I HAVE JUST THE IDEA. ISN'T THAT RIGHT, BETSY?

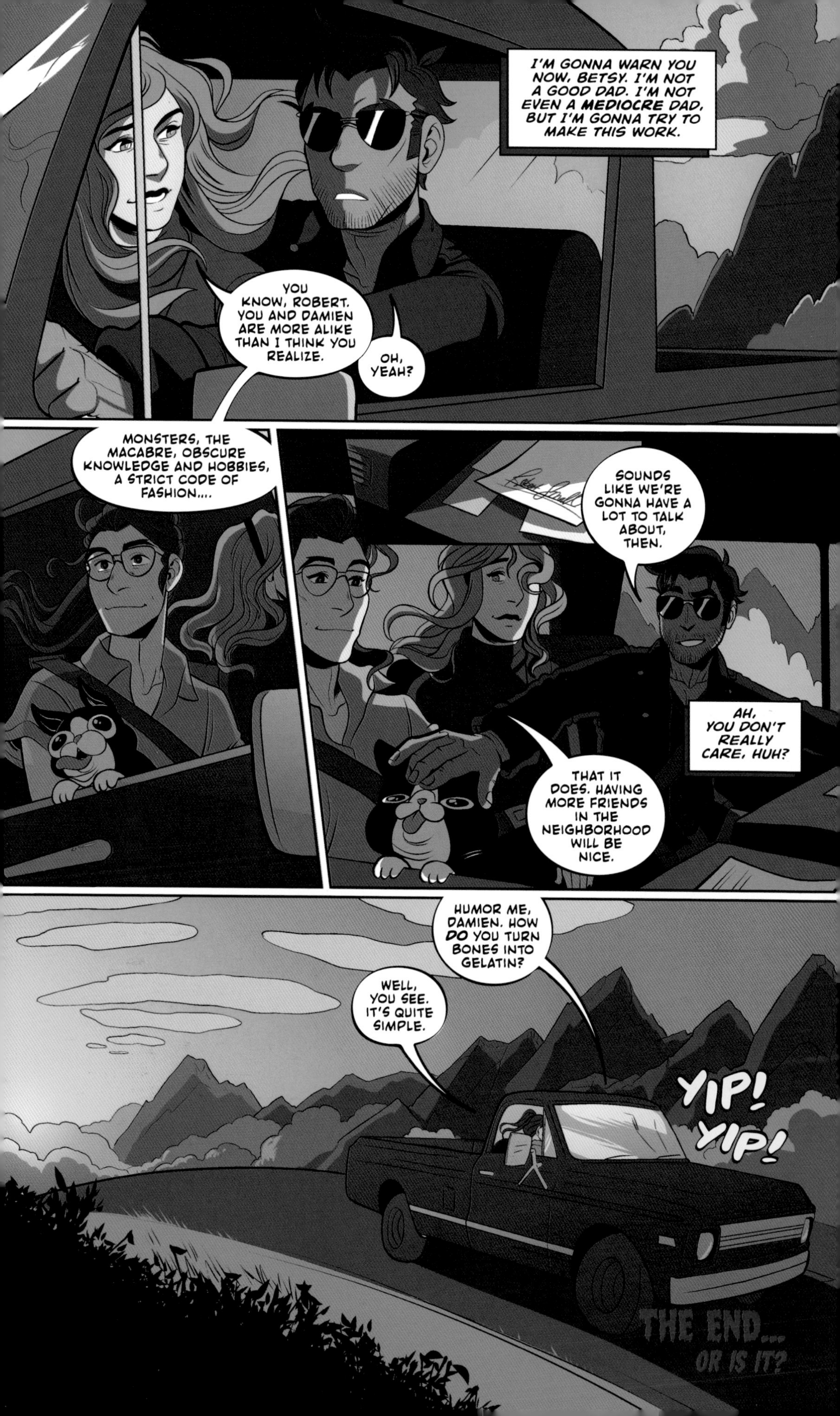
I'M GONNA WARN YOU NOW, BETSY. I'M NOT A GOOD DAD. I'M NOT EVEN A MEDIOCRE DAD, BUT I'M GONNA TRY TO MAKE THIS WORK.
YOU KNOW, ROBERT. YOU AND DAMIEN ARE MORE ALIKE THAN I THINK YOU REALIZE.
OH, YEAH?
MONSTERS, THE MACABRE, OBSCURE KNOWLEDGE AND HOBBIES, A STRICT CODE OF FASHION....
SOUNDS LIKE WE'RE GONNA HAVE A LOT TO TALK ABOUT, THEN.
AH, YOU DON'T REALLY CARE, HUH?
THAT IT DOES. HAVING MORE FRIENDS IN THE NEIGHBORHOOD WILL BE NICE.
HUMOR ME, DAMIEN. HOW DO YOU TURN BONES INTO GELATIN?
WELL, YOU SEE. IT'S QUITE SIMPLE.
YIP! YIP!
THE END...
OR IS IT?

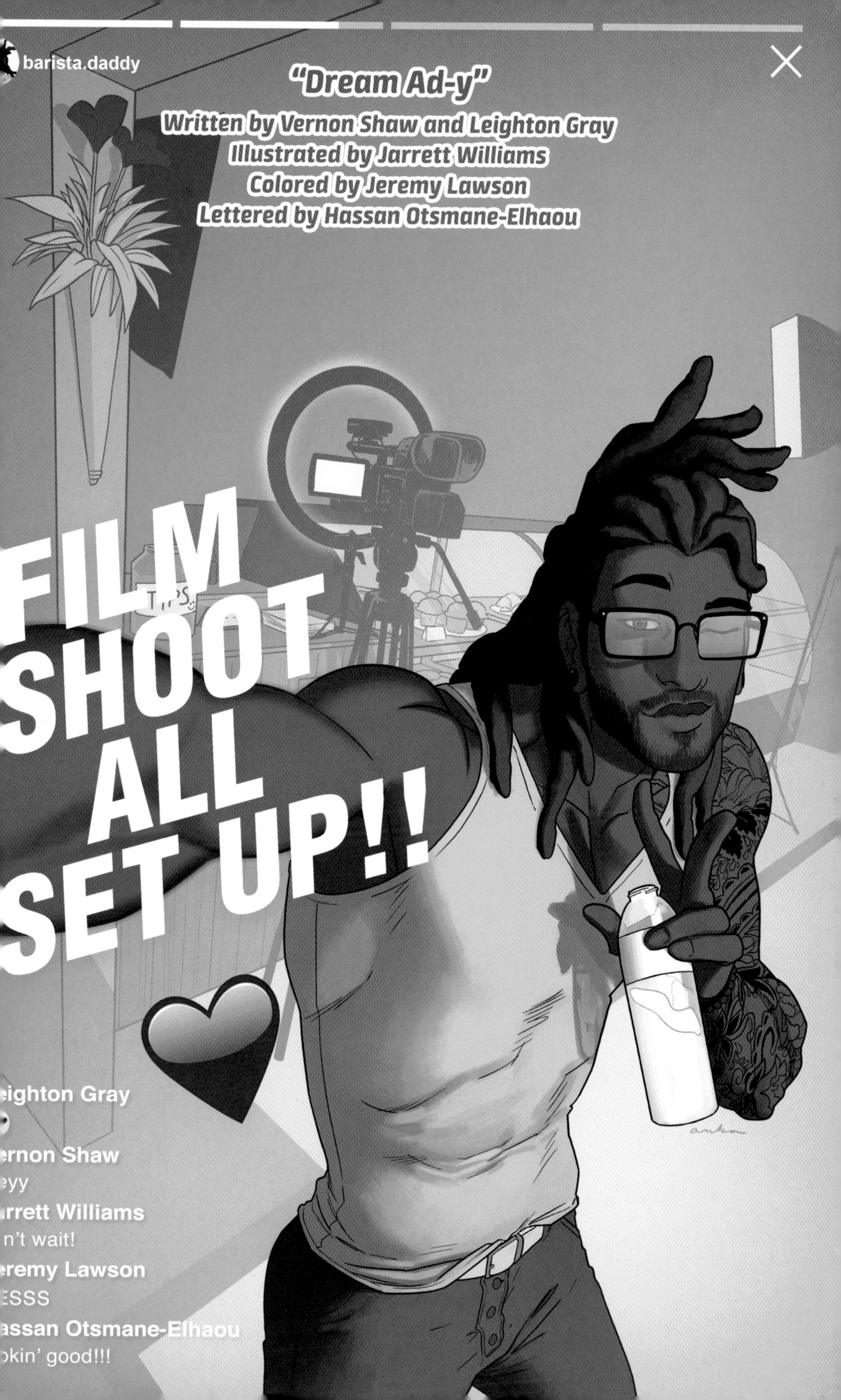
barista.daddy
“Dream Ad-y”
Written by Vernon Shaw and Leighton Gray
Illustrated by Jarrett Williams
Colored by Jeremy Lawson
Lettered by Hassan Otsmane-Elhaou
TIPS
FILM SHOOT ALL SET UP!!
ighton Gray
rnon Shaw
yy
rrett Williams
n't wait!
remy Lawson
SSS
ssan Otsmane-Elhaou
kin' good!!!

Cover by Jarrett Williams and Jeremy Lawson

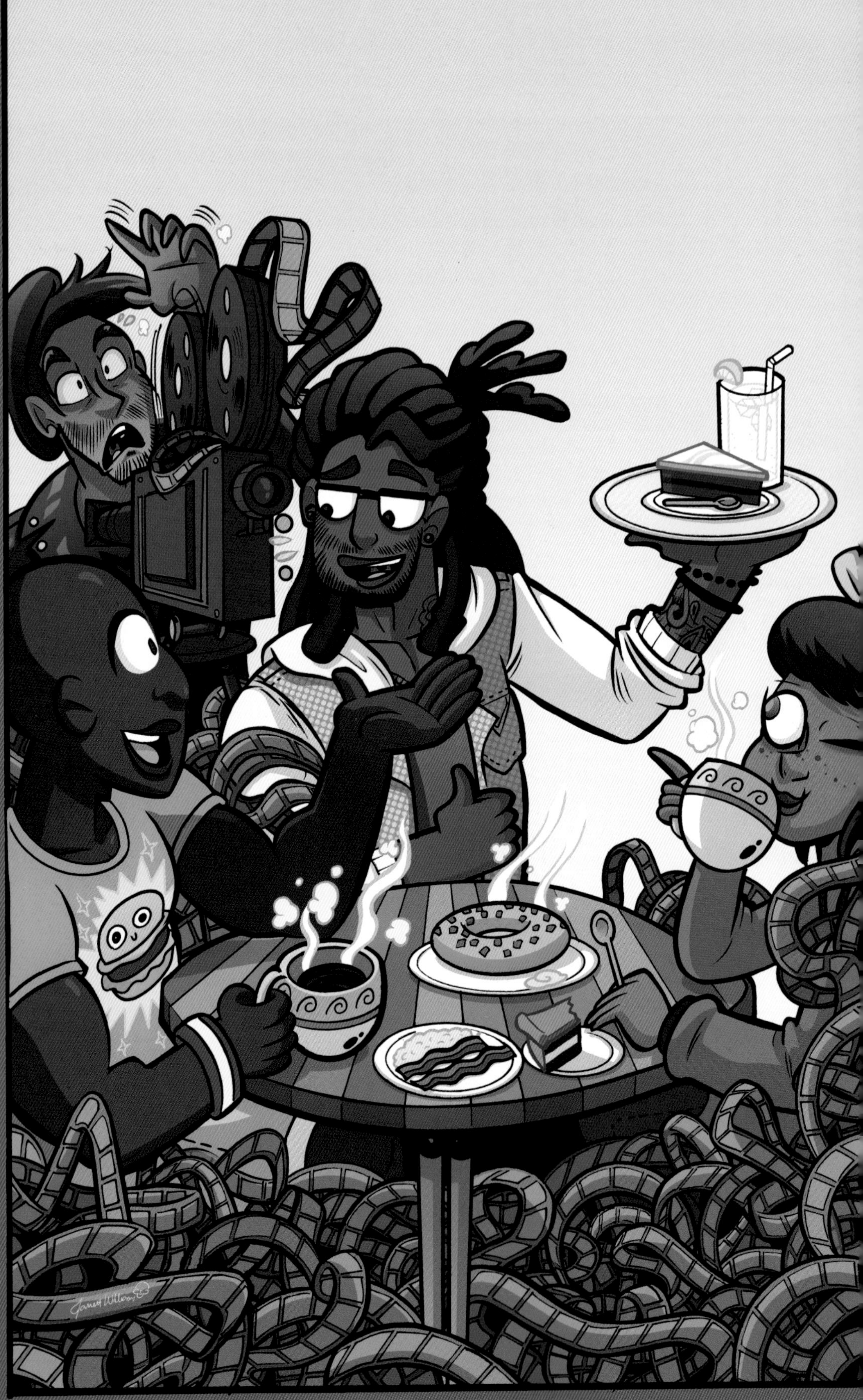

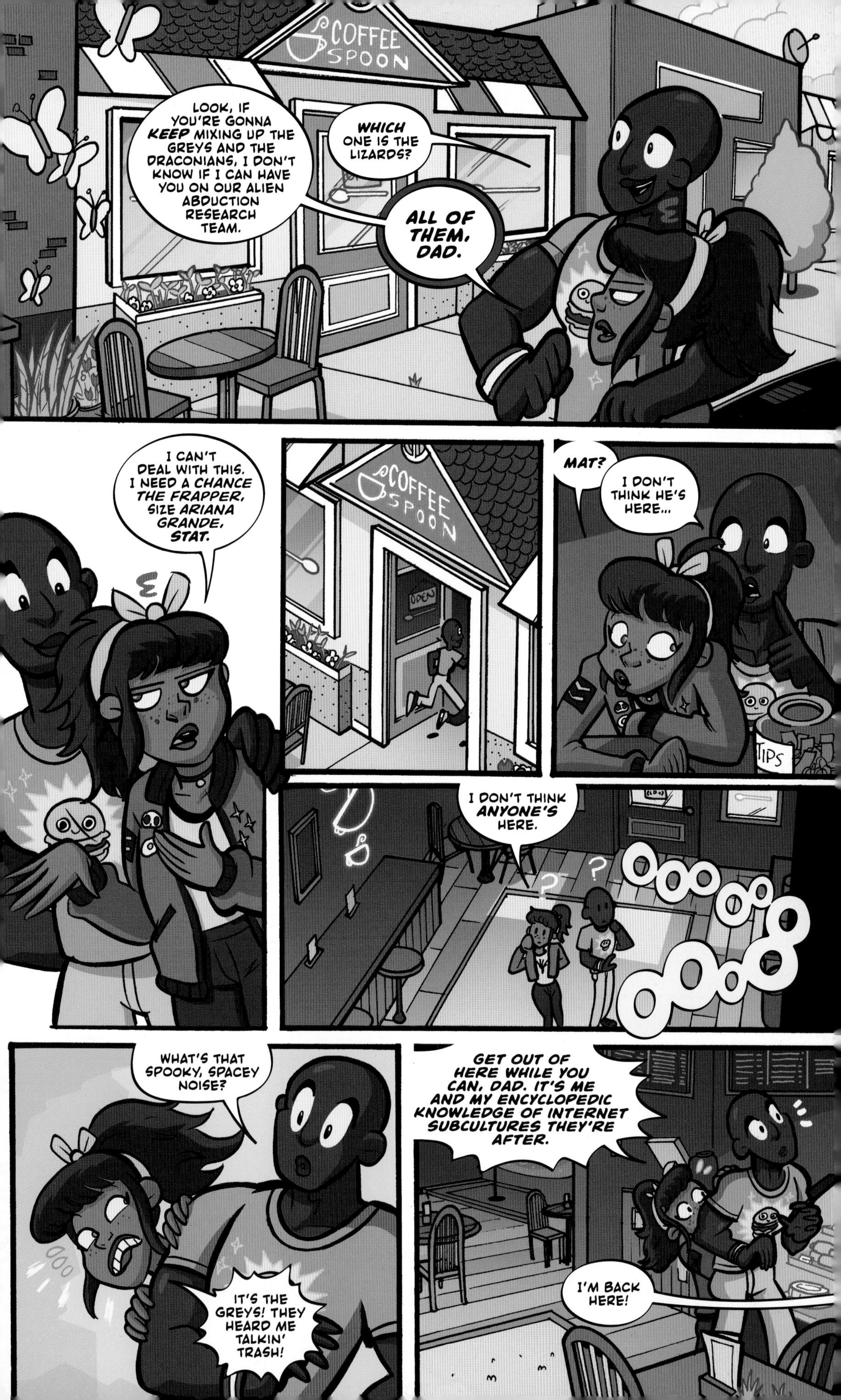
COFFEE SPOON
LOOK, IF YOU'RE GONNA KEEP MIXING UP THE GREYS AND THE DRACONIANS, I DON'T KNOW IF I CAN HAVE YOU ON OUR ALIEN ABDUCTION RESEARCH TEAM.
WHICH ONE IS THE LIZARDS?
ALL OF THEM, DAD.
I CAN'T DEAL WITH THIS. I NEED A CHANCE THE FRAPPER, SIZE ARIANA GRANDE, STAT.
COFFEE SPOON
OPEN
MAT?
I DON'T THINK HE'S HERE...
TIPS
I DON'T THINK ANYONE'S HERE.
WHAT'S THAT SPOOKY, SPACEY NOISE?
IT'S THE GREYS! THEY HEARD ME TALKIN' TRASH!
GET OUT OF HERE WHILE YOU CAN, DAD. IT'S ME AND MY ENCYCLOPEDIC KNOWLEDGE OF INTERNET SUBCULTURES THEY'RE AFTER.
I'M BACK HERE!

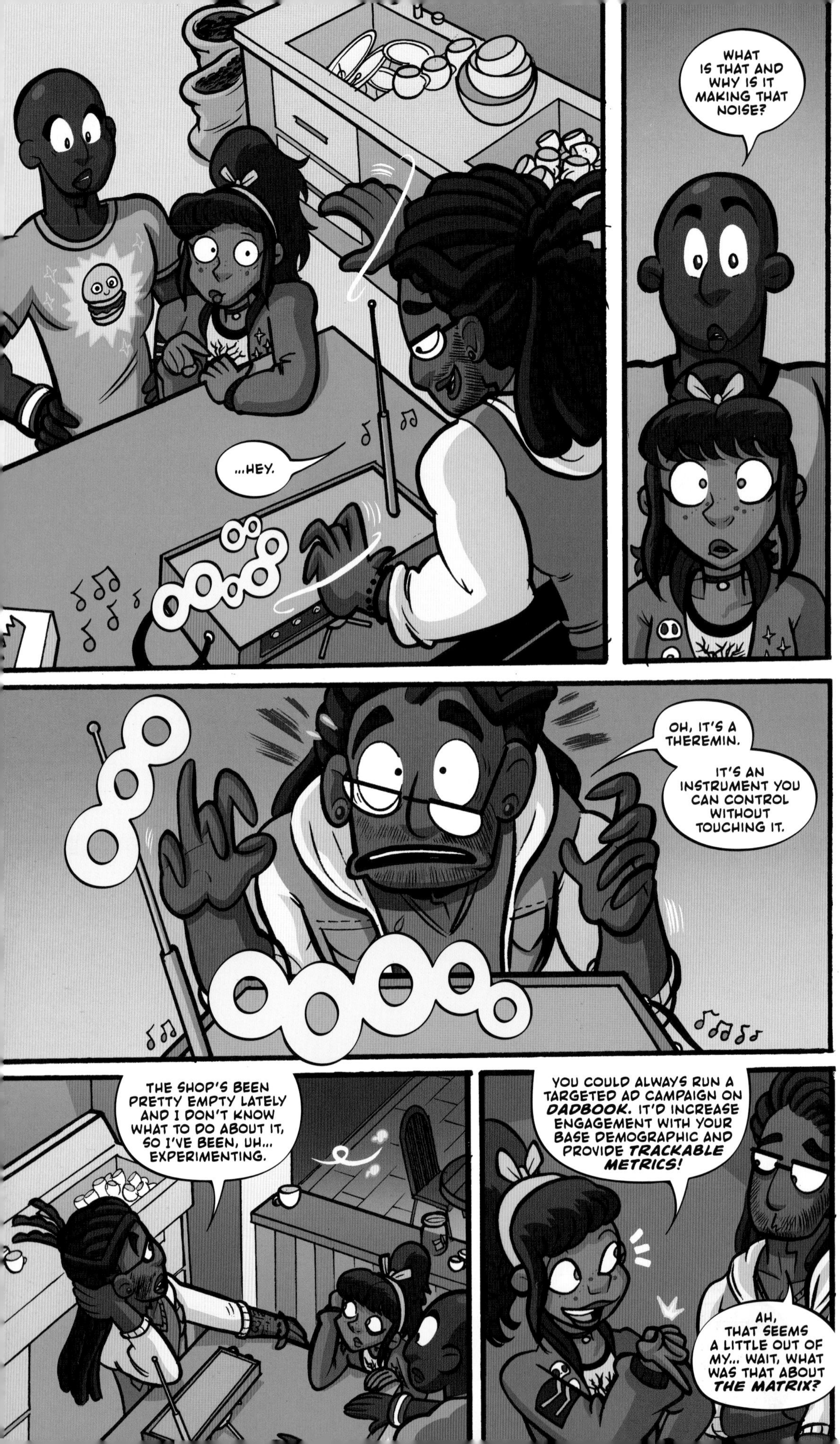
...HEY.
WHAT IS THAT AND WHY IS IT MAKING THAT NOISE?
OH, IT'S A THEREMIN.
IT'S AN INSTRUMENT YOU CAN CONTROL WITHOUT TOUCHING IT.
THE SHOP'S BEEN PRETTY EMPTY LATELY AND I DON'T KNOW WHAT TO DO ABOUT IT, SO I'VE BEEN, UH... EXPERIMENTING.
YOU COULD ALWAYS RUN A TARGETED AD CAMPAIGN ON *DADBOOK*. IT'D INCREASE ENGAGEMENT WITH YOUR BASE DEMOGRAPHIC AND PROVIDE ***TRACKABLE METRICS!***
AH, THAT SEEMS A LITTLE OUT OF MY... WAIT, WHAT WAS THAT ABOUT ***THE MATRIX?***

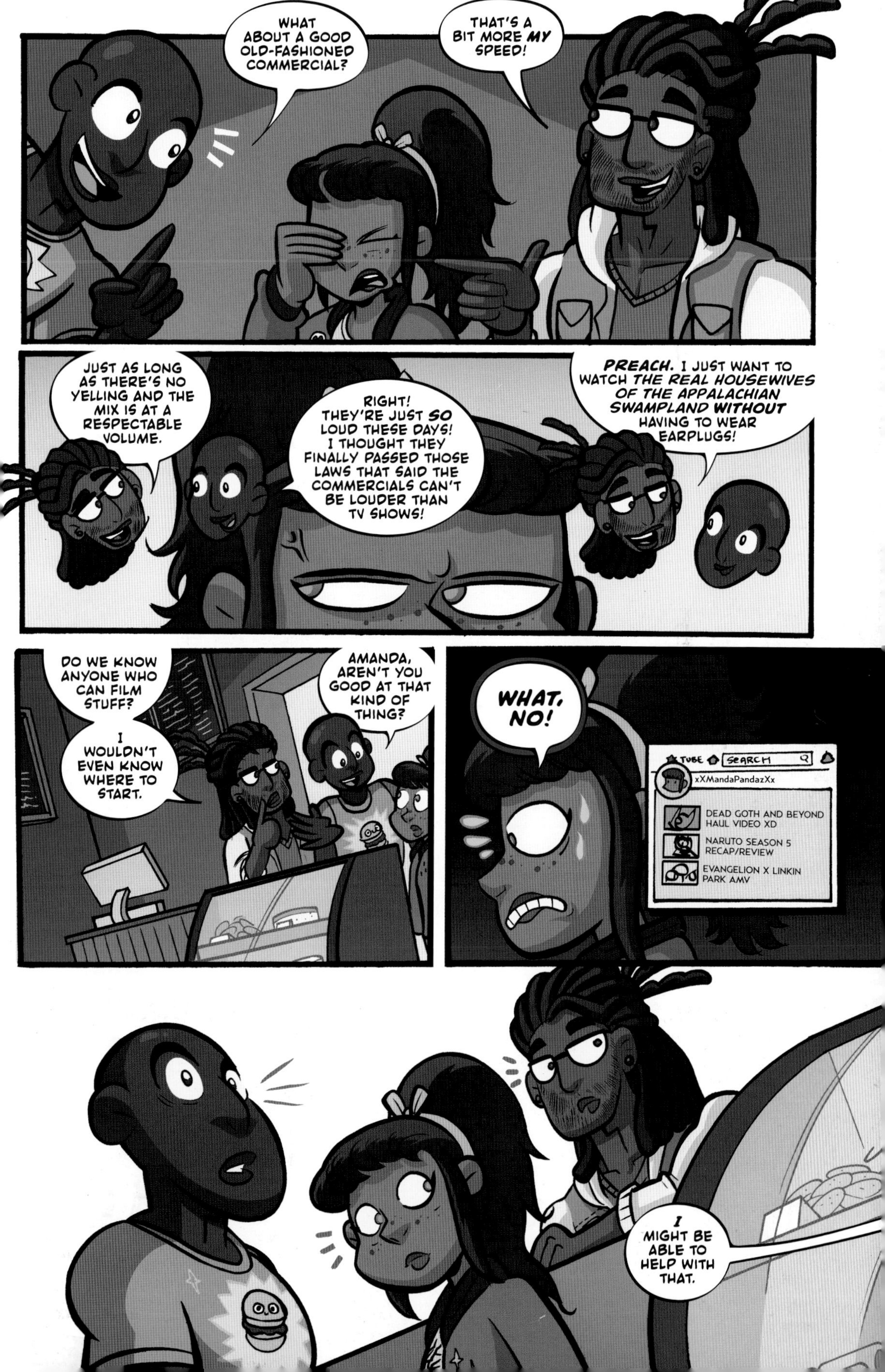
WHAT ABOUT A GOOD OLD-FASHIONED COMMERCIAL?
THAT'S A BIT MORE MY SPEED!
JUST AS LONG AS THERE'S NO YELLING AND THE MIX IS AT A RESPECTABLE VOLUME.
RIGHT! THEY'RE JUST SO LOUD THESE DAYS! I THOUGHT THEY FINALLY PASSED THOSE LAWS THAT SAID THE COMMERCIALS CAN'T BE LOUDER THAN TV SHOWS!
PREACH. I JUST WANT TO WATCH THE REAL HOUSEWIVES OF THE APPALACHIAN SWAMPLAND WITHOUT HAVING TO WEAR EARPLUGS!
DO WE KNOW ANYONE WHO CAN FILM STUFF?
I WOULDN'T EVEN KNOW WHERE TO START.
AMANDA, AREN'T YOU GOOD AT THAT KIND OF THING?
WHAT, NO!
TUBE
SEARCH
xXMandaPandazXx
DEAD GOTH AND BEYOND HAUL VIDEO XD
NARUTO SEASON 5 RECAP/REVIEW
EVANGELION X LINKIN PARK AMV
I MIGHT BE ABLE TO HELP WITH THAT.

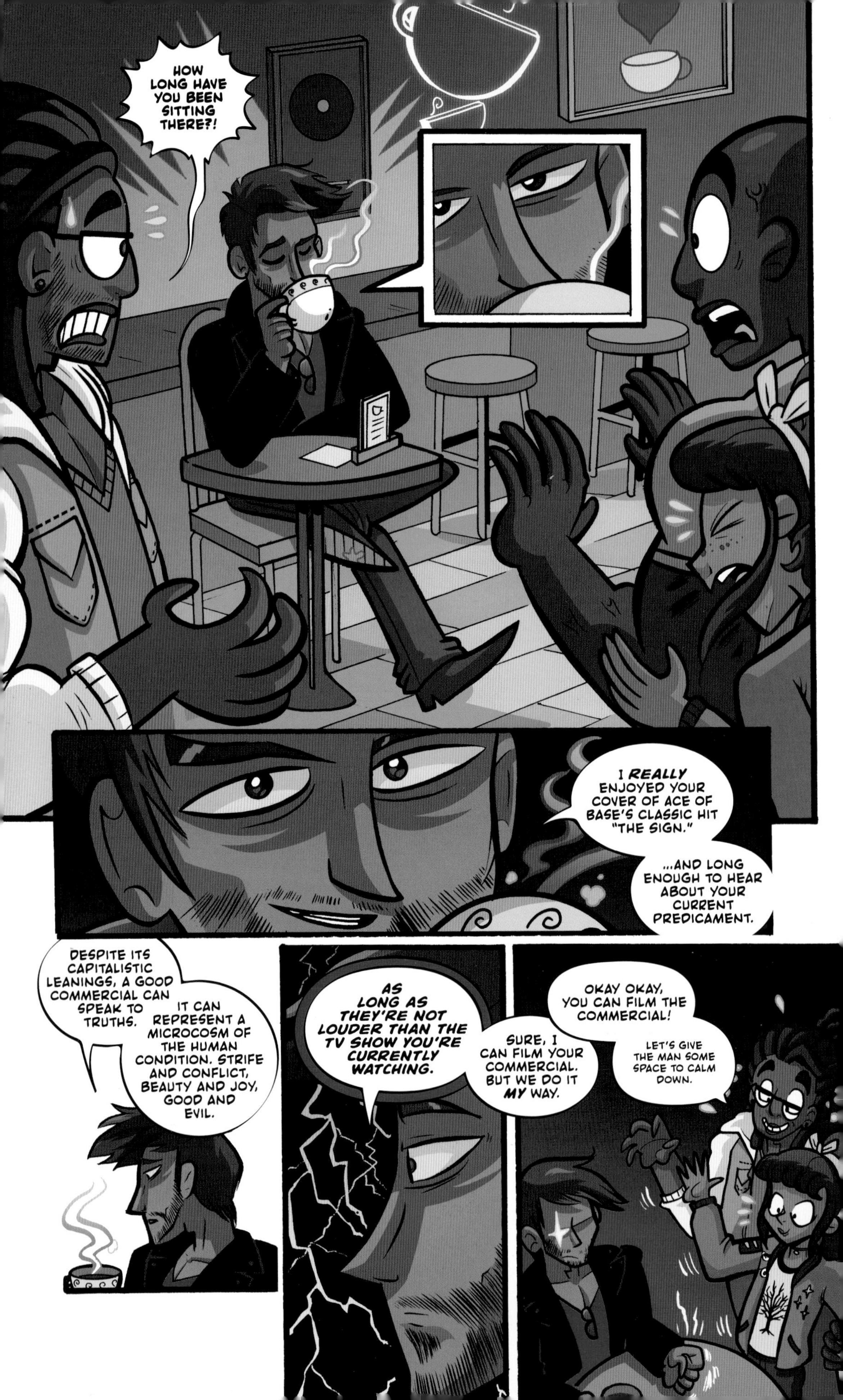
HOW LONG HAVE YOU BEEN SITTING THERE?!
I *REALLY* ENJOYED YOUR COVER OF ACE OF BASE'S CLASSIC HIT "THE SIGN."
...AND LONG ENOUGH TO HEAR ABOUT YOUR CURRENT PREDICAMENT.
DESPITE ITS CAPITALISTIC LEANINGS, A GOOD COMMERCIAL CAN SPEAK TO TRUTHS.
IT CAN REPRESENT A MICROCOSM OF THE HUMAN CONDITION. STRIFE AND CONFLICT, BEAUTY AND JOY, GOOD AND EVIL.
AS LONG AS THEY'RE NOT LOUDER THAN THE TV SHOW YOU'RE CURRENTLY WATCHING.
SURE, I CAN FILM YOUR COMMERCIAL. BUT WE DO IT *MY* WAY.
OKAY OKAY, YOU CAN FILM THE COMMERCIAL!
LET'S GIVE THE MAN SOME SPACE TO CALM DOWN.

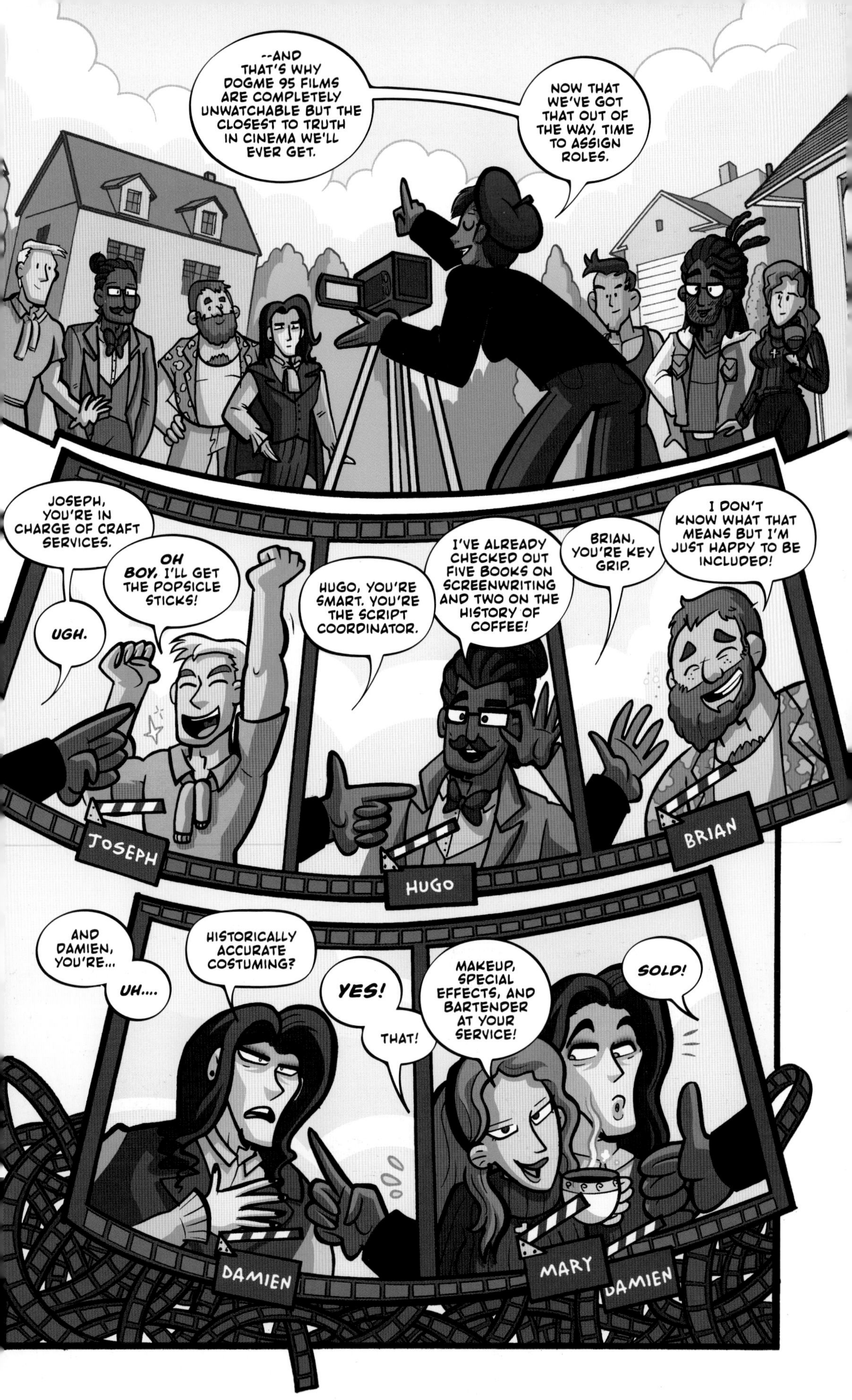
--AND THAT'S WHY DOGME 95 FILMS ARE COMPLETELY UNWATCHABLE BUT THE CLOSEST TO TRUTH IN CINEMA WE'LL EVER GET.
NOW THAT WE'VE GOT THAT OUT OF THE WAY, TIME TO ASSIGN ROLES.
JOSEPH, YOU'RE IN CHARGE OF CRAFT SERVICES.
OH BOY. I'LL GET THE POPSICLE STICKS!
UGH.
JOSEPH
HUGO, YOU'RE SMART. YOU'RE THE SCRIPT COORDINATOR.
I'VE ALREADY CHECKED OUT FIVE BOOKS ON SCREENWRITING AND TWO ON THE HISTORY OF COFFEE!
HUGO
BRIAN, YOU'RE KEY GRIP.
I DON'T KNOW WHAT THAT MEANS BUT I'M JUST HAPPY TO BE INCLUDED!
BRIAN
AND DAMIEN, YOU'RE...
UH....
HISTORICALLY ACCURATE COSTUMING?
YES!
THAT!
DAMIEN
MAKEUP, SPECIAL EFFECTS, AND BARTENDER AT YOUR SERVICE!
SOLD!
MARY
DAMIEN

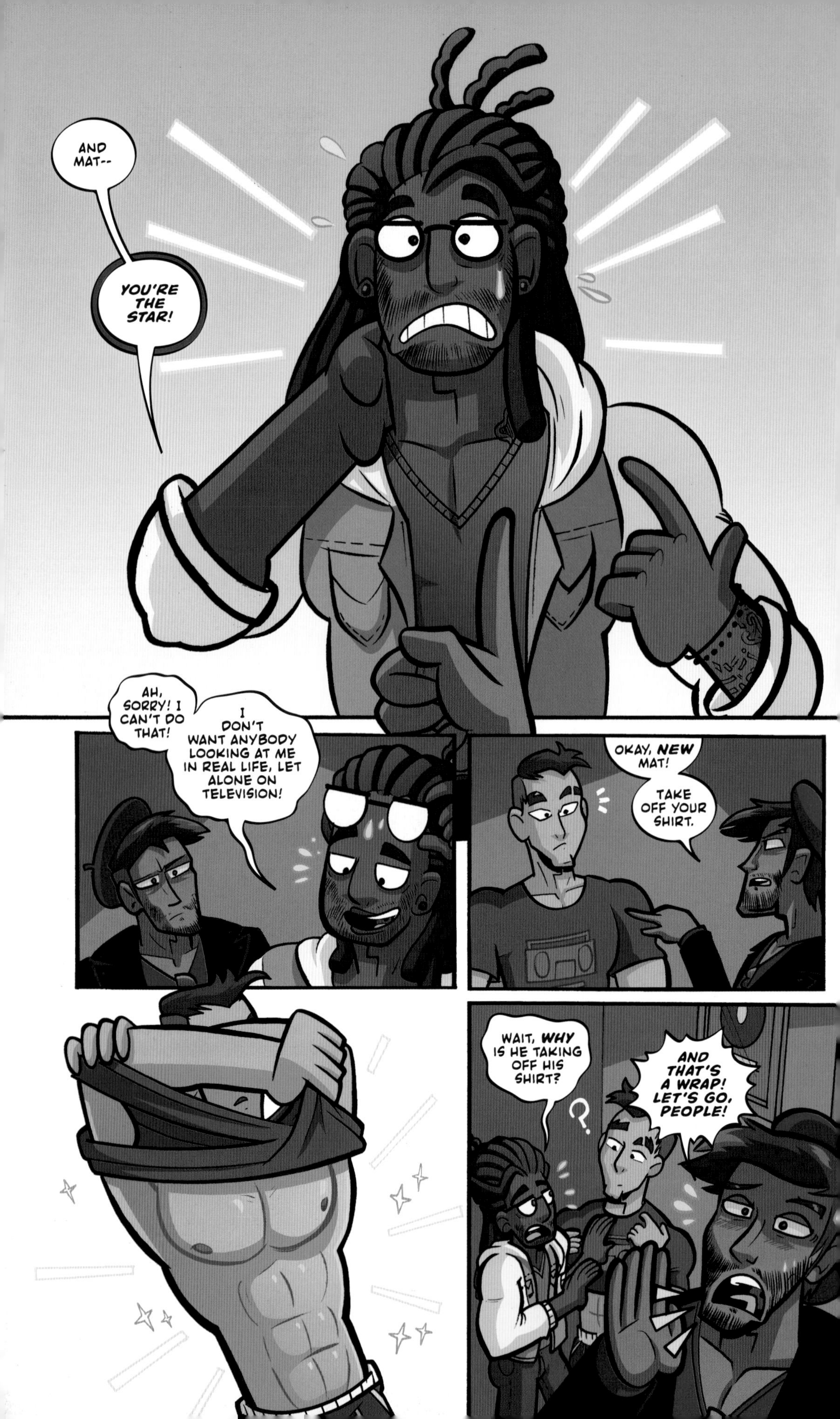
AND MAT--
YOU'RE THE STAR!
AH, SORRY! I CAN'T DO THAT!
I DON'T WANT ANYBODY LOOKING AT ME IN REAL LIFE, LET ALONE ON TELEVISION!
OKAY, NEW MAT!
TAKE OFF YOUR SHIRT.
WAIT, WHY IS HE TAKING OFF HIS SHIRT?
?
AND THAT'S A WRAP! LET'S GO, PEOPLE!

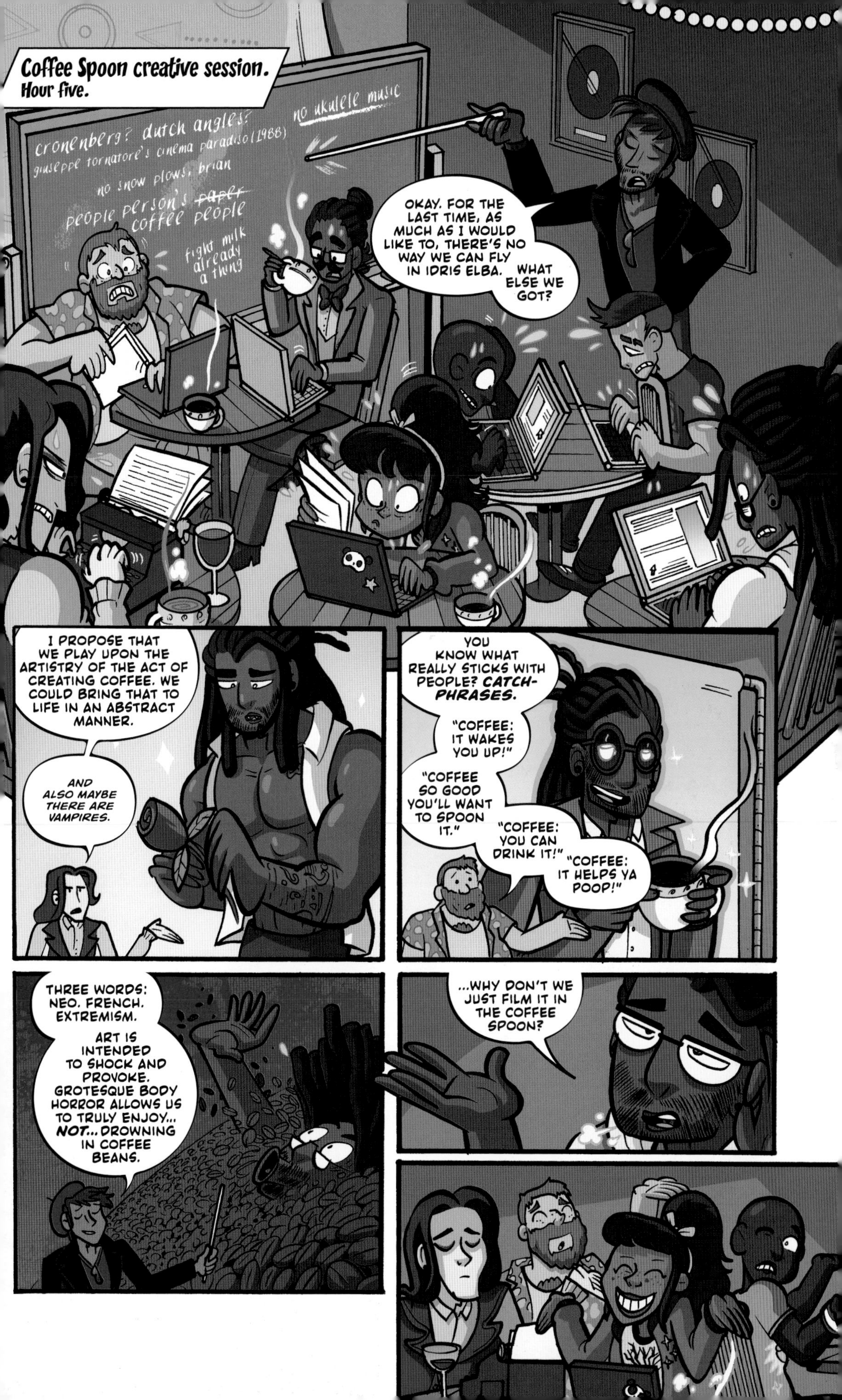
Coffee Spoon creative session. Hour five.
cronenberg? dutch angles?
giuseppe tornatore's cinema paradiso (1988)
no snow plows, brian
people person's ~~paper~~ coffee people
fight milk already a thing
no ukulele music
OKAY. FOR THE LAST TIME, AS MUCH AS I WOULD LIKE TO, THERE'S NO WAY WE CAN FLY IN IDRIS ELBA.
WHAT ELSE WE GOT?
I PROPOSE THAT WE PLAY UPON THE ARTISTRY OF THE ACT OF CREATING COFFEE. WE COULD BRING THAT TO LIFE IN AN ABSTRACT MANNER.
AND ALSO MAYBE THERE ARE VAMPIRES.
YOU KNOW WHAT REALLY STICKS WITH PEOPLE? CATCH-PHRASES.
"COFFEE: IT WAKES YOU UP!"
"COFFEE SO GOOD YOU'LL WANT TO SPOON IT."
"COFFEE: YOU CAN DRINK IT!"
"COFFEE: IT HELPS YA POOP!"
THREE WORDS: NEO. FRENCH. EXTREMISM.
ART IS INTENDED TO SHOCK AND PROVOKE. GROTESQUE BODY HORROR ALLOWS US TO TRULY ENJOY... NOT... DROWNING IN COFFEE BEANS.
...WHY DON'T WE JUST FILM IT IN THE COFFEE SPOON?

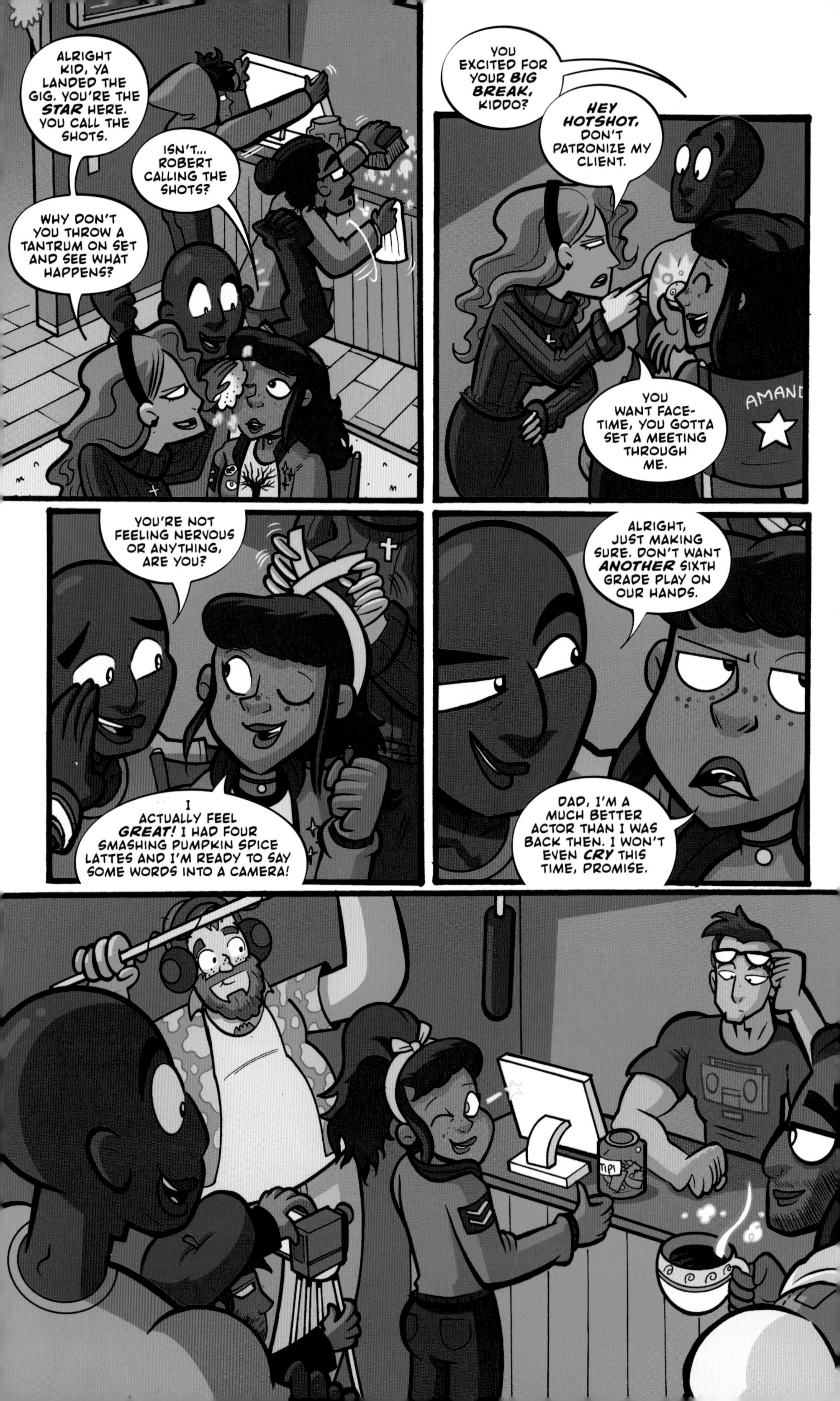
ALRIGHT KID, YA LANDED THE GIG. YOU'RE THE STAR HERE. YOU CALL THE SHOTS.
ISN'T... ROBERT CALLING THE SHOTS?
WHY DON'T YOU THROW A TANTRUM ON SET AND SEE WHAT HAPPENS?
YOU EXCITED FOR YOUR BIG BREAK, KIDDO?
HEY HOTSHOT, DON'T PATRONIZE MY CLIENT.
AMAND
YOU WANT FACE-TIME, YOU GOTTA SET A MEETING THROUGH ME.
YOU'RE NOT FEELING NERVOUS OR ANYTHING, ARE YOU?
I ACTUALLY FEEL GREAT! I HAD FOUR SMASHING PUMPKIN SPICE LATTES AND I'M READY TO SAY SOME WORDS INTO A CAMERA!
ALRIGHT, JUST MAKING SURE. DON'T WANT ANOTHER SIXTH GRADE PLAY ON OUR HANDS.
DAD, I'M A MUCH BETTER ACTOR THAN I WAS BACK THEN. I WON'T EVEN CRY THIS TIME, PROMISE.
TIPS

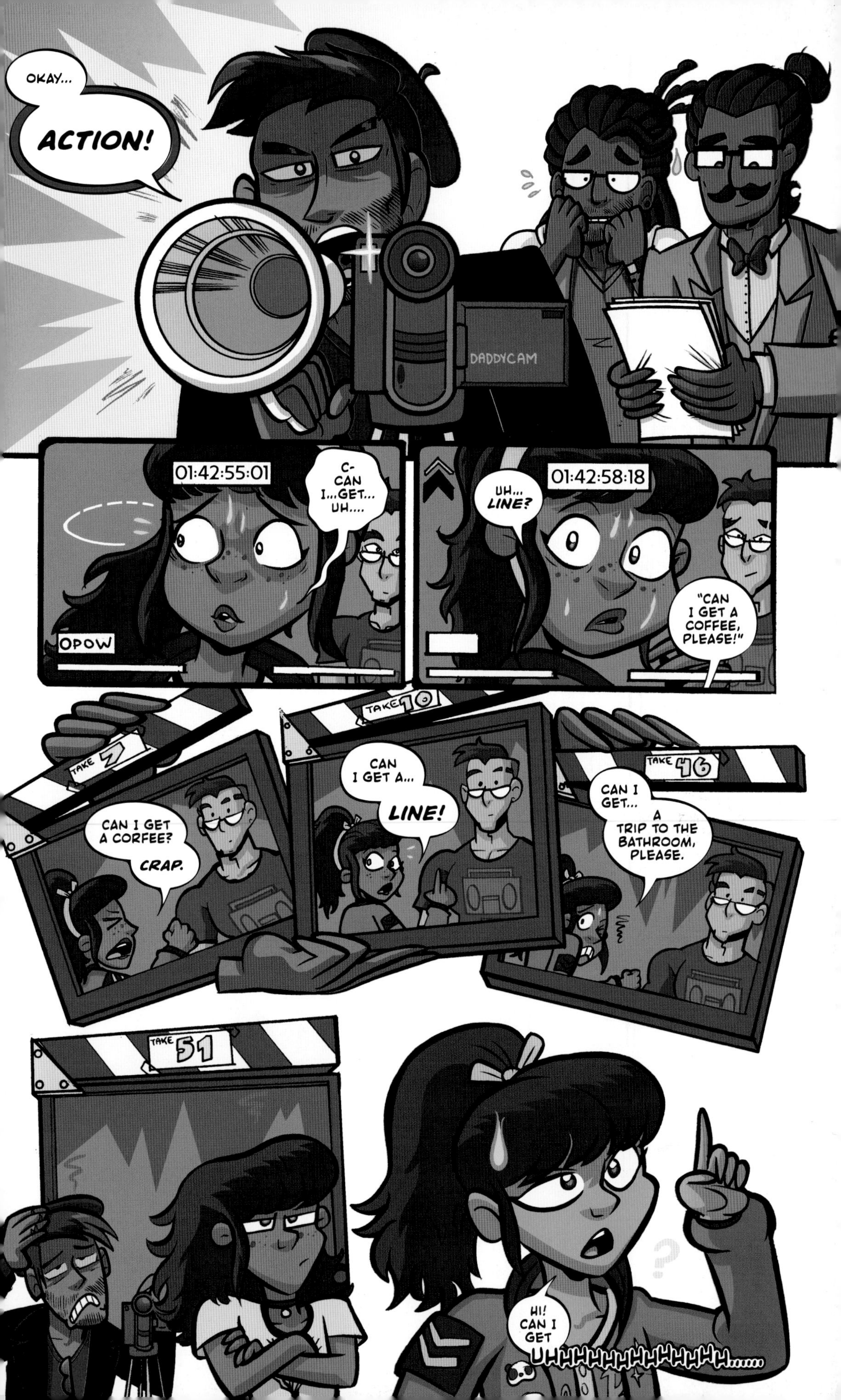
OKAY...
ACTION!
DADDYCAM
01:42:55:01
C- CAN I...GET... UH....
OPOW
01:42:58:18
UH... LINE?
"CAN I GET A COFFEE, PLEASE!"
TAKE 7
CAN I GET A CORFEE?
CRAP.
TAKE 10
CAN I GET A...
LINE!
TAKE 46
CAN I GET...
A TRIP TO THE BATHROOM, PLEASE.
TAKE 51
HI! CAN I GET
UHHHHHHHHHHHHH......

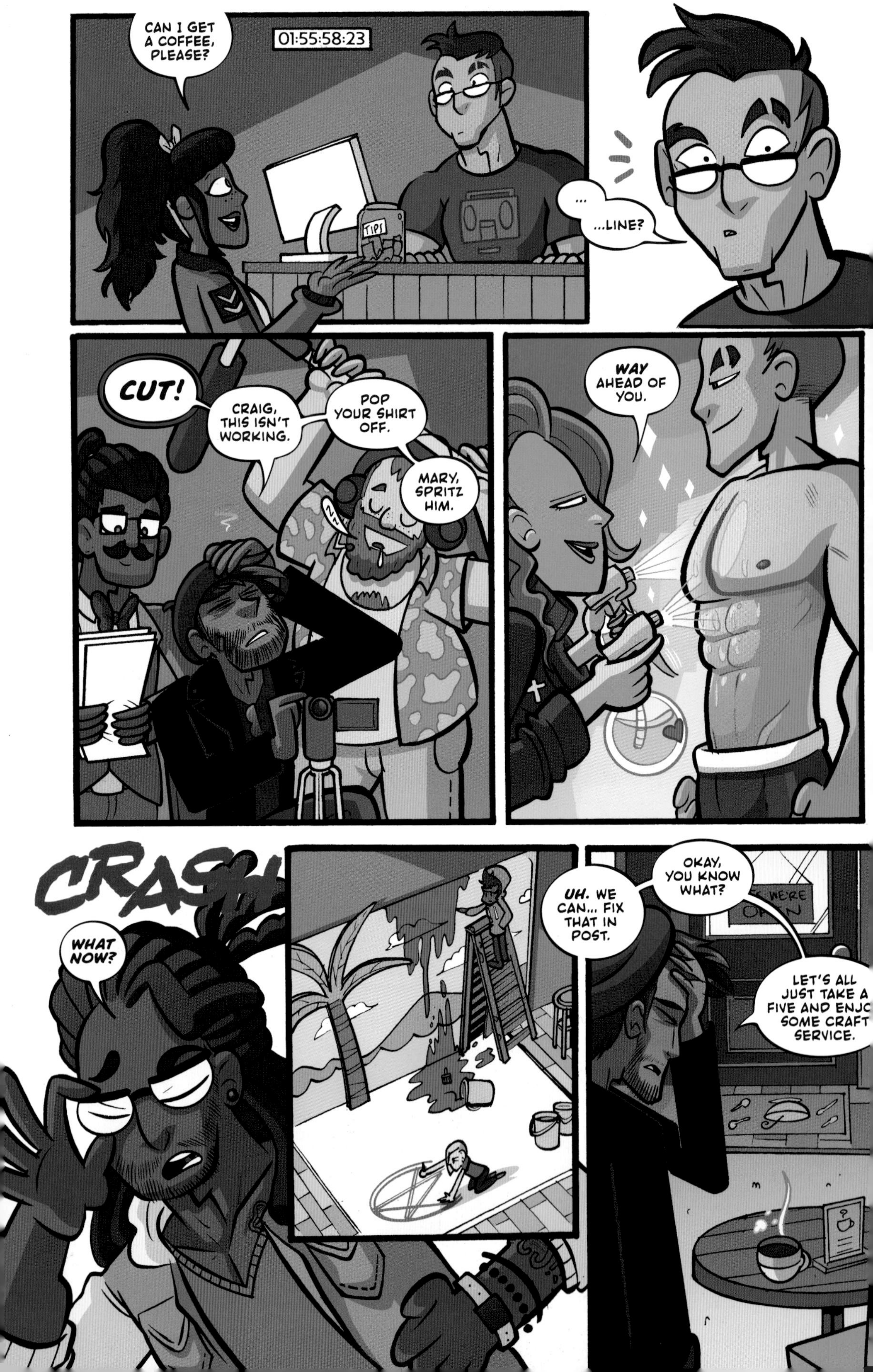
CAN I GET A COFFEE, PLEASE?
01:55:58:23
TIPS
...
...LINE?
CUT!
CRAIG, THIS ISN'T WORKING.
POP YOUR SHIRT OFF.
MARY, SPRITZ HIM.
WAY AHEAD OF YOU.
CRASH
WHAT NOW?
UH. WE CAN... FIX THAT IN POST.
OKAY, YOU KNOW WHAT?
LET'S ALL JUST TAKE A FIVE AND ENJO SOME CRAFT SERVICE.
WE'RE OPEN

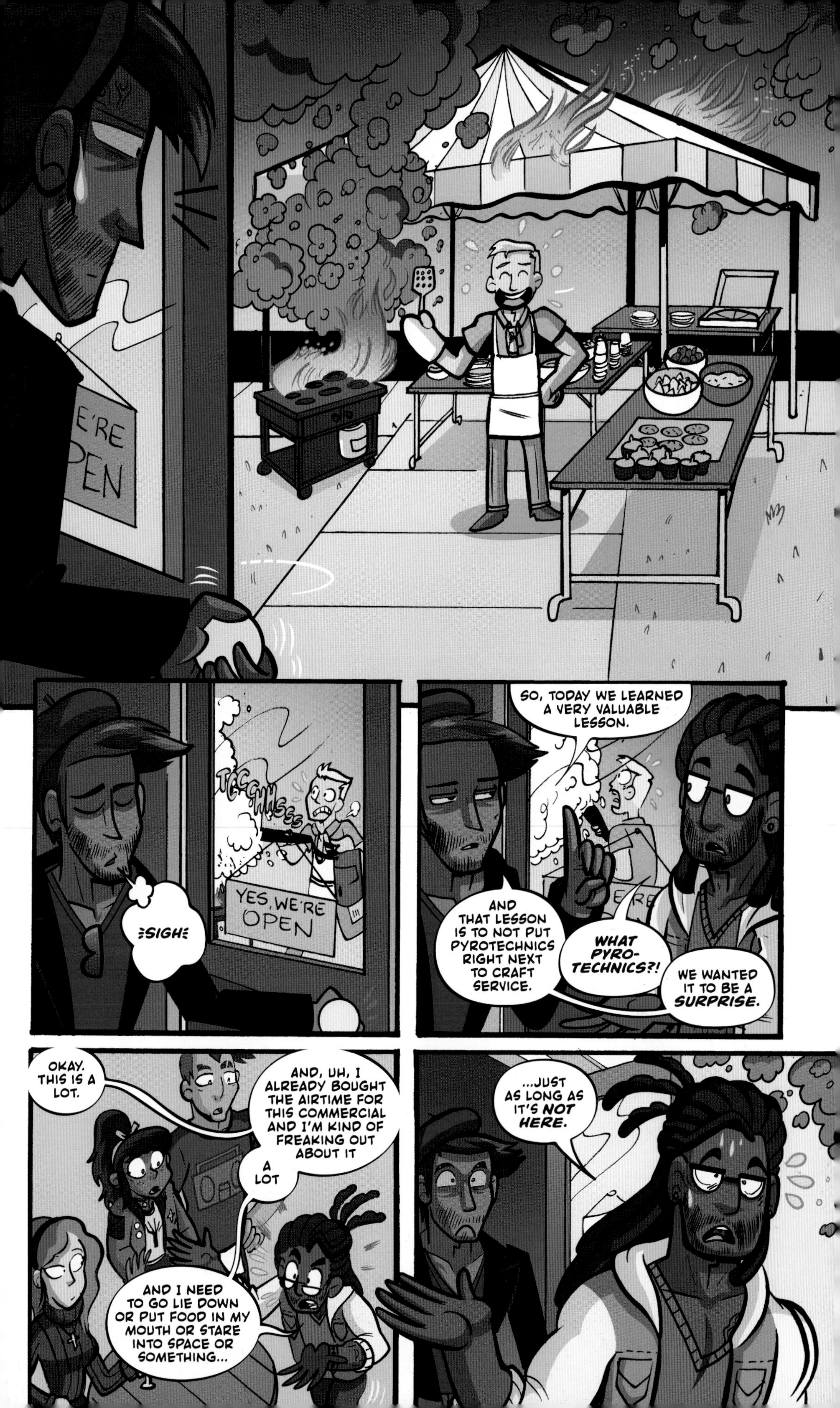
E'RE
OPEN
TCCCHHSSS
YES, WE'RE OPEN
SIGH
SO, TODAY WE LEARNED A VERY VALUABLE LESSON.
AND THAT LESSON IS TO NOT PUT PYROTECHNICS RIGHT NEXT TO CRAFT SERVICE.
WHAT PYRO-TECHNICS?!
WE WANTED IT TO BE A SURPRISE.
OKAY. THIS IS A LOT.
AND, UH, I ALREADY BOUGHT THE AIRTIME FOR THIS COMMERCIAL AND I'M KIND OF FREAKING OUT ABOUT IT
A LOT
AND I NEED TO GO LIE DOWN OR PUT FOOD IN MY MOUTH OR STARE INTO SPACE OR SOMETHING...
...JUST AS LONG AS IT'S NOT HERE.

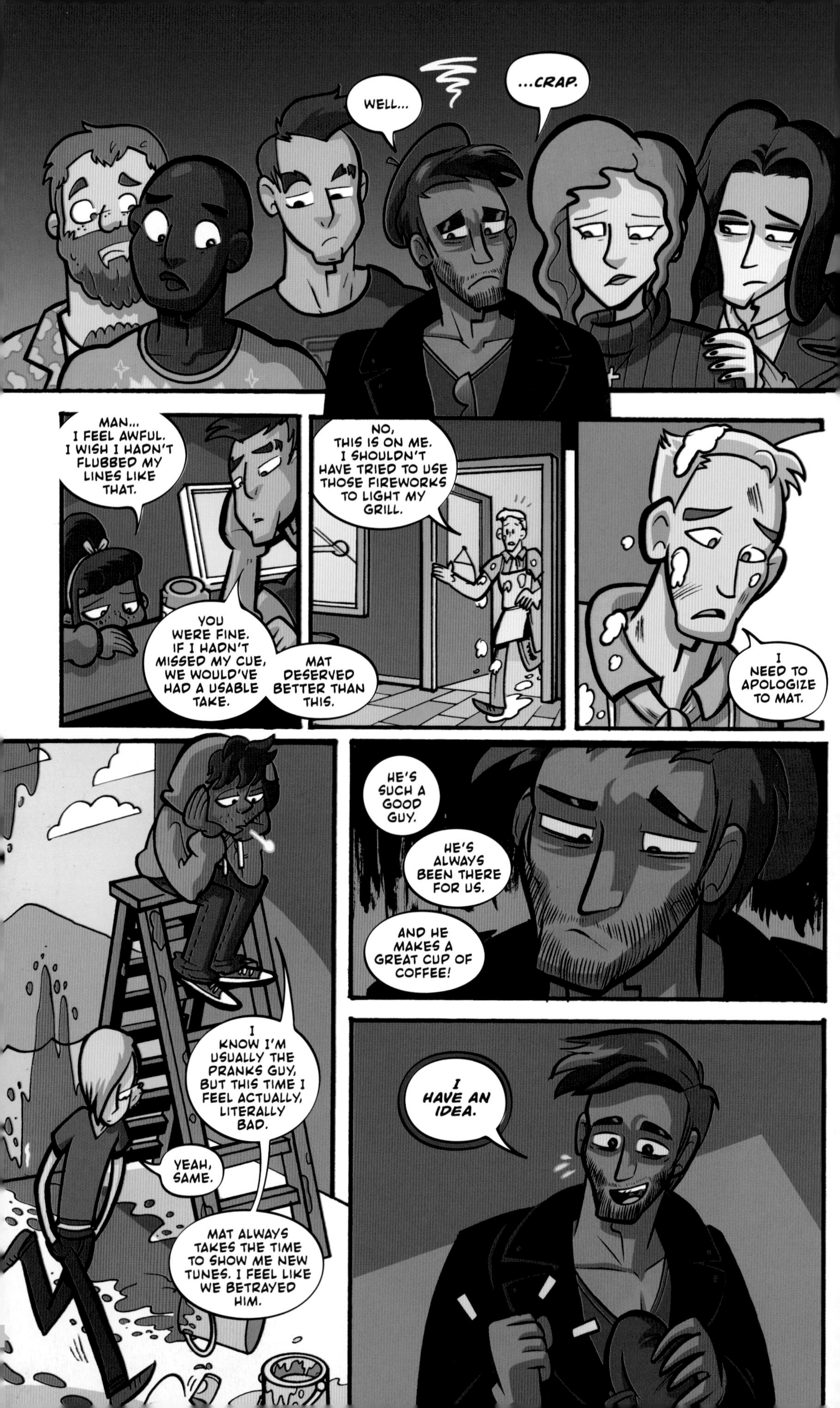
WELL...
...CRAP.
MAN... I FEEL AWFUL. I WISH I HADN'T FLUBBED MY LINES LIKE THAT.
YOU WERE FINE. IF I HADN'T MISSED MY CUE, WE WOULD'VE HAD A USABLE TAKE.
NO, THIS IS ON ME. I SHOULDN'T HAVE TRIED TO USE THOSE FIREWORKS TO LIGHT MY GRILL.
MAT DESERVED BETTER THAN THIS.
I NEED TO APOLOGIZE TO MAT.
I KNOW I'M USUALLY THE PRANKS GUY, BUT THIS TIME I FEEL ACTUALLY, LITERALLY BAD.
YEAH, SAME.
MAT ALWAYS TAKES THE TIME TO SHOW ME NEW TUNES. I FEEL LIKE WE BETRAYED HIM.
HE'S SUCH A GOOD GUY.
HE'S ALWAYS BEEN THERE FOR US.
AND HE MAKES A GREAT CUP OF COFFEE!
I HAVE AN IDEA.

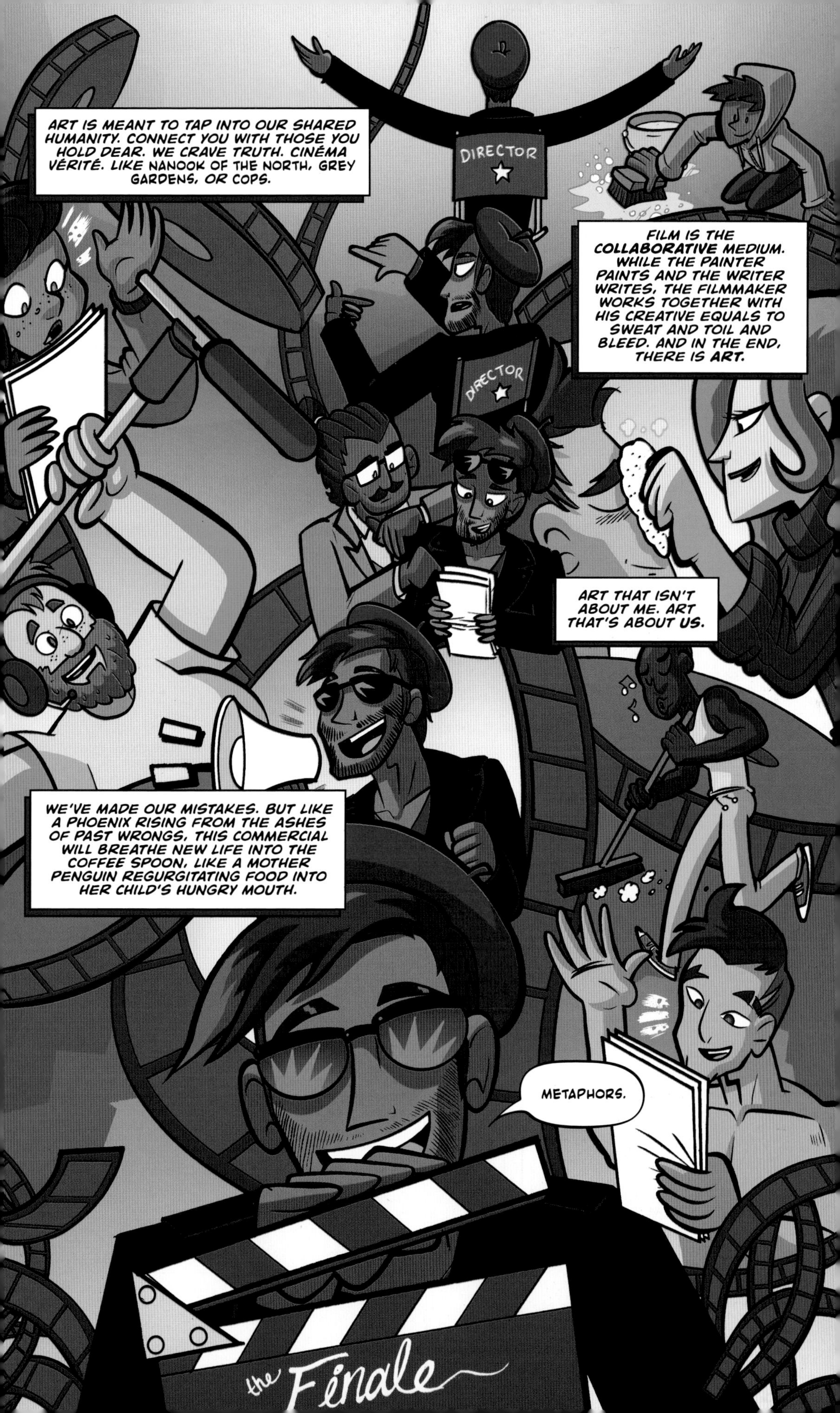
ART IS MEANT TO TAP INTO OUR SHARED HUMANITY. CONNECT YOU WITH THOSE YOU HOLD DEAR. WE CRAVE TRUTH. CINÉMA VÉRITÉ. LIKE NANOOK OF THE NORTH, GREY GARDENS, OR COPS.
DIRECTOR
FILM IS THE **COLLABORATIVE** MEDIUM. WHILE THE PAINTER PAINTS AND THE WRITER WRITES, THE FILMMAKER WORKS TOGETHER WITH HIS CREATIVE EQUALS TO SWEAT AND TOIL AND BLEED. AND IN THE END, THERE IS **ART**.
DIRECTOR
ART THAT ISN'T ABOUT ME. ART THAT'S ABOUT **US**.
WE'VE MADE OUR MISTAKES. BUT LIKE A PHOENIX RISING FROM THE ASHES OF PAST WRONGS, THIS COMMERCIAL WILL BREATHE NEW LIFE INTO THE COFFEE SPOON, LIKE A MOTHER PENGUIN REGURGITATING FOOD INTO HER CHILD'S HUNGRY MOUTH.
METAPHORS.
the Finale

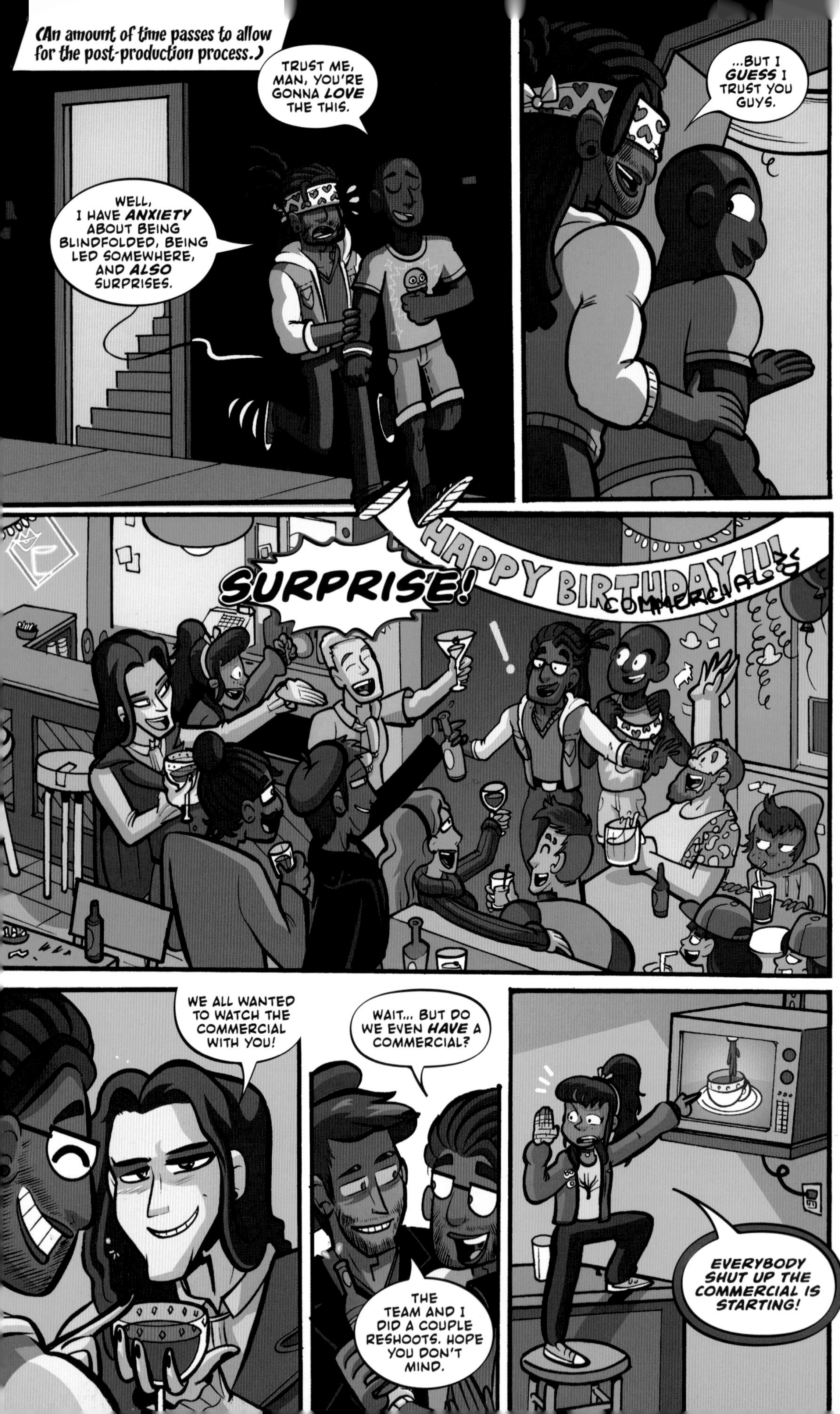
(An amount of time passes to allow for the post-production process.)
TRUST ME, MAN, YOU'RE GONNA LOVE THE THIS.
WELL, I HAVE ANXIETY ABOUT BEING BLINDFOLDED, BEING LED SOMEWHERE, AND ALSO SURPRISES.
...BUT I GUESS I TRUST YOU GUYS.
SURPRISE!
HAPPY BIRTHDAY!!!
COMMERCIAL
WE ALL WANTED TO WATCH THE COMMERCIAL WITH YOU!
WAIT... BUT DO WE EVEN HAVE A COMMERCIAL?
THE TEAM AND I DID A COUPLE RESHOOTS. HOPE YOU DON'T MIND.
EVERYBODY SHUT UP THE COMMERCIAL IS STARTING!

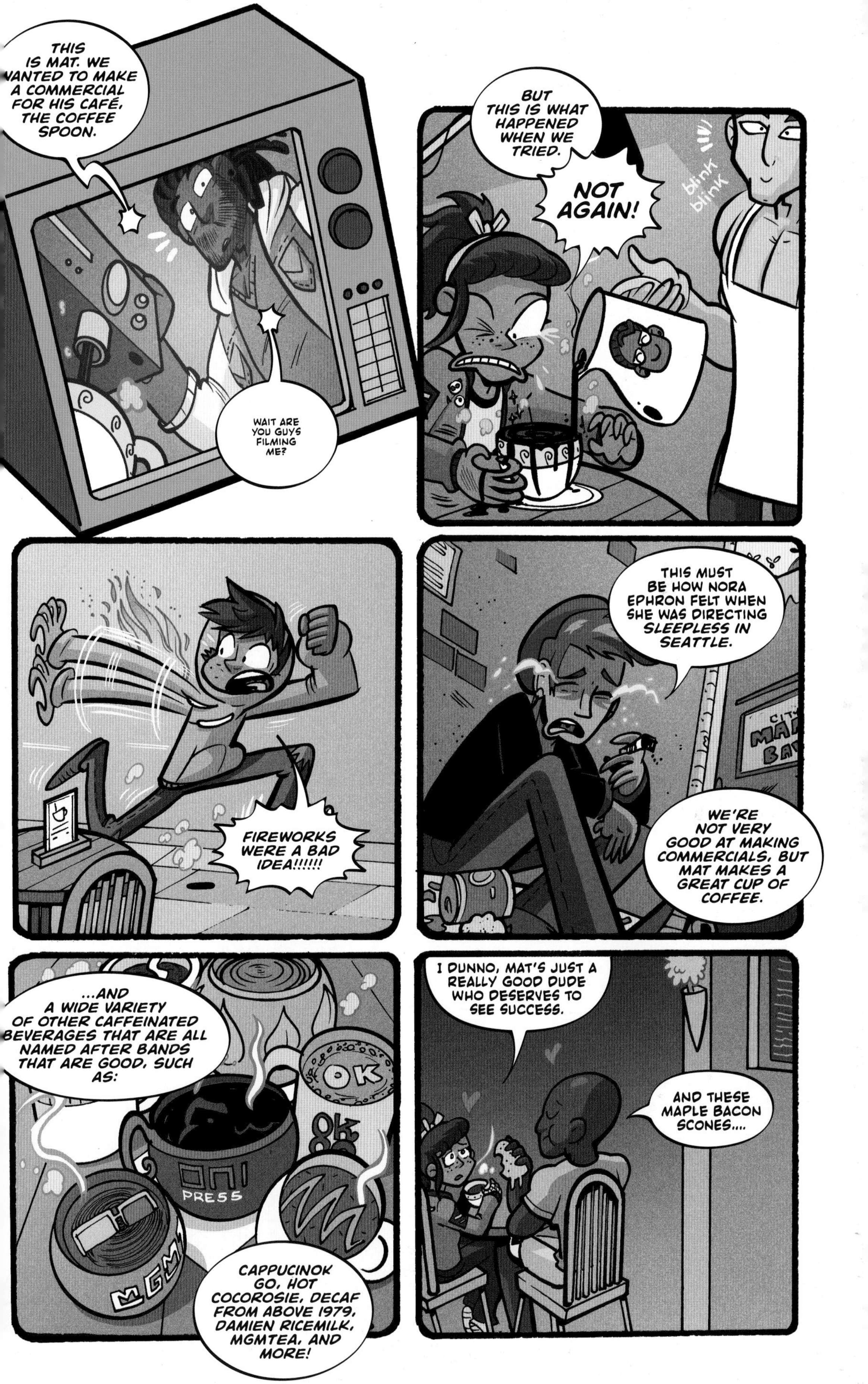

THIS IS MAT. WE WANTED TO MAKE A COMMERCIAL FOR HIS CAFÉ, THE COFFEE SPOON.
WAIT ARE YOU GUYS FILMING ME?
BUT THIS IS WHAT HAPPENED WHEN WE TRIED.
NOT AGAIN!
blink blink
FIREWORKS WERE A BAD IDEA!!!!!!
THIS MUST BE HOW NORA EPHRON FELT WHEN SHE WAS DIRECTING *SLEEPLESS IN SEATTLE.*
WE'RE NOT VERY GOOD AT MAKING COMMERCIALS, BUT MAT MAKES A GREAT CUP OF COFFEE.
...AND A WIDE VARIETY OF OTHER CAFFEINATED BEVERAGES THAT ARE ALL NAMED AFTER BANDS THAT ARE GOOD, SUCH AS:
OK
ONI PRESS
CAPPUCINOK GO, HOT COCOROSIE, DECAF FROM ABOVE 1979, DAMIEN RICEMILK, MGMTEA, AND MORE!
I DUNNO, MAT'S JUST A REALLY GOOD DUDE WHO DESERVES TO SEE SUCCESS.
AND THESE MAPLE BACON SCONES....

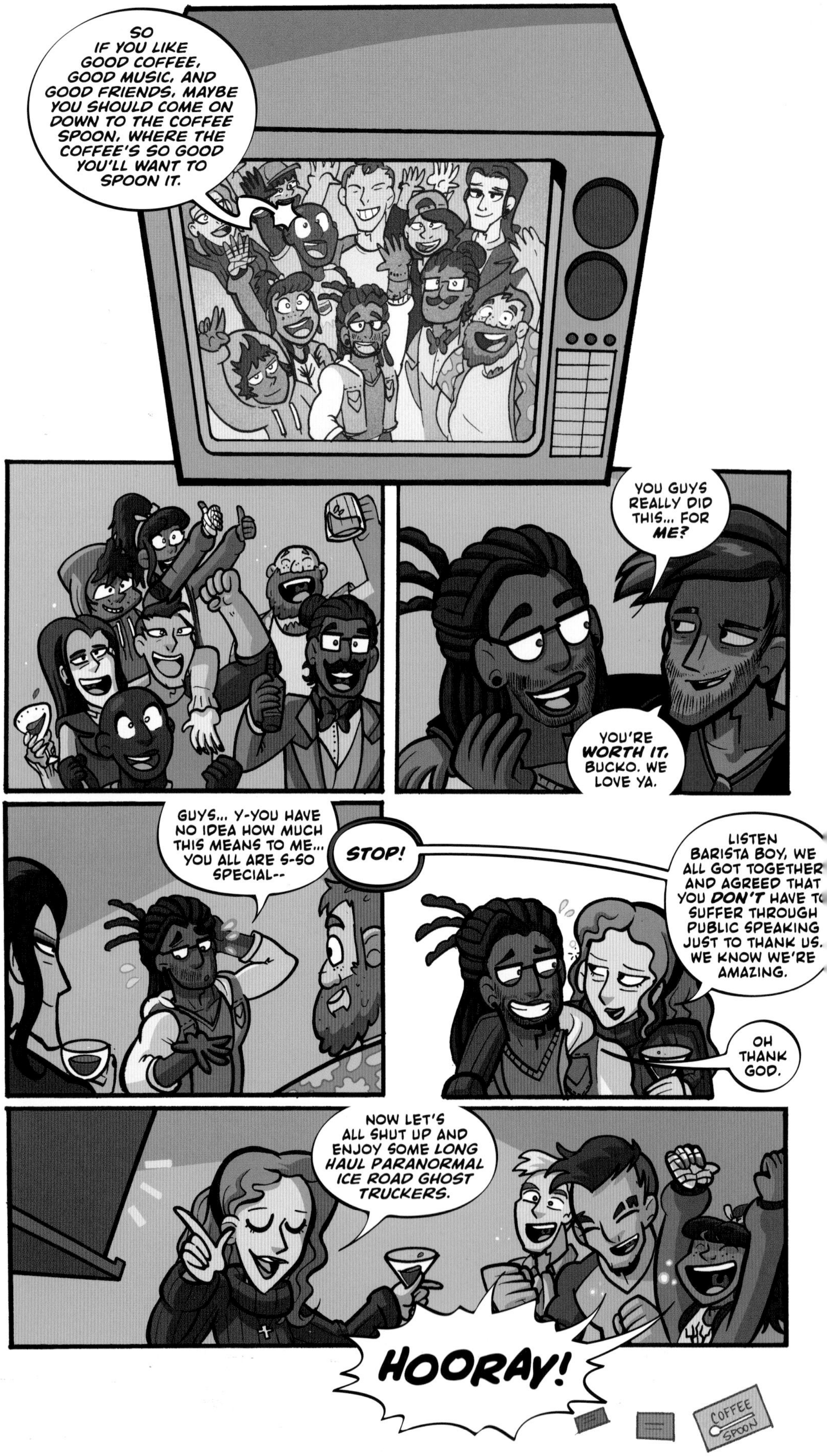
SO IF YOU LIKE GOOD COFFEE, GOOD MUSIC, AND GOOD FRIENDS, MAYBE YOU SHOULD COME ON DOWN TO THE COFFEE SPOON, WHERE THE COFFEE'S SO GOOD YOU'LL WANT TO SPOON IT.
YOU GUYS REALLY DID THIS... FOR ME?
YOU'RE WORTH IT, BUCKO. WE LOVE YA.
GUYS... Y-YOU HAVE NO IDEA HOW MUCH THIS MEANS TO ME... YOU ALL ARE S-SO SPECIAL--
STOP!
LISTEN BARISTA BOY, WE ALL GOT TOGETHER AND AGREED THAT YOU DON'T HAVE TO SUFFER THROUGH PUBLIC SPEAKING JUST TO THANK US. WE KNOW WE'RE AMAZING.
OH THANK GOD.
NOW LET'S ALL SHUT UP AND ENJOY SOME LONG HAUL PARANORMAL ICE ROAD GHOST TRUCKERS.
HOORAY!
COFFEE SPOON

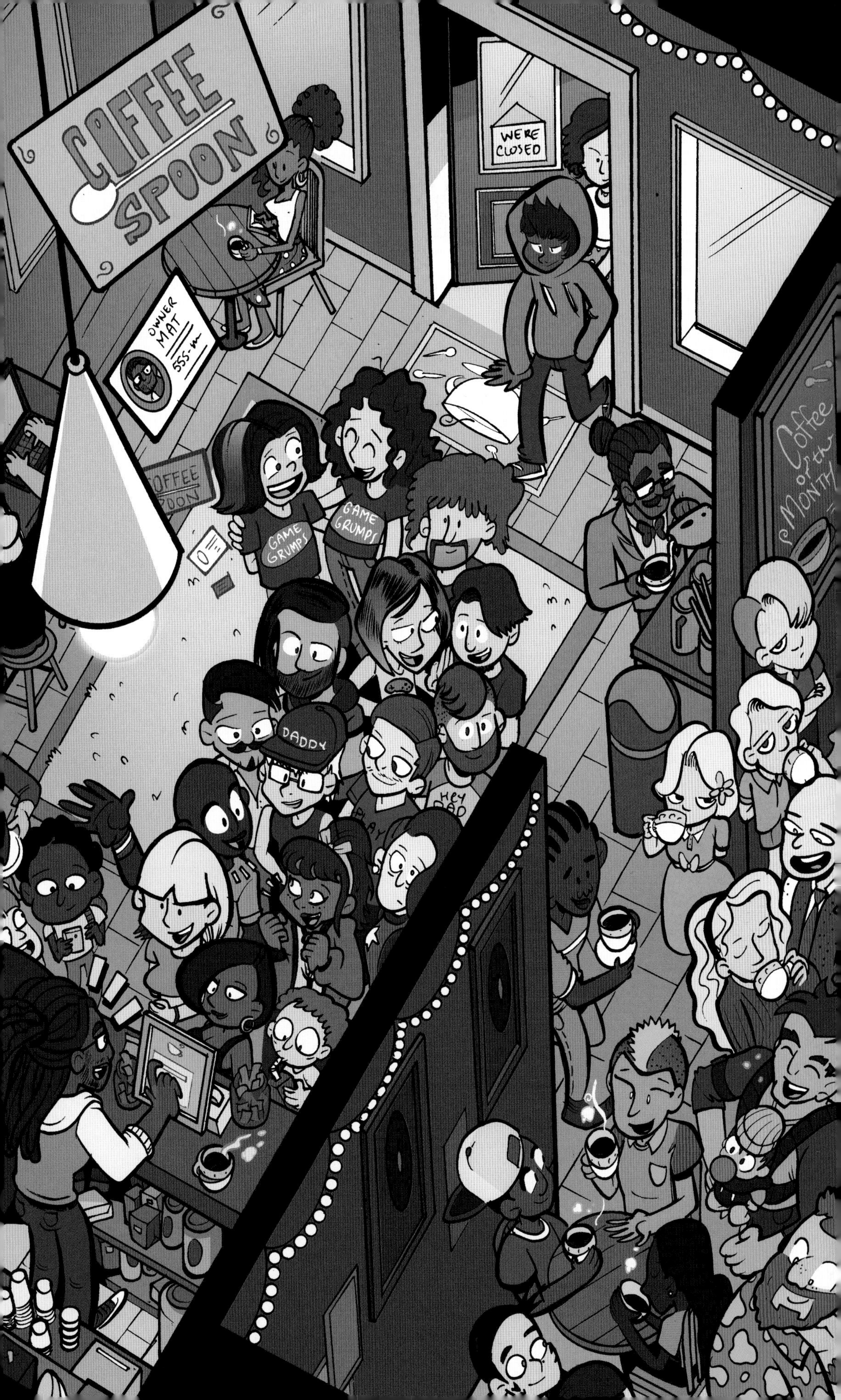

COFFEE SPOON
WE'RE CLOSED
OWNER MAT 555-
COFFEE SPOON
GAME GRUMPS
GAME GRUMPS
Coffee of the MONTH
DADDY
HEY DAD

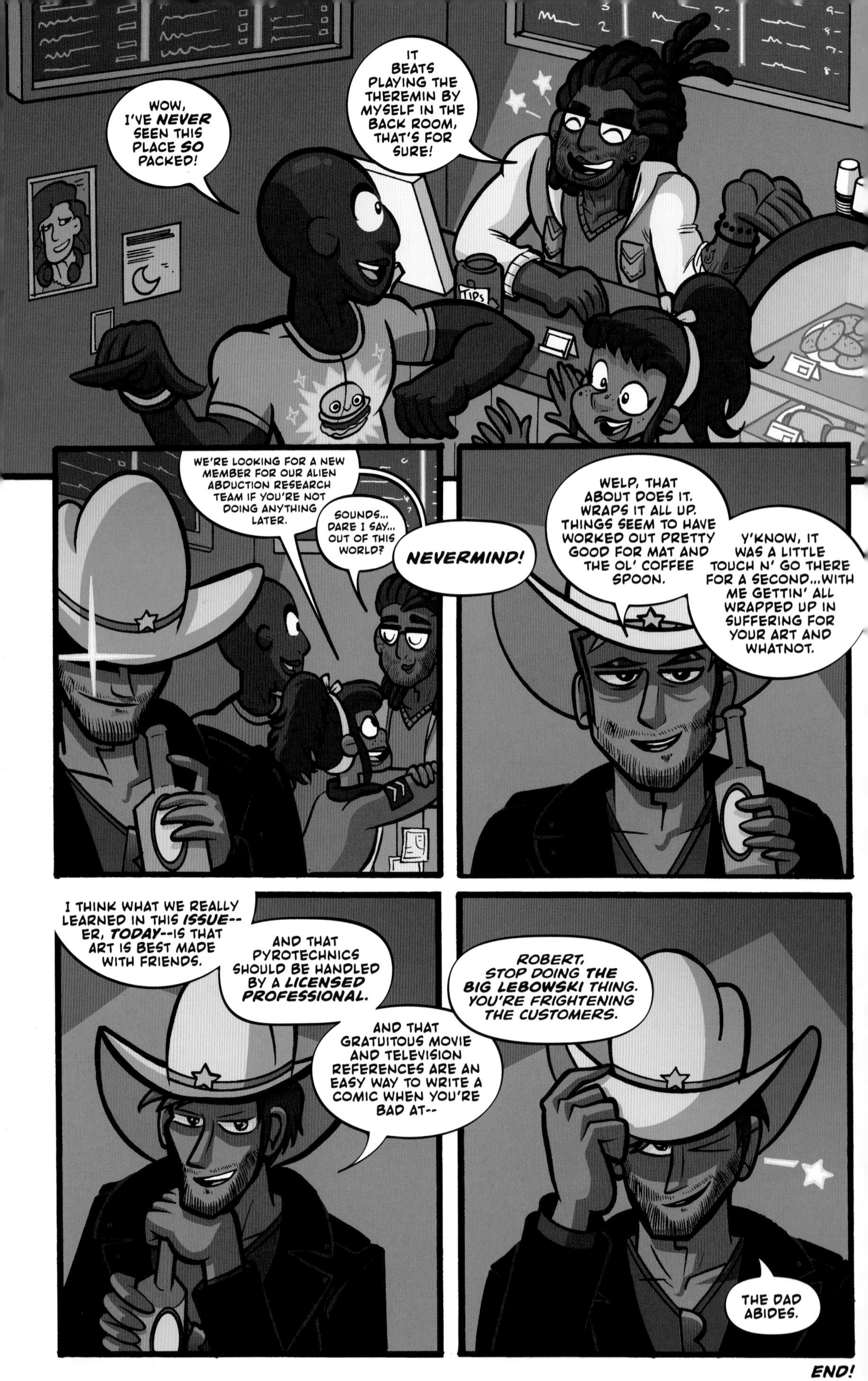
WOW, I'VE NEVER SEEN THIS PLACE SO PACKED!
IT BEATS PLAYING THE THEREMIN BY MYSELF IN THE BACK ROOM, THAT'S FOR SURE!
TIPS
WE'RE LOOKING FOR A NEW MEMBER FOR OUR ALIEN ABDUCTION RESEARCH TEAM IF YOU'RE NOT DOING ANYTHING LATER.
SOUNDS... DARE I SAY... OUT OF THIS WORLD?
NEVERMIND!
WELP, THAT ABOUT DOES IT. WRAPS IT ALL UP. THINGS SEEM TO HAVE WORKED OUT PRETTY GOOD FOR MAT AND THE OL' COFFEE SPOON.
Y'KNOW, IT WAS A LITTLE TOUCH N' GO THERE FOR A SECOND...WITH ME GETTIN' ALL WRAPPED UP IN SUFFERING FOR YOUR ART AND WHATNOT.
I THINK WHAT WE REALLY LEARNED IN THIS ISSUE-- ER, TODAY--IS THAT ART IS BEST MADE WITH FRIENDS.
AND THAT PYROTECHNICS SHOULD BE HANDLED BY A LICENSED PROFESSIONAL.
AND THAT GRATUITOUS MOVIE AND TELEVISION REFERENCES ARE AN EASY WAY TO WRITE A COMIC WHEN YOU'RE BAD AT--
ROBERT, STOP DOING THE BIG LEBOWSKI THING. YOU'RE FRIGHTENING THE CUSTOMERS.
THE DAD ABIDES.

END!

"Fair Deal"

Written by C. Spike Trotman
Illustrated by Drew Green
Colored by Reed Black
Lettered by Hassan Otsmane-Elhaou
Cover by Kris Anka

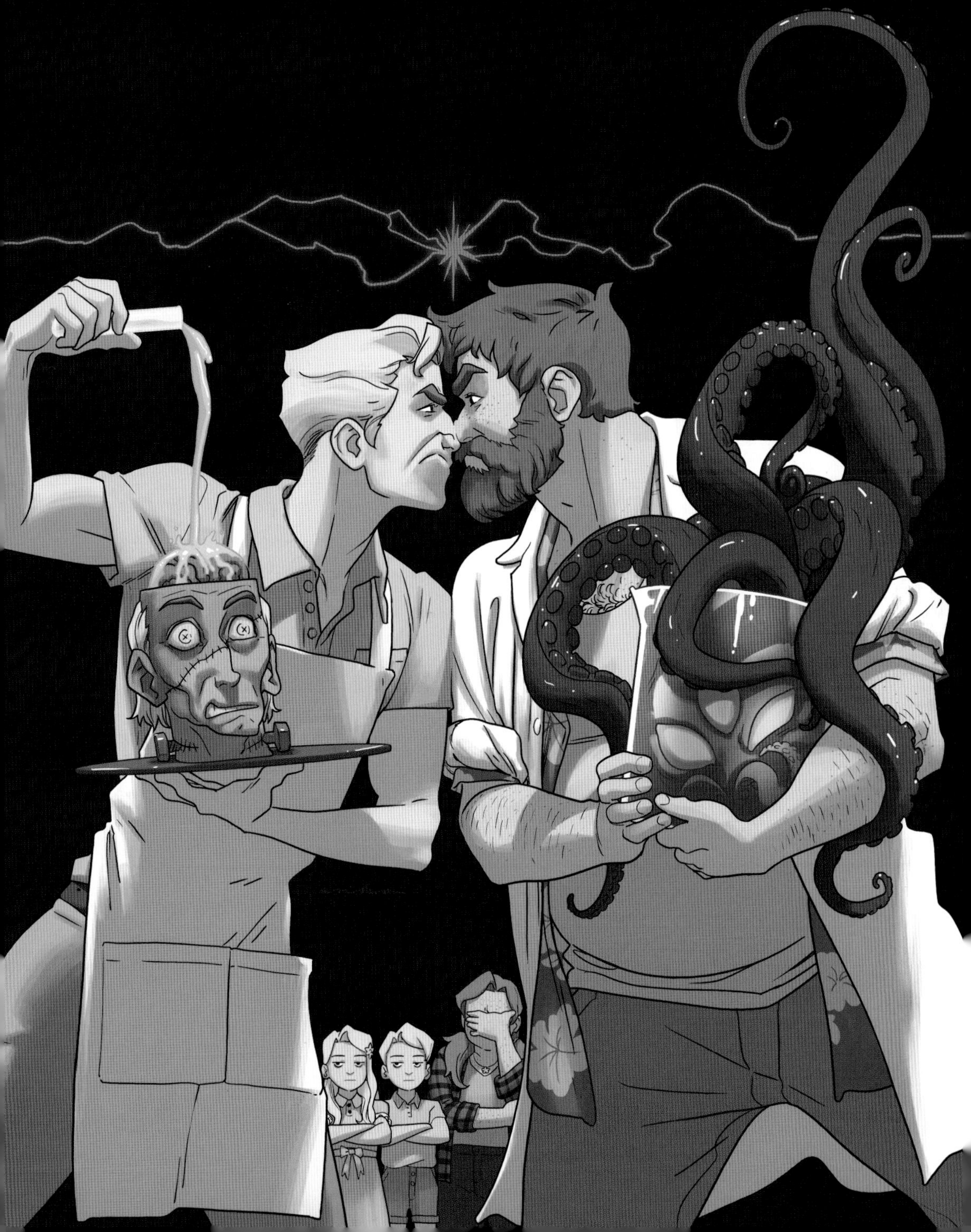

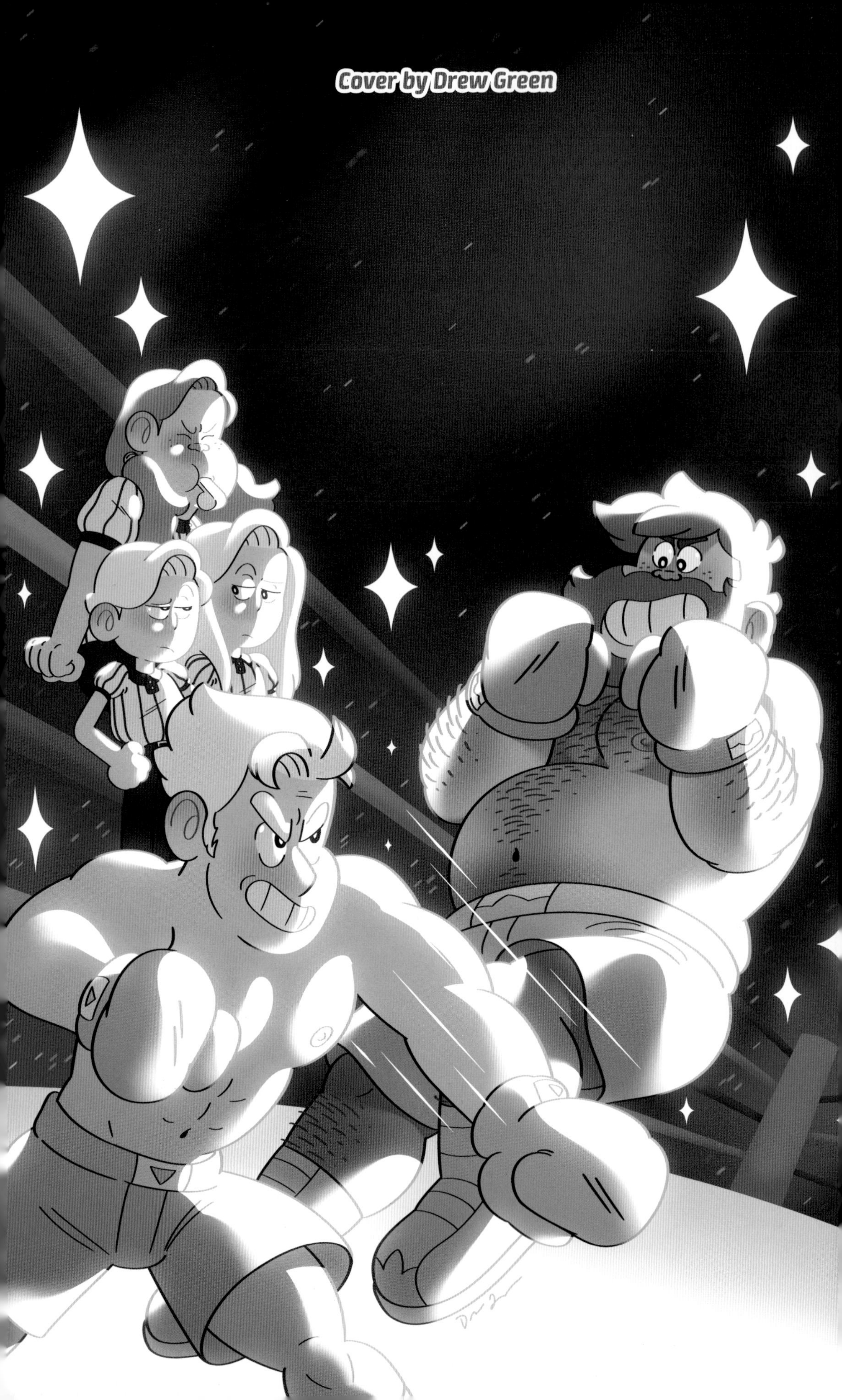

Cover by Drew Green

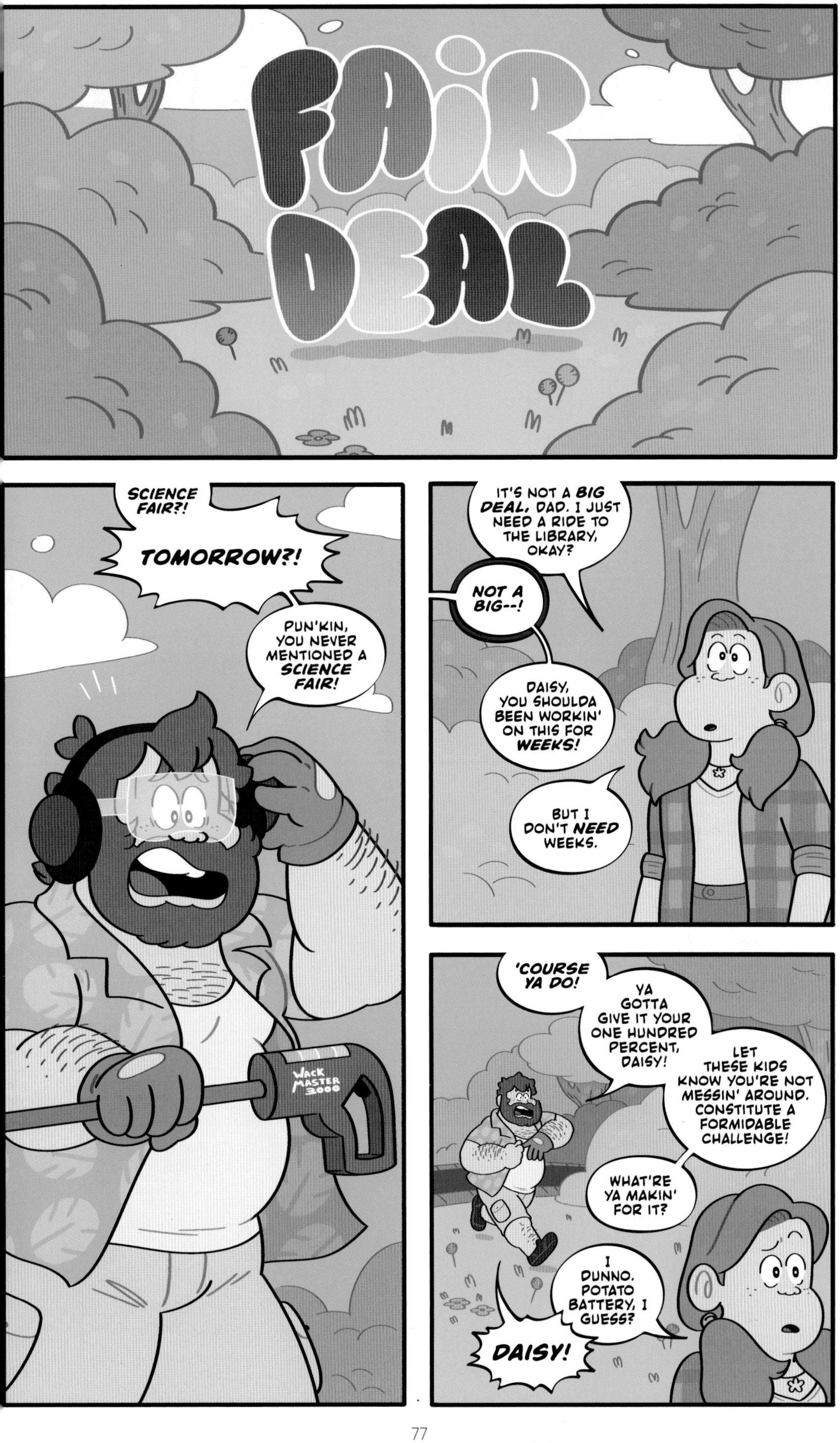
FAIR DEAL
SCIENCE FAIR?!
TOMORROW?!
PUN'KIN, YOU NEVER MENTIONED A SCIENCE FAIR!
WACK MASTER 3000
IT'S NOT A BIG DEAL, DAD. I JUST NEED A RIDE TO THE LIBRARY, OKAY?
NOT A BIG--!
DAISY, YOU SHOULDA BEEN WORKIN' ON THIS FOR WEEKS!
BUT I DON'T NEED WEEKS.
'COURSE YA DO!
YA GOTTA GIVE IT YOUR ONE HUNDRED PERCENT, DAISY!
LET THESE KIDS KNOW YOU'RE NOT MESSIN' AROUND. CONSTITUTE A FORMIDABLE CHALLENGE!
WHAT'RE YA MAKIN' FOR IT?
I DUNNO. POTATO BATTERY, I GUESS?
DAISY!

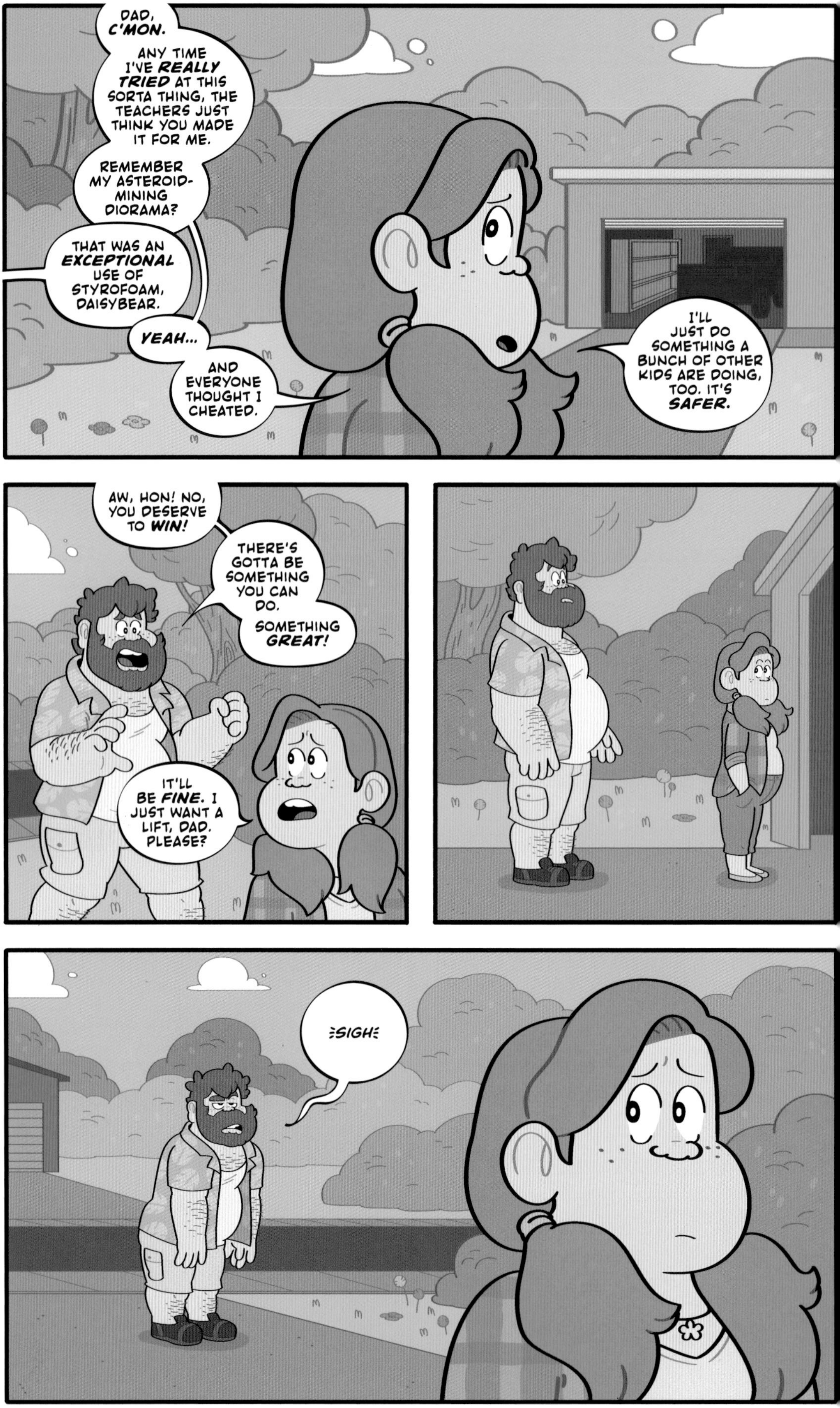
DAD, **C'MON.**
ANY TIME I'VE ***REALLY TRIED*** AT THIS SORTA THING, THE TEACHERS JUST THINK YOU MADE IT FOR ME.
REMEMBER MY ASTEROID-MINING DIORAMA?
THAT WAS AN ***EXCEPTIONAL*** USE OF STYROFOAM, DAISYBEAR.
YEAH...
AND EVERYONE THOUGHT I CHEATED.
I'LL JUST DO SOMETHING A BUNCH OF OTHER KIDS ARE DOING, TOO. IT'S ***SAFER.***
AW, HON! NO, YOU DESERVE TO ***WIN!***
THERE'S GOTTA BE SOMETHING YOU CAN DO.
SOMETHING ***GREAT!***
IT'LL BE ***FINE.*** I JUST WANT A LIFT, DAD. PLEASE?
SIGH

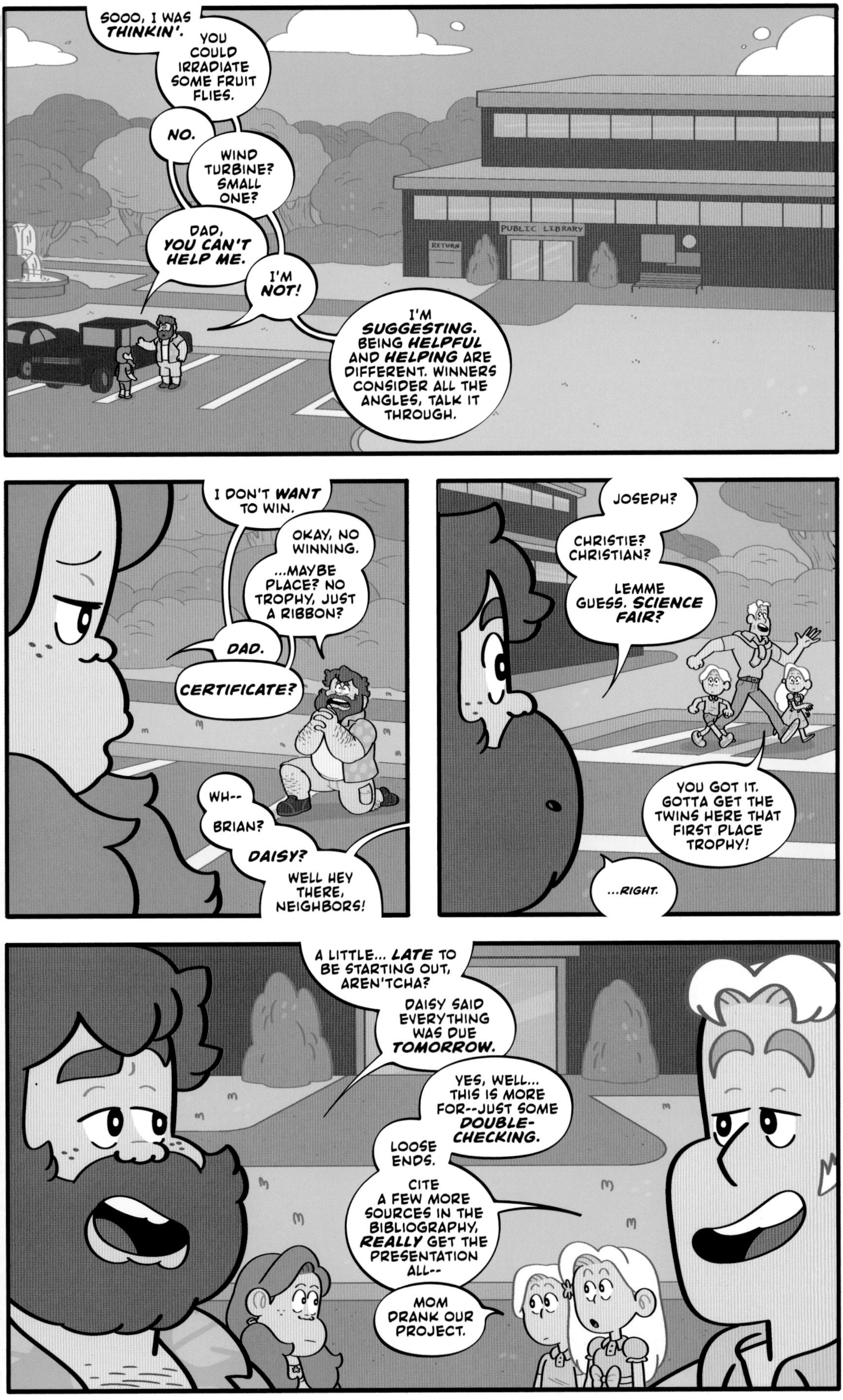
SOOO, I WAS THINKIN'.
YOU COULD IRRADIATE SOME FRUIT FLIES.
NO.
WIND TURBINE? SMALL ONE?
DAD, YOU CAN'T HELP ME.
I'M NOT!
I'M SUGGESTING. BEING HELPFUL AND HELPING ARE DIFFERENT. WINNERS CONSIDER ALL THE ANGLES, TALK IT THROUGH.
PUBLIC LIBRARY
RETURN
I DON'T WANT TO WIN.
OKAY, NO WINNING.
...MAYBE PLACE? NO TROPHY, JUST A RIBBON?
DAD.
CERTIFICATE?
WH--
BRIAN?
DAISY?
WELL HEY THERE, NEIGHBORS!
JOSEPH?
CHRISTIE? CHRISTIAN?
LEMME GUESS. SCIENCE FAIR?
YOU GOT IT. GOTTA GET THE TWINS HERE THAT FIRST PLACE TROPHY!
...RIGHT.
A LITTLE... LATE TO BE STARTING OUT, AREN'TCHA?
DAISY SAID EVERYTHING WAS DUE TOMORROW.
YES, WELL... THIS IS MORE FOR--JUST SOME DOUBLE-CHECKING.
LOOSE ENDS.
CITE A FEW MORE SOURCES IN THE BIBLIOGRAPHY, REALLY GET THE PRESENTATION ALL--
MOM DRANK OUR PROJECT.

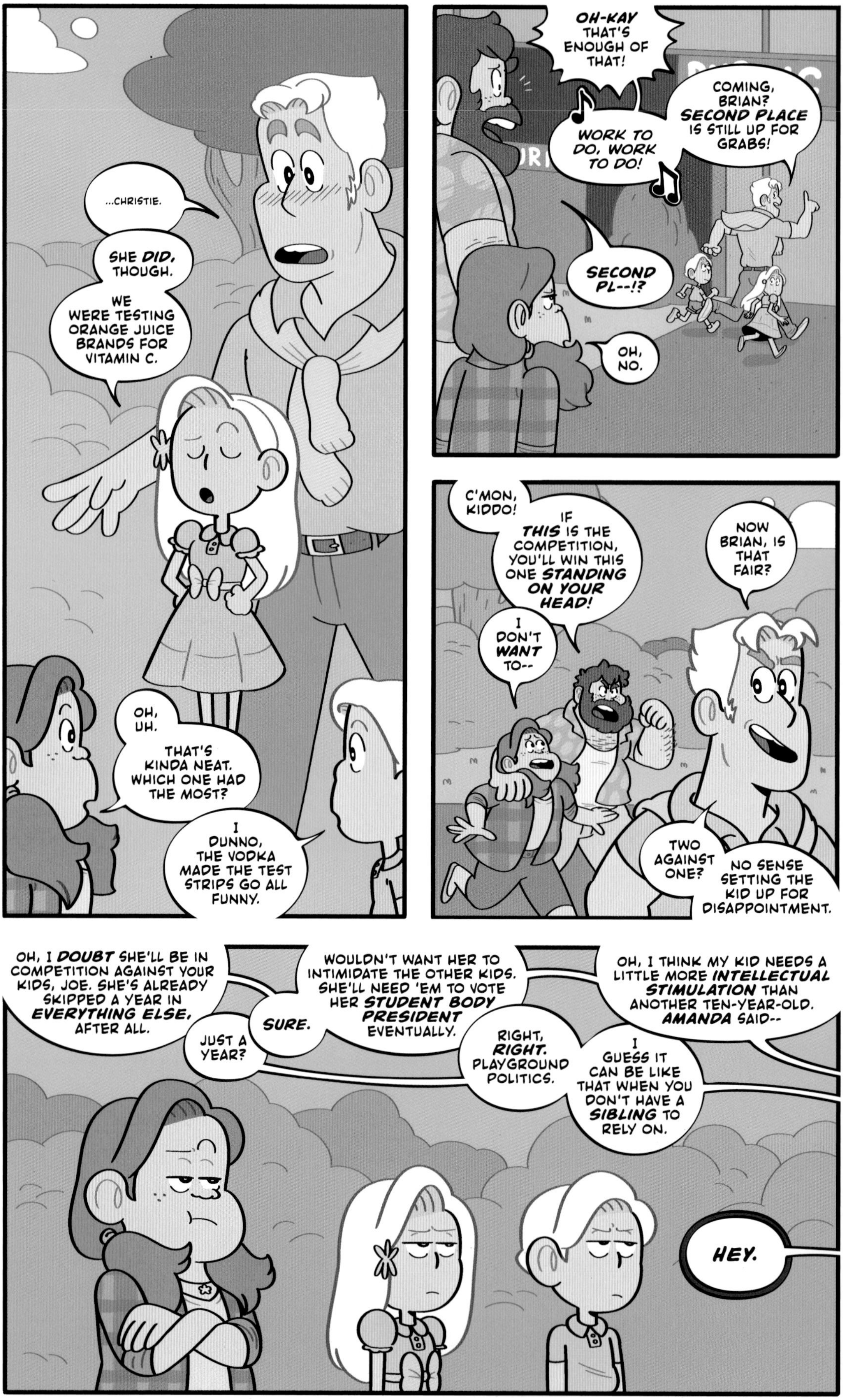
...CHRISTIE.
SHE *DID,* THOUGH.
WE WERE TESTING ORANGE JUICE BRANDS FOR VITAMIN C.
OH, UH.
THAT'S KINDA NEAT. WHICH ONE HAD THE MOST?
I DUNNO, THE VODKA MADE THE TEST STRIPS GO ALL FUNNY.
OH-KAY THAT'S ENOUGH OF THAT!
WORK TO DO, WORK TO DO!
COMING, BRIAN? ***SECOND PLACE*** IS STILL UP FOR GRABS!
SECOND PL--!?
OH, NO.
C'MON, KIDDO!
IF ***THIS*** IS THE COMPETITION, YOU'LL WIN THIS ONE ***STANDING ON YOUR HEAD!***
I DON'T ***WANT*** TO--
NOW BRIAN, IS THAT FAIR?
TWO AGAINST ONE?
NO SENSE SETTING THE KID UP FOR DISAPPOINTMENT.
OH, I ***DOUBT*** SHE'LL BE IN COMPETITION AGAINST YOUR KIDS, JOE. SHE'S ALREADY SKIPPED A YEAR IN ***EVERYTHING ELSE,*** AFTER ALL.
JUST A YEAR?
SURE.
WOULDN'T WANT HER TO INTIMIDATE THE OTHER KIDS. SHE'LL NEED 'EM TO VOTE HER ***STUDENT BODY PRESIDENT*** EVENTUALLY.
RIGHT, ***RIGHT.*** PLAYGROUND POLITICS.
OH, I THINK MY KID NEEDS A LITTLE MORE ***INTELLECTUAL STIMULATION*** THAN ANOTHER TEN-YEAR-OLD. ***AMANDA*** SAID--
I GUESS IT CAN BE LIKE THAT WHEN YOU DON'T HAVE A ***SIBLING*** TO RELY ON.
HEY.

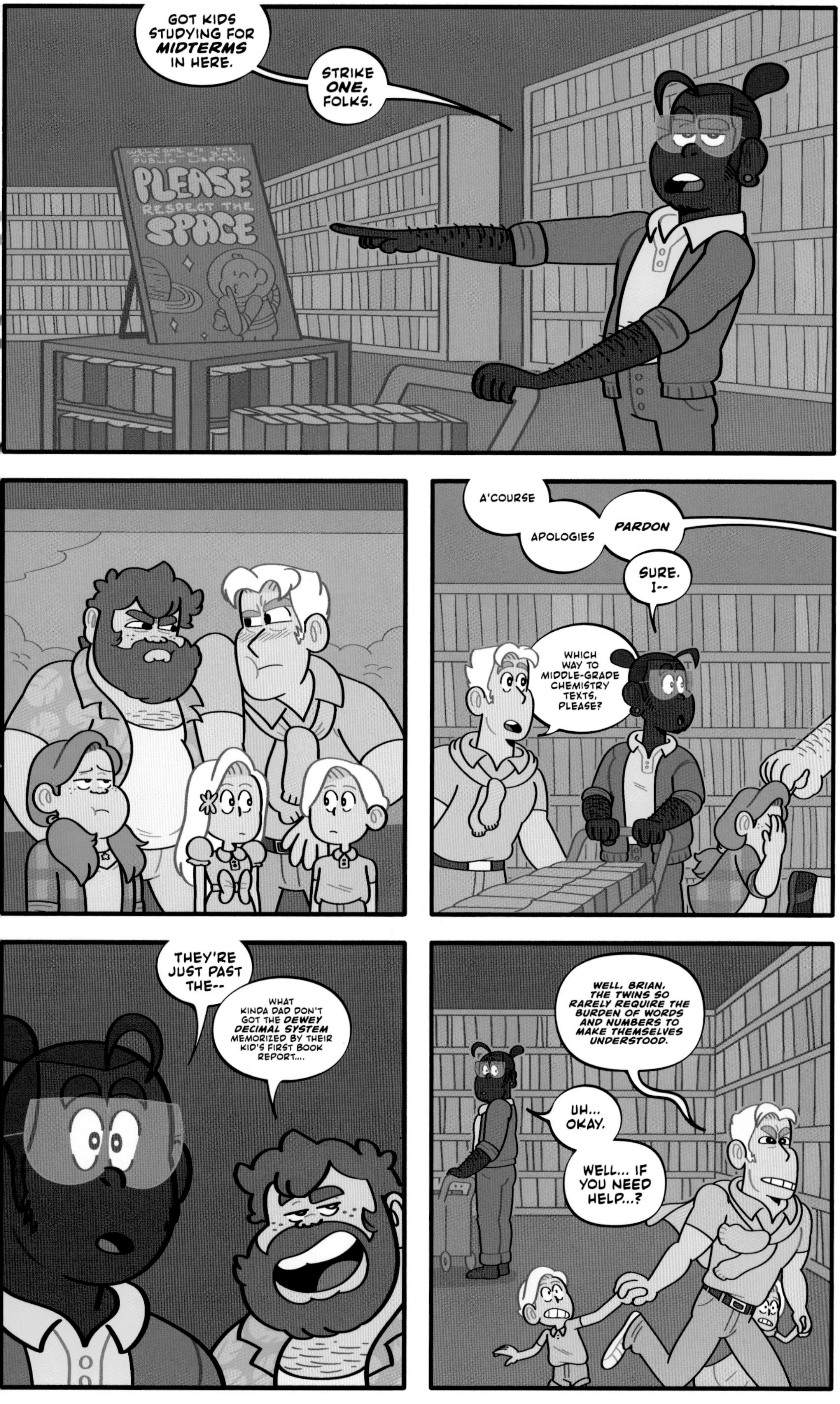
GOT KIDS STUDYING FOR *MIDTERMS* IN HERE.
STRIKE *ONE,* FOLKS.
PLEASE RESPECT THE SPACE
A'COURSE
APOLOGIES
PARDON
SURE. I--
WHICH WAY TO MIDDLE-GRADE CHEMISTRY TEXTS, PLEASE?
THEY'RE JUST PAST THE--
WHAT KINDA DAD DON'T GOT THE *DEWEY DECIMAL SYSTEM* MEMORIZED BY THEIR KID'S FIRST BOOK REPORT....
WELL, BRIAN, THE TWINS SO RARELY REQUIRE THE BURDEN OF WORDS AND NUMBERS TO MAKE THEMSELVES UNDERSTOOD.
UH... OKAY.
WELL... IF YOU NEED HELP...?

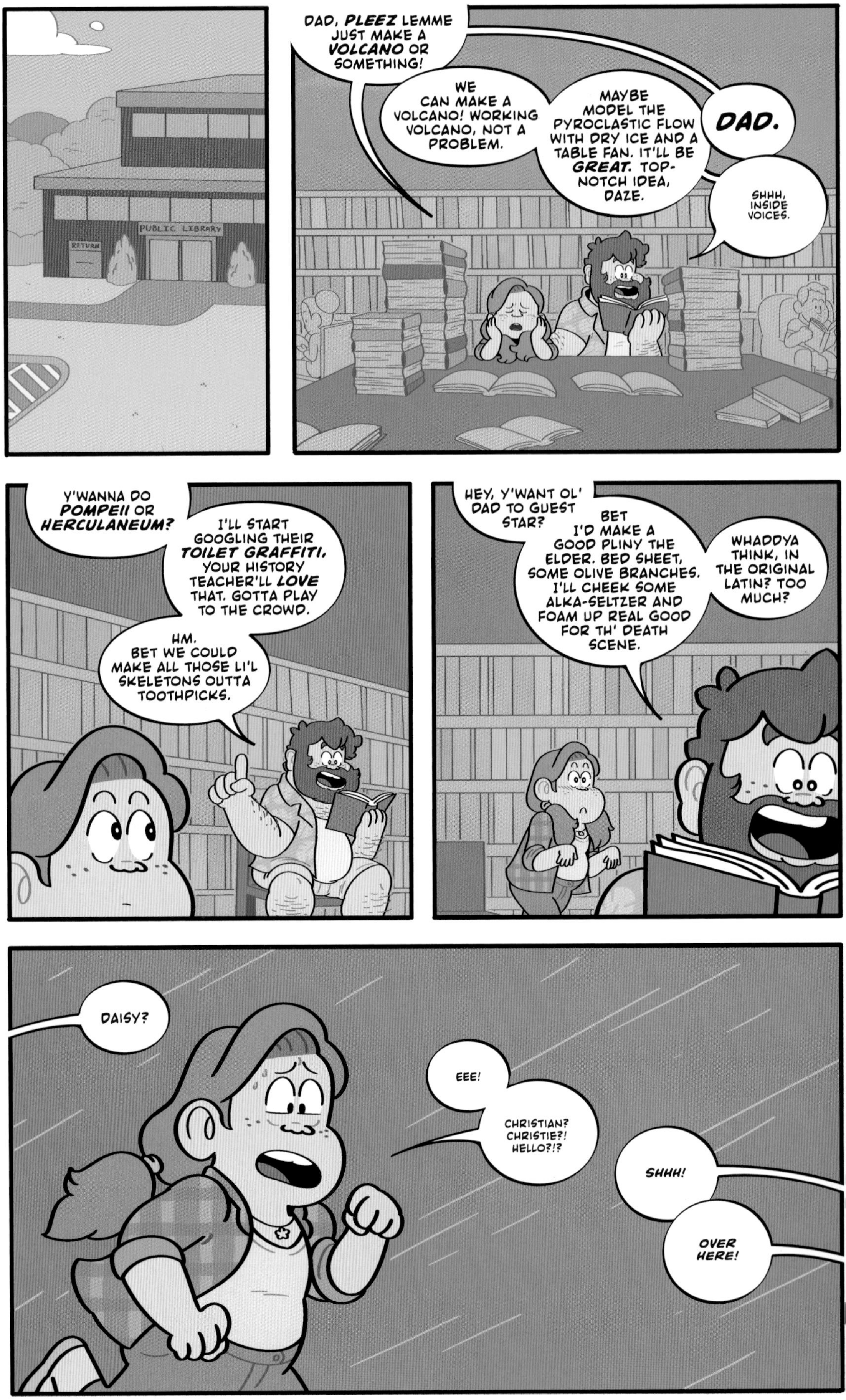
PUBLIC LIBRARY
RETURN
DAD, PLEEZ LEMME JUST MAKE A VOLCANO OR SOMETHING!
WE CAN MAKE A VOLCANO! WORKING VOLCANO, NOT A PROBLEM.
MAYBE MODEL THE PYROCLASTIC FLOW WITH DRY ICE AND A TABLE FAN. IT'LL BE GREAT. TOP-NOTCH IDEA, DAZE.
DAD.
SHHH, INSIDE VOICES.
Y'WANNA DO POMPEII OR HERCULANEUM?
I'LL START GOOGLING THEIR TOILET GRAFFITI. YOUR HISTORY TEACHER'LL LOVE THAT. GOTTA PLAY TO THE CROWD.
HM. BET WE COULD MAKE ALL THOSE LI'L SKELETONS OUTTA TOOTHPICKS.
HEY, Y'WANT OL' DAD TO GUEST STAR?
BET I'D MAKE A GOOD PLINY THE ELDER. BED SHEET, SOME OLIVE BRANCHES. I'LL CHEEK SOME ALKA-SELTZER AND FOAM UP REAL GOOD FOR TH' DEATH SCENE.
WHADDYA THINK, IN THE ORIGINAL LATIN? TOO MUCH?
DAISY?
EEE!
CHRISTIAN? CHRISTIE?! HELLO?!?
SHHH!
OVER HERE!

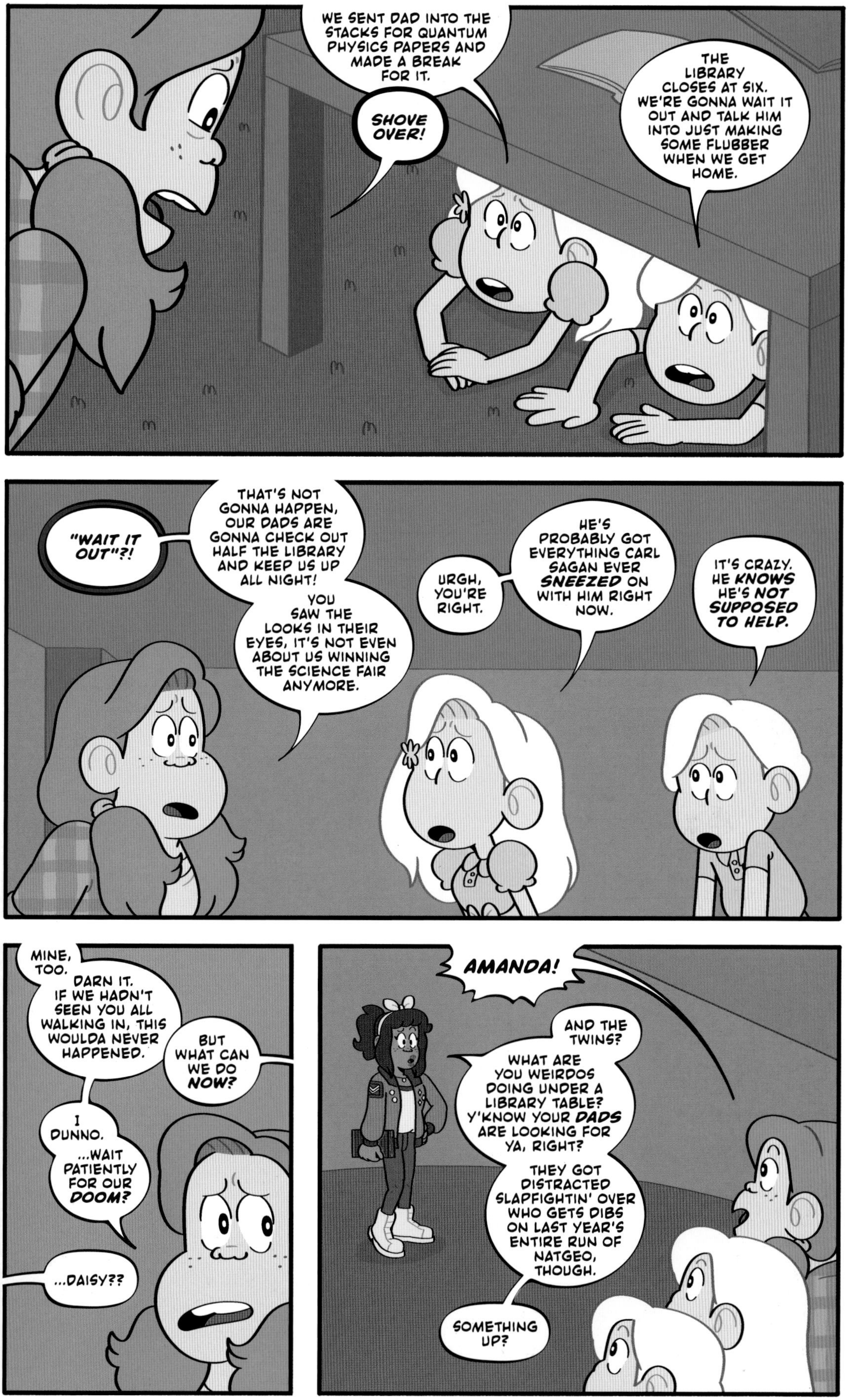
WE SENT DAD INTO THE STACKS FOR QUANTUM PHYSICS PAPERS AND MADE A BREAK FOR IT.
SHOVE OVER!
THE LIBRARY CLOSES AT SIX. WE'RE GONNA WAIT IT OUT AND TALK HIM INTO JUST MAKING SOME FLUBBER WHEN WE GET HOME.
"WAIT IT OUT"?!
THAT'S NOT GONNA HAPPEN, OUR DADS ARE GONNA CHECK OUT HALF THE LIBRARY AND KEEP US UP ALL NIGHT!
YOU SAW THE LOOKS IN THEIR EYES, IT'S NOT EVEN ABOUT US WINNING THE SCIENCE FAIR ANYMORE.
URGH, YOU'RE RIGHT.
HE'S PROBABLY GOT EVERYTHING CARL SAGAN EVER SNEEZED ON WITH HIM RIGHT NOW.
IT'S CRAZY. HE KNOWS HE'S NOT SUPPOSED TO HELP.
MINE, TOO. DARN IT. IF WE HADN'T SEEN YOU ALL WALKING IN, THIS WOULDA NEVER HAPPENED.
BUT WHAT CAN WE DO NOW?
I DUNNO. ...WAIT PATIENTLY FOR OUR DOOM?
...DAISY??
AMANDA!
AND THE TWINS?
WHAT ARE YOU WEIRDOS DOING UNDER A LIBRARY TABLE? Y'KNOW YOUR DADS ARE LOOKING FOR YA, RIGHT?
THEY GOT DISTRACTED SLAPFIGHTIN' OVER WHO GETS DIBS ON LAST YEAR'S ENTIRE RUN OF NATGEO, THOUGH.
SOMETHING UP?

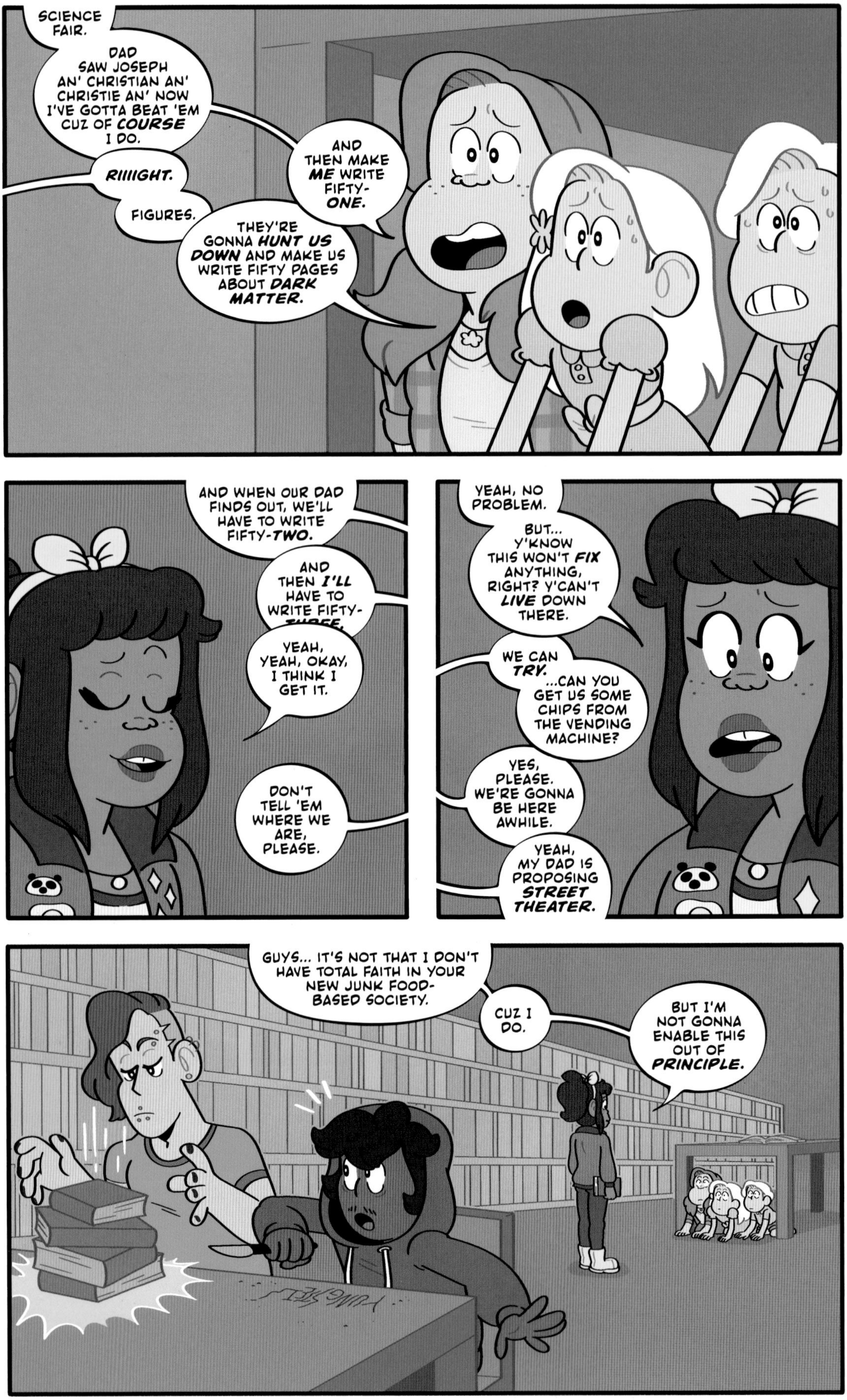
SCIENCE FAIR.
DAD SAW JOSEPH AN' CHRISTIAN AN' CHRISTIE AN' NOW I'VE GOTTA BEAT 'EM CUZ OF COURSE I DO.
RIIIIGHT.
FIGURES.
AND THEN MAKE ME WRITE FIFTY-ONE.
THEY'RE GONNA HUNT US DOWN AND MAKE US WRITE FIFTY PAGES ABOUT DARK MATTER.
AND WHEN OUR DAD FINDS OUT, WE'LL HAVE TO WRITE FIFTY-TWO.
AND THEN I'LL HAVE TO WRITE FIFTY-
YEAH, YEAH, OKAY, I THINK I GET IT.
DON'T TELL 'EM WHERE WE ARE, PLEASE.
YEAH, NO PROBLEM.
BUT... Y'KNOW THIS WON'T FIX ANYTHING, RIGHT? Y'CAN'T LIVE DOWN THERE.
WE CAN TRY.
...CAN YOU GET US SOME CHIPS FROM THE VENDING MACHINE?
YES, PLEASE. WE'RE GONNA BE HERE AWHILE.
YEAH, MY DAD IS PROPOSING STREET THEATER.
GUYS... IT'S NOT THAT I DON'T HAVE TOTAL FAITH IN YOUR NEW JUNK FOOD-BASED SOCIETY.
CUZ I DO.
BUT I'M NOT GONNA ENABLE THIS OUT OF PRINCIPLE.

LOOK, YOU WANT SOME ADVICE FROM SOMEONE WHO'S WEATHERED THE DAD-STORM AND LIVED TO TELL THE TALE?

WHEN THEY WON'T LISTEN TO REASON, AND IT'S REALLY *IMPORTANT?* YOUR BEST BET IS GETTIN' *UN-REASONABLE.*

Y'MEAN, LIKE... CRY?

I'M NOT GONNA *CRY!*

I'M NOT A *BABY!*

CRYING DOESN'T MEAN--

LOOK, Y'DON'T *HAVE* TO CRY. YOU JUST HAVE TO... *BE KIDS.*

I'M NOT SUPPOSED TO TELL YOU THIS, REAL-DEAL ADULT SECRET STUFF.

BUT THEY REALLY, *REALLY* DO CARE ABOUT YOU. THAT'S WHY THEY'RE *DOING* THIS.

YOU JUST HAVE TO SHOW 'EM IT'S THE WRONG THING TO BE CARING ABOUT.

Y-YOU MEAN...

MISBEHAVE?

HAHA.

YOU UP TO THE CHALLENGE, KID?

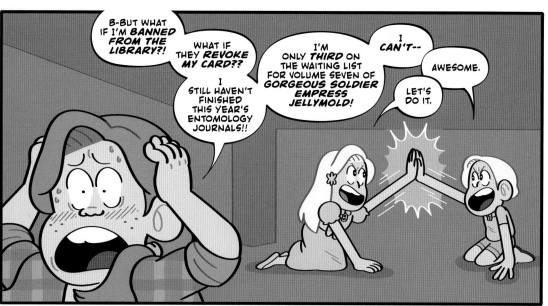

B-BUT WHAT IF I'M *BANNED FROM THE LIBRARY?!*

WHAT IF THEY *REVOKE MY CARD??*

I STILL HAVEN'T FINISHED THIS YEAR'S ENTOMOLOGY JOURNALS!!

I'M ONLY *THIRD* ON THE WAITING LIST FOR VOLUME SEVEN OF *GORGEOUS SOLDIER EMPRESS JELLYMOLD!*

I *CAN'T--*

AWESOME.

LET'S DO IT.

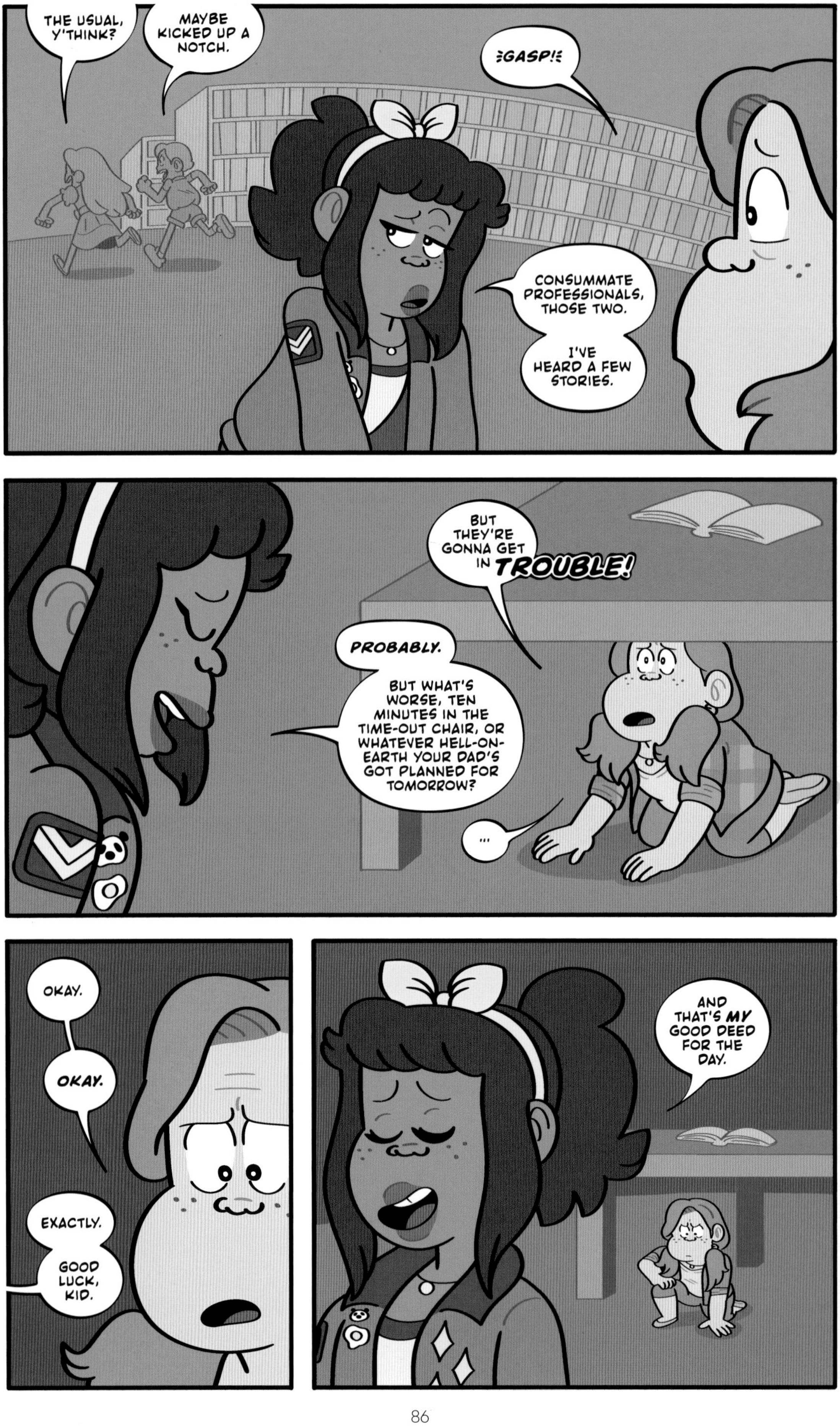
THE USUAL, Y'THINK?
MAYBE KICKED UP A NOTCH.
GASP!
CONSUMMATE PROFESSIONALS, THOSE TWO.
I'VE HEARD A FEW STORIES.
BUT THEY'RE GONNA GET IN TROUBLE!
PROBABLY.
BUT WHAT'S WORSE, TEN MINUTES IN THE TIME-OUT CHAIR, OR WHATEVER HELL-ON-EARTH YOUR DAD'S GOT PLANNED FOR TOMORROW?
...
OKAY.
OKAY.
EXACTLY.
GOOD LUCK, KID.
AND THAT'S MY GOOD DEED FOR THE DAY.

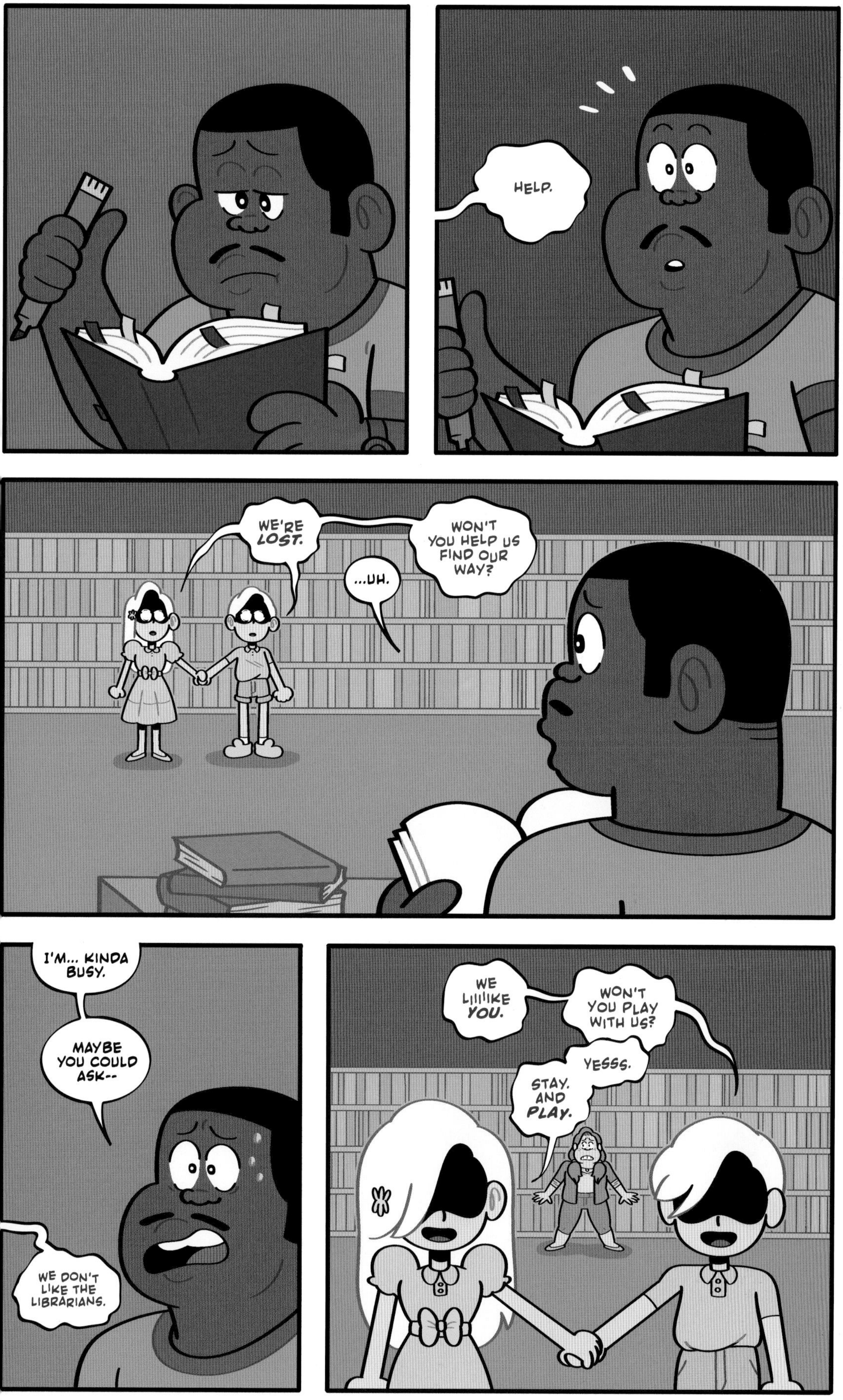
HELP.
WE'RE LOST.
...UH.
WON'T YOU HELP US FIND OUR WAY?
I'M... KINDA BUSY.
MAYBE YOU COULD ASK--
WE DON'T LIKE THE LIBRARIANS.
WE LIIIIIKE YOU.
WON'T YOU PLAY WITH US?
YESSS.
STAY. AND PLAY.

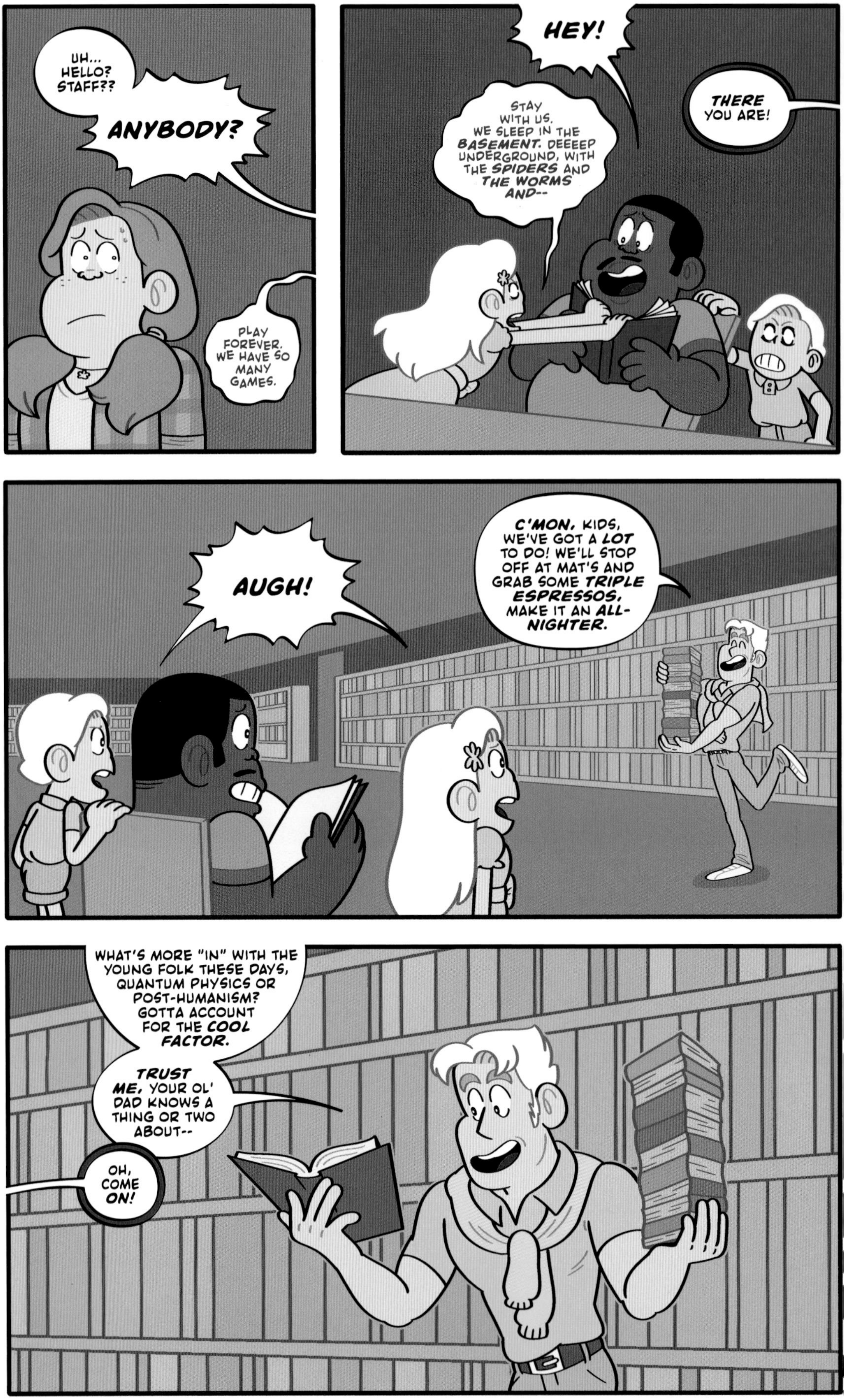

UH... HELLO? STAFF??
ANYBODY?
PLAY FOREVER. WE HAVE SO MANY GAMES.
HEY!
STAY WITH US. WE SLEEP IN THE BASEMENT. DEEEEP UNDERGROUND, WITH THE SPIDERS AND THE WORMS AND--
THERE YOU ARE!
AUGH!
C'MON, KIDS, WE'VE GOT A LOT TO DO! WE'LL STOP OFF AT MAT'S AND GRAB SOME TRIPLE ESPRESSOS, MAKE IT AN ALL-NIGHTER.
WHAT'S MORE "IN" WITH THE YOUNG FOLK THESE DAYS, QUANTUM PHYSICS OR POST-HUMANISM? GOTTA ACCOUNT FOR THE COOL FACTOR.
TRUST ME, YOUR OL' DAD KNOWS A THING OR TWO ABOUT--
OH, COME ON!

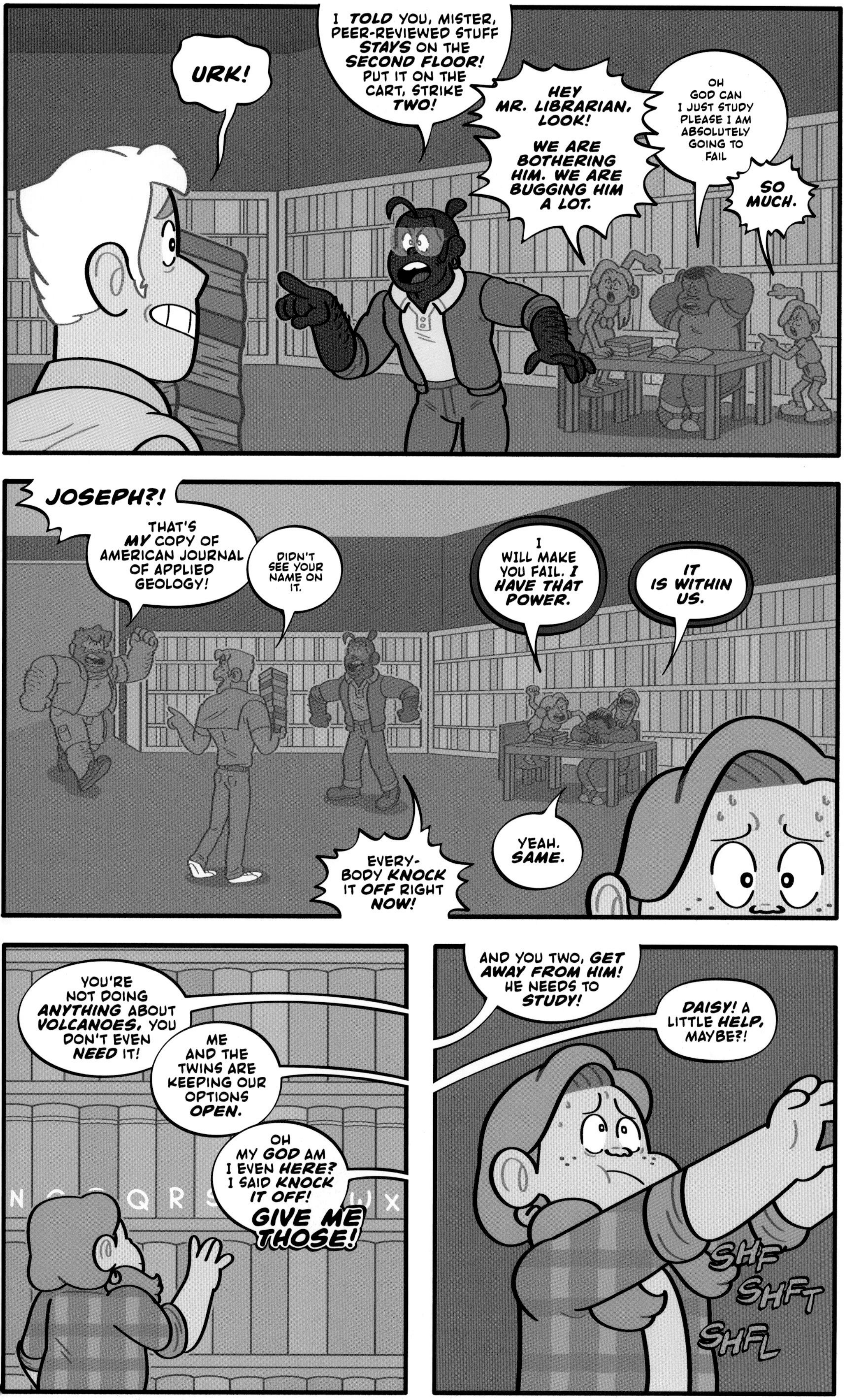
URK!
I TOLD YOU, MISTER, PEER-REVIEWED STUFF STAYS ON THE SECOND FLOOR! PUT IT ON THE CART, STRIKE TWO!
HEY MR. LIBRARIAN, LOOK! WE ARE BOTHERING HIM. WE ARE BUGGING HIM A LOT.
OH GOD CAN I JUST STUDY PLEASE I AM ABSOLUTELY GOING TO FAIL
SO MUCH.
JOSEPH?!
THAT'S MY COPY OF AMERICAN JOURNAL OF APPLIED GEOLOGY!
DIDN'T SEE YOUR NAME ON IT.
I WILL MAKE YOU FAIL. I HAVE THAT POWER.
IT IS WITHIN US.
EVERY-BODY KNOCK IT OFF RIGHT NOW!
YEAH. SAME.
YOU'RE NOT DOING ANYTHING ABOUT VOLCANOES, YOU DON'T EVEN NEED IT!
ME AND THE TWINS ARE KEEPING OUR OPTIONS OPEN.
OH MY GOD AM I EVEN HERE? I SAID KNOCK IT OFF!
GIVE ME THOSE!
AND YOU TWO, GET AWAY FROM HIM! HE NEEDS TO STUDY!
DAISY! A LITTLE HELP, MAYBE?!
SHF
SHFT
SHFL

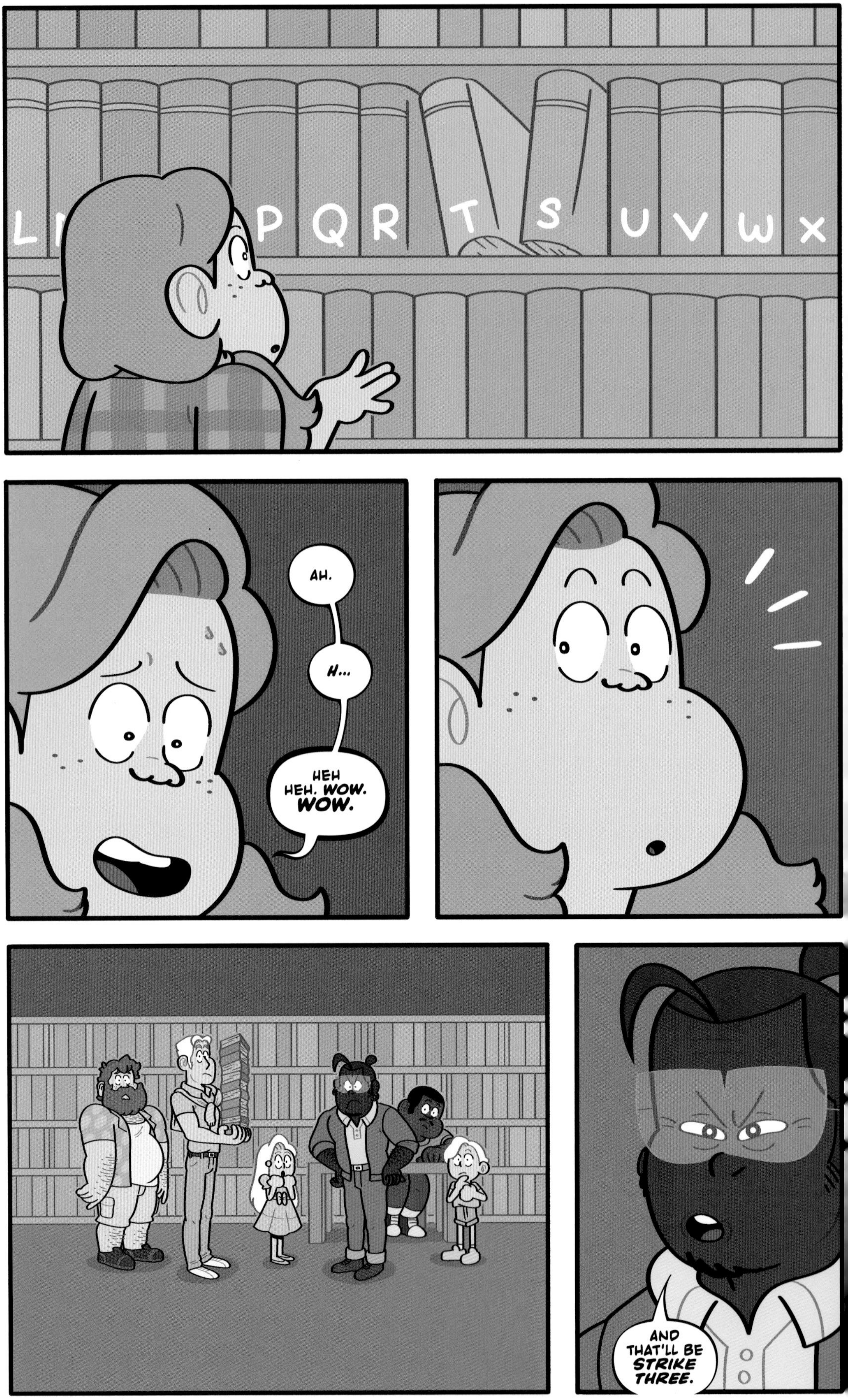
L
P Q R T S U V W X
AH.
H...
HEH HEH. WOW. WOW.
AND THAT'LL BE STRIKE THREE.

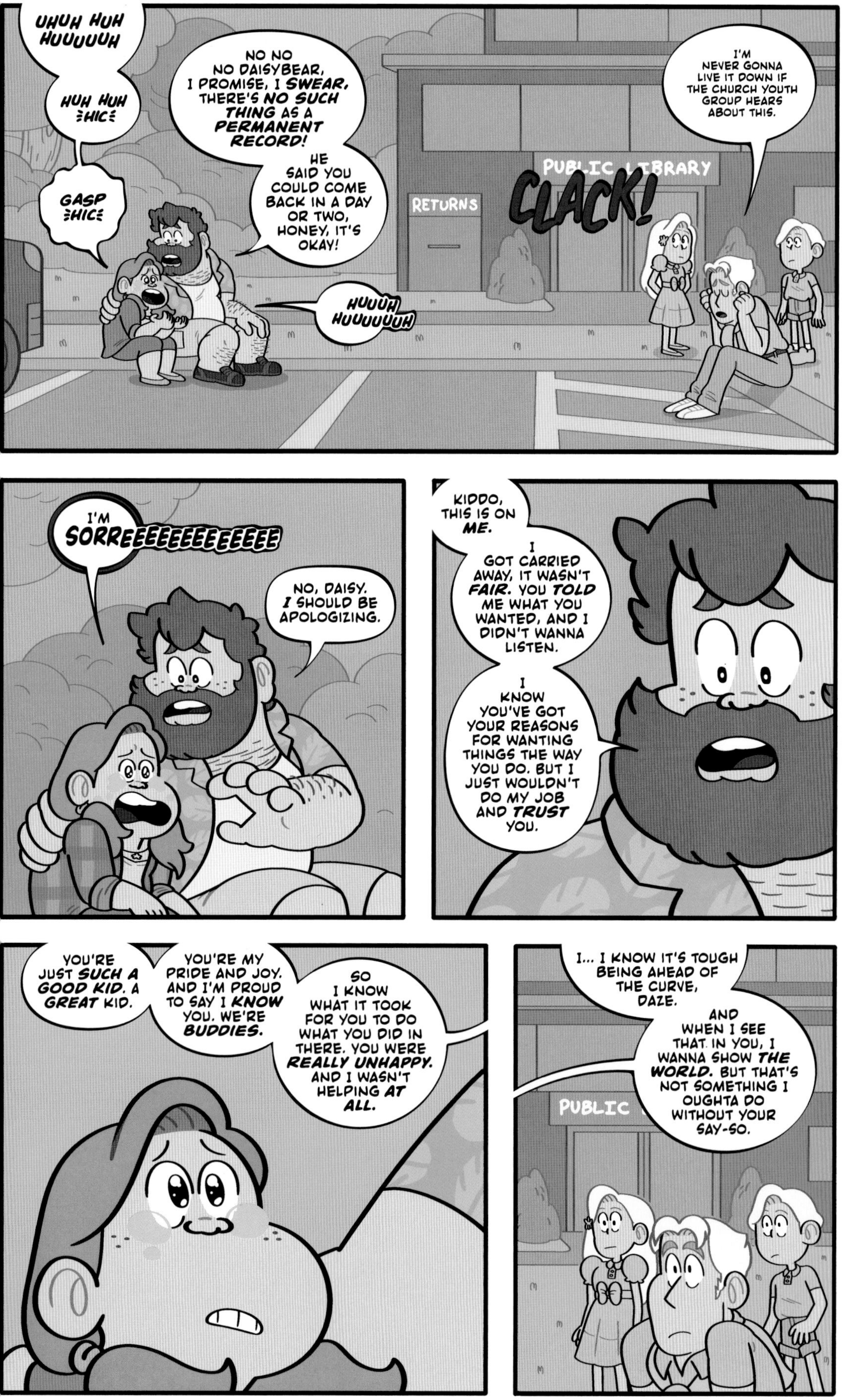
UHUH HUH HUUUUUH
HUH HUH HIC
GASP HIC
NO NO NO DAISYBEAR, I PROMISE, I SWEAR, THERE'S NO SUCH THING AS A PERMANENT RECORD!
HE SAID YOU COULD COME BACK IN A DAY OR TWO, HONEY, IT'S OKAY!
HUUUH HUUUUUUH
RETURNS
PUBLIC LIBRARY
CLACK!
I'M NEVER GONNA LIVE IT DOWN IF THE CHURCH YOUTH GROUP HEARS ABOUT THIS.
I'M SORREEEEEEEEEEEEE
NO, DAISY. I SHOULD BE APOLOGIZING.
KIDDO, THIS IS ON ME.
I GOT CARRIED AWAY, IT WASN'T FAIR. YOU TOLD ME WHAT YOU WANTED, AND I DIDN'T WANNA LISTEN.
I KNOW YOU'VE GOT YOUR REASONS FOR WANTING THINGS THE WAY YOU DO. BUT I JUST WOULDN'T DO MY JOB AND TRUST YOU.
YOU'RE JUST SUCH A GOOD KID. A GREAT KID.
YOU'RE MY PRIDE AND JOY. AND I'M PROUD TO SAY I KNOW YOU. WE'RE BUDDIES.
SO I KNOW WHAT IT TOOK FOR YOU TO DO WHAT YOU DID IN THERE. YOU WERE REALLY UNHAPPY. AND I WASN'T HELPING AT ALL.
I... I KNOW IT'S TOUGH BEING AHEAD OF THE CURVE, DAZE.
PUBLIC
AND WHEN I SEE THAT IN YOU, I WANNA SHOW THE WORLD. BUT THAT'S NOT SOMETHING I OUGHTA DO WITHOUT YOUR SAY-SO.

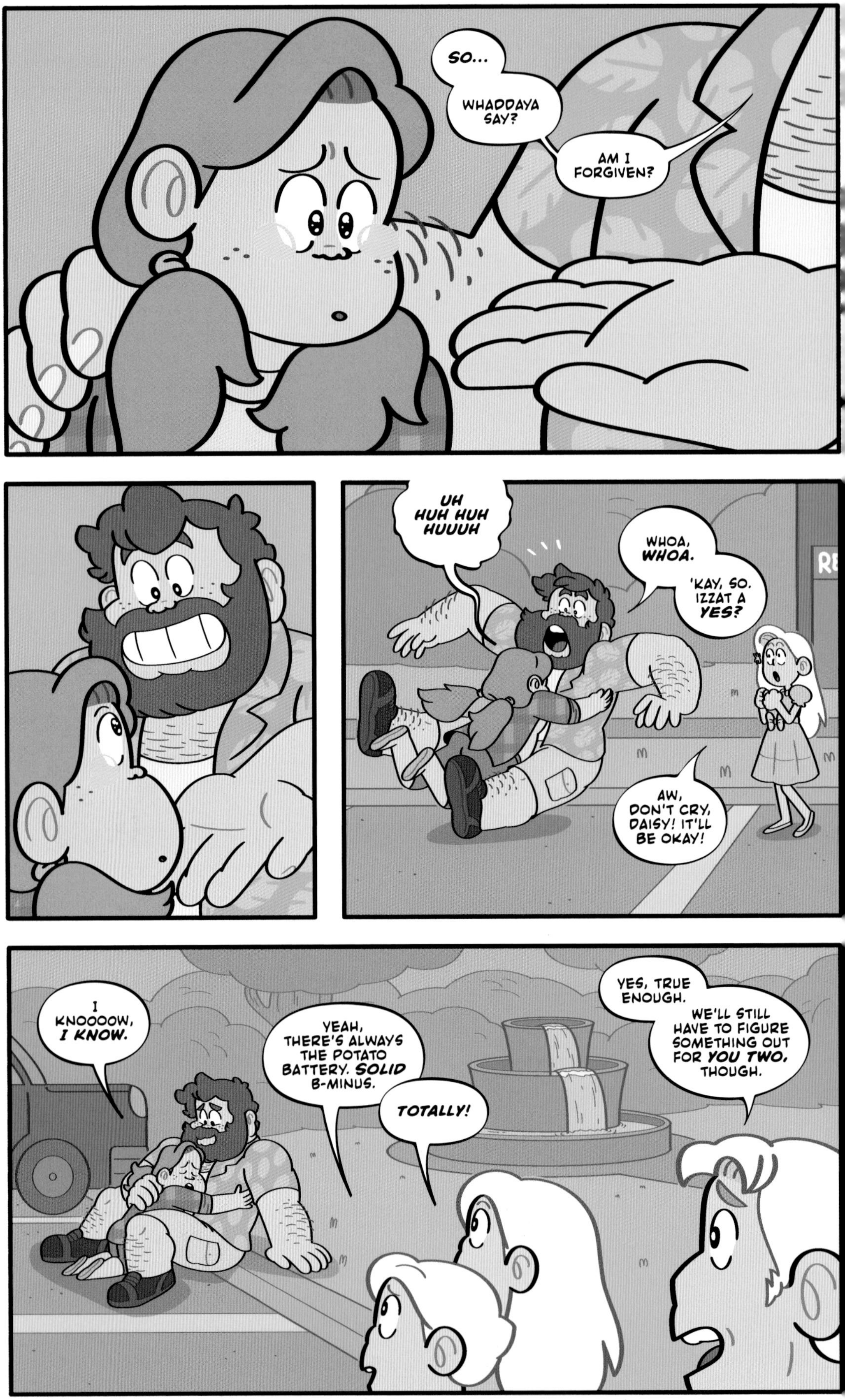
SO...
WHADDAYA SAY?
AM I FORGIVEN?
UH HUH HUH HUUUH
WHOA, **WHOA.**
'KAY, SO. IZZAT A ***YES?***
AW, DON'T CRY, DAISY! IT'LL BE OKAY!
I KNOOOOW, ***I KNOW.***
YEAH, THERE'S ALWAYS THE POTATO BATTERY. ***SOLID*** B-MINUS.
TOTALLY!
YES, TRUE ENOUGH.
WE'LL STILL HAVE TO FIGURE SOMETHING OUT FOR ***YOU TWO,*** THOUGH.

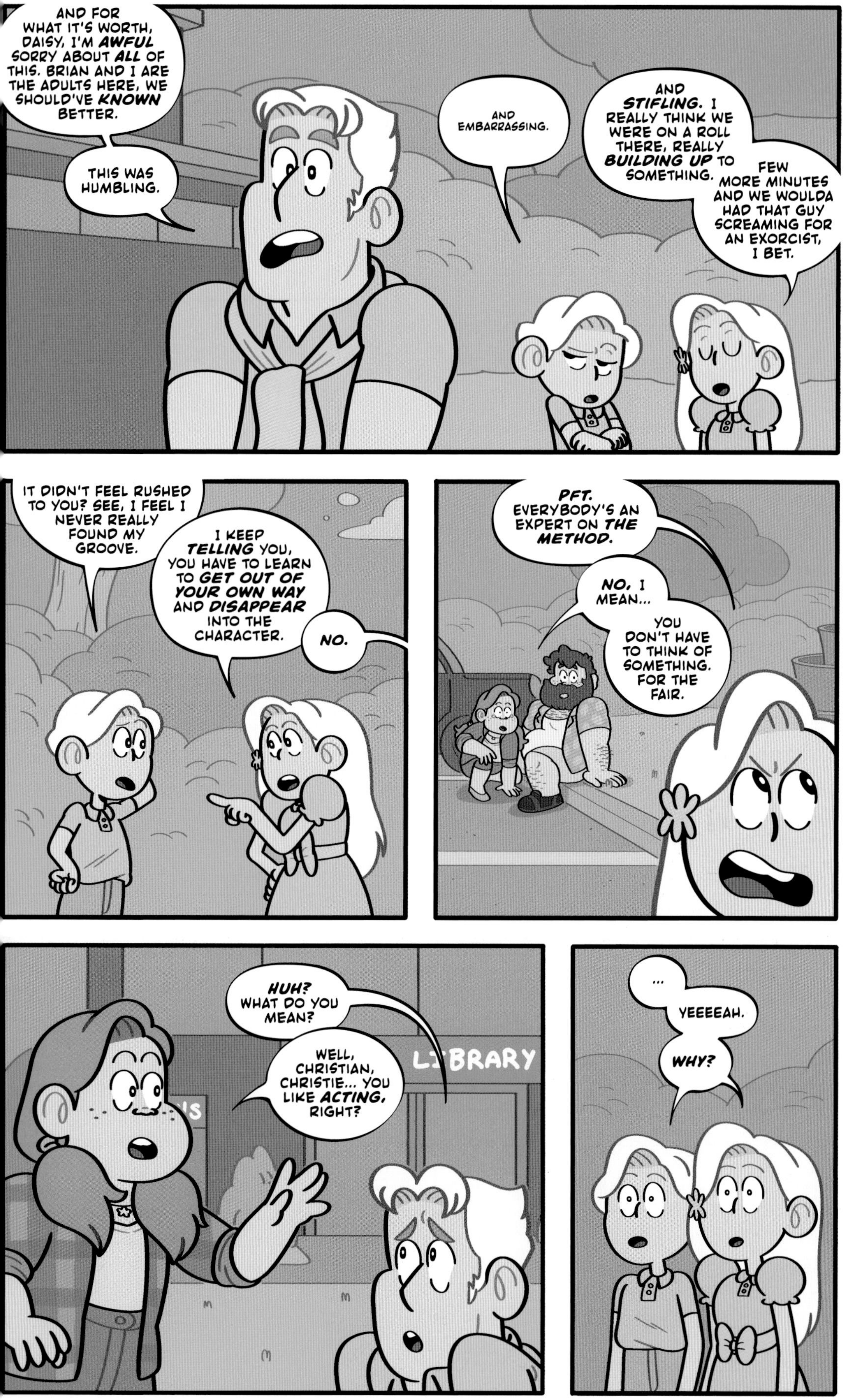

AND FOR WHAT IT'S WORTH, DAISY, I'M **AWFUL** SORRY ABOUT **ALL** OF THIS. BRIAN AND I ARE THE ADULTS HERE, WE SHOULD'VE **KNOWN** BETTER.
THIS WAS HUMBLING.
AND EMBARRASSING.
AND **STIFLING.** I REALLY THINK WE WERE ON A ROLL THERE, REALLY **BUILDING UP** TO SOMETHING.
FEW MORE MINUTES AND WE WOULDA HAD THAT GUY SCREAMING FOR AN EXORCIST, I BET.
IT DIDN'T FEEL RUSHED TO YOU? SEE, I FEEL I NEVER REALLY FOUND MY GROOVE.
I KEEP **TELLING** YOU, YOU HAVE TO LEARN TO **GET OUT OF YOUR OWN WAY** AND **DISAPPEAR** INTO THE CHARACTER.
NO.
PFT. EVERYBODY'S AN EXPERT ON **THE METHOD.**
NO, I MEAN...
YOU DON'T HAVE TO THINK OF SOMETHING. FOR THE FAIR.
HUH? WHAT DO YOU MEAN?
WELL, CHRISTIAN, CHRISTIE... YOU LIKE **ACTING,** RIGHT?
LIBRARY
...
YEEEEAH.
WHY?

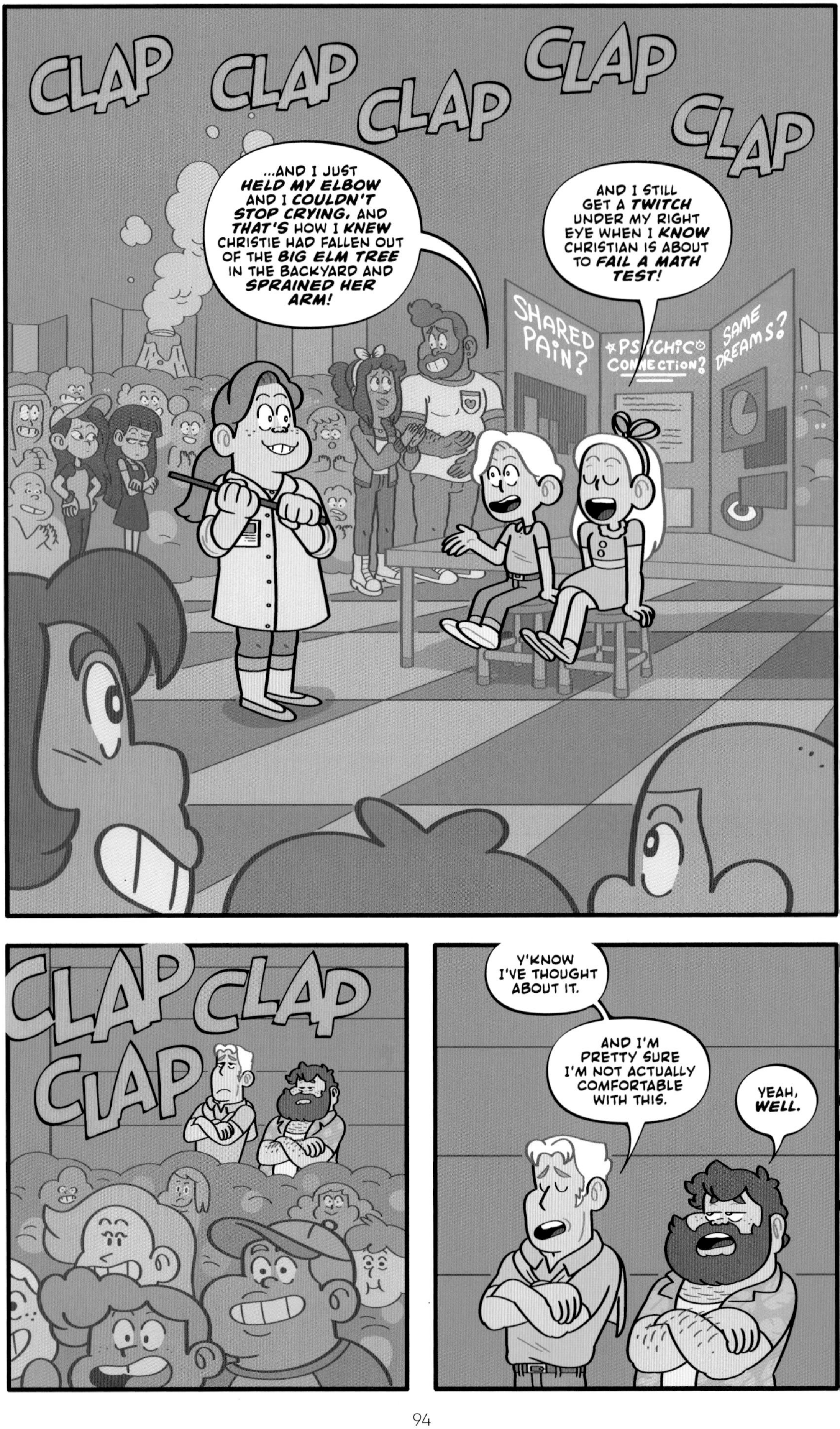
CLAP CLAP CLAP CLAP CLAP
...AND I JUST HELD MY ELBOW AND I COULDN'T STOP CRYING, AND THAT'S HOW I KNEW CHRISTIE HAD FALLEN OUT OF THE BIG ELM TREE IN THE BACKYARD AND SPRAINED HER ARM!
AND I STILL GET A TWITCH UNDER MY RIGHT EYE WHEN I KNOW CHRISTIAN IS ABOUT TO FAIL A MATH TEST!
SHARED PAIN?
PSYCHIC CONNECTION?
SAME DREAMS?
CLAP CLAP CLAP
Y'KNOW I'VE THOUGHT ABOUT IT.
AND I'M PRETTY SURE I'M NOT ACTUALLY COMFORTABLE WITH THIS.
YEAH, WELL.

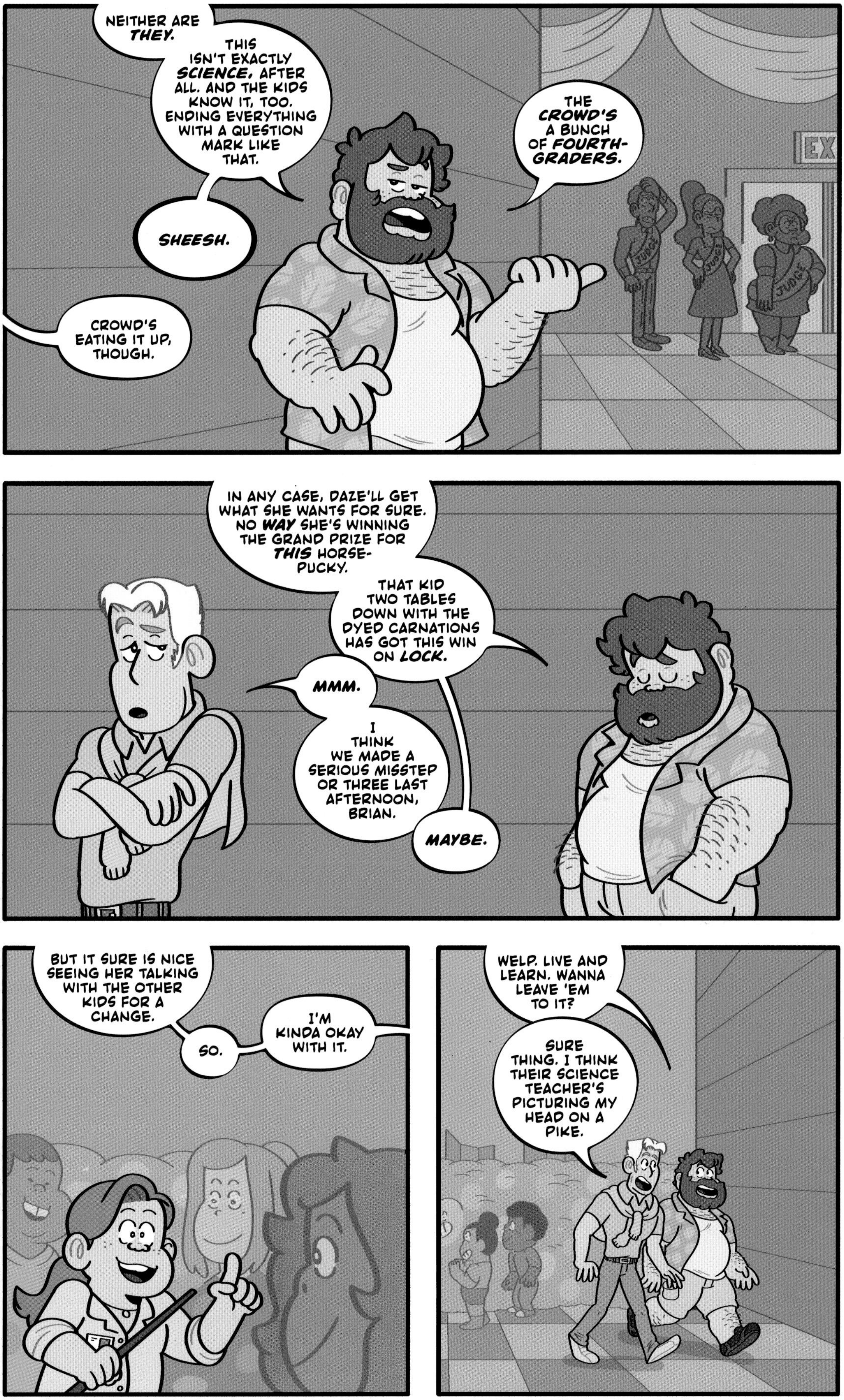
NEITHER ARE THEY.
THIS ISN'T EXACTLY SCIENCE, AFTER ALL. AND THE KIDS KNOW IT, TOO. ENDING EVERYTHING WITH A QUESTION MARK LIKE THAT.
SHEESH.
THE CROWD'S A BUNCH OF FOURTH-GRADERS.
EX
JUDGE
JUDGE
JUDGE
CROWD'S EATING IT UP, THOUGH.
IN ANY CASE, DAZE'LL GET WHAT SHE WANTS FOR SURE. NO WAY SHE'S WINNING THE GRAND PRIZE FOR THIS HORSE-PUCKY.
THAT KID TWO TABLES DOWN WITH THE DYED CARNATIONS HAS GOT THIS WIN ON LOCK.
MMM.
I THINK WE MADE A SERIOUS MISSTEP OR THREE LAST AFTERNOON, BRIAN.
MAYBE.
BUT IT SURE IS NICE SEEING HER TALKING WITH THE OTHER KIDS FOR A CHANGE.
SO.
I'M KINDA OKAY WITH IT.
WELP. LIVE AND LEARN. WANNA LEAVE 'EM TO IT?
SURE THING. I THINK THEIR SCIENCE TEACHER'S PICTURING MY HEAD ON A PIKE.

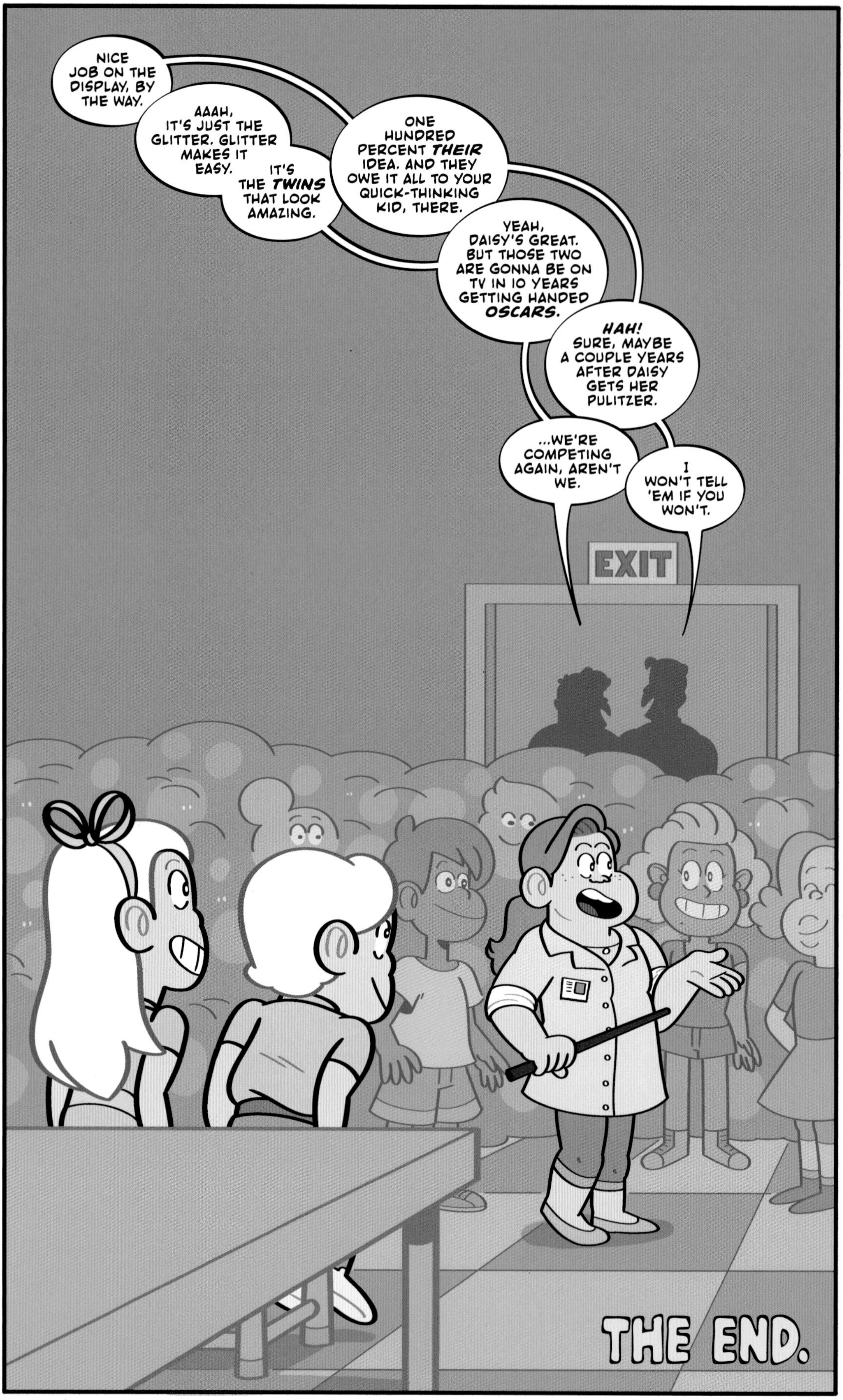
NICE JOB ON THE DISPLAY, BY THE WAY.
AAAH, IT'S JUST THE GLITTER. GLITTER MAKES IT EASY.
IT'S THE *TWINS* THAT LOOK AMAZING.
ONE HUNDRED PERCENT *THEIR* IDEA. AND THEY OWE IT ALL TO YOUR QUICK-THINKING KID, THERE.
YEAH, DAISY'S GREAT. BUT THOSE TWO ARE GONNA BE ON TV IN 10 YEARS GETTING HANDED *OSCARS.*
HAH! SURE, MAYBE A COUPLE YEARS AFTER DAISY GETS HER PULITZER.
...WE'RE COMPETING AGAIN, AREN'T WE.
I WON'T TELL 'EM IF YOU WON'T.
EXIT
THE END.

"Dungeons & Daddies"
Written by Josh Trujillo
Illustrated by D.J. Kirkland
Colored by Matt Herms
Lettered by Hassan Otsmane-Elhaou
Cover by Kris Anka

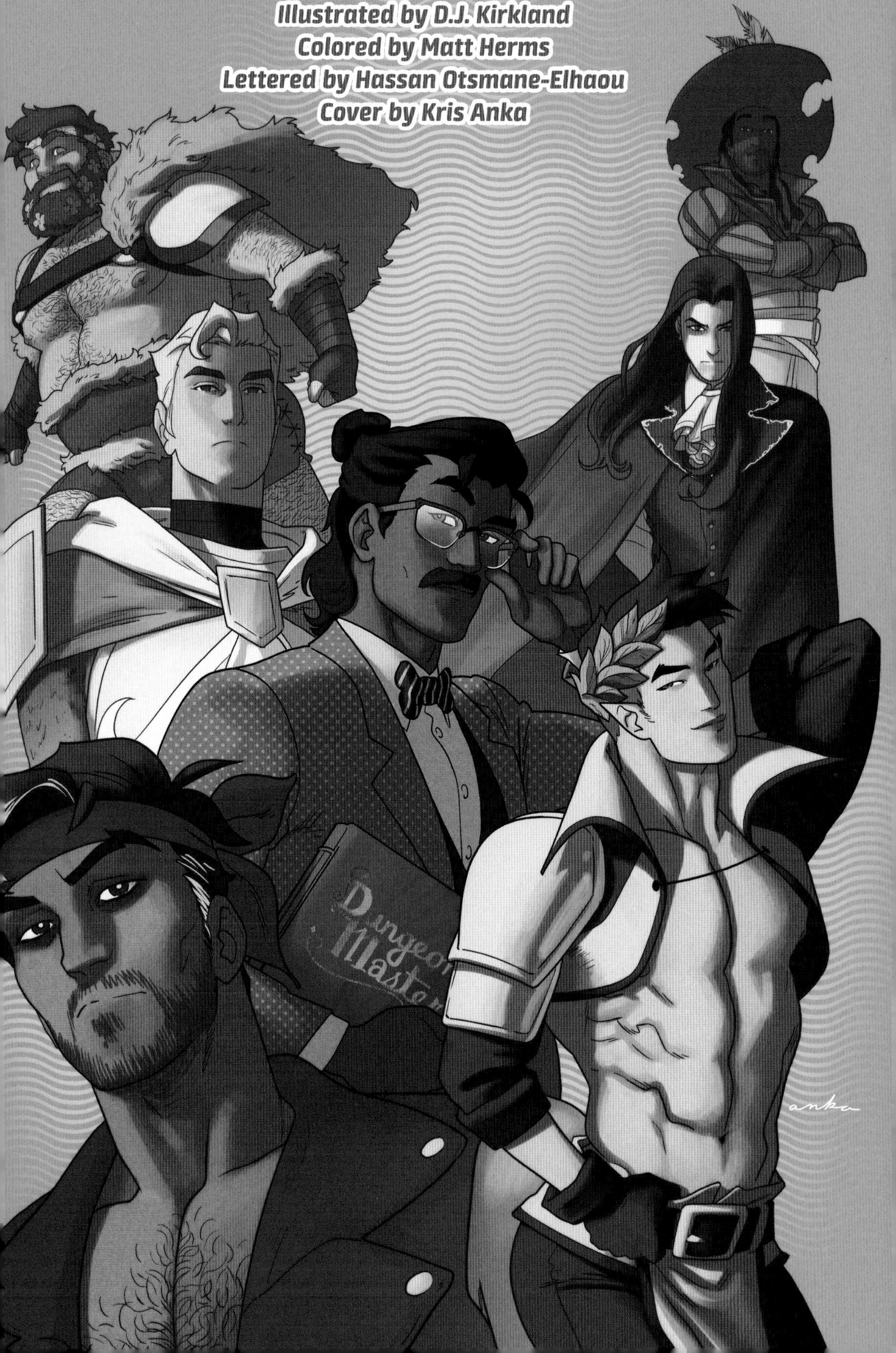
Dungeon Master
anka

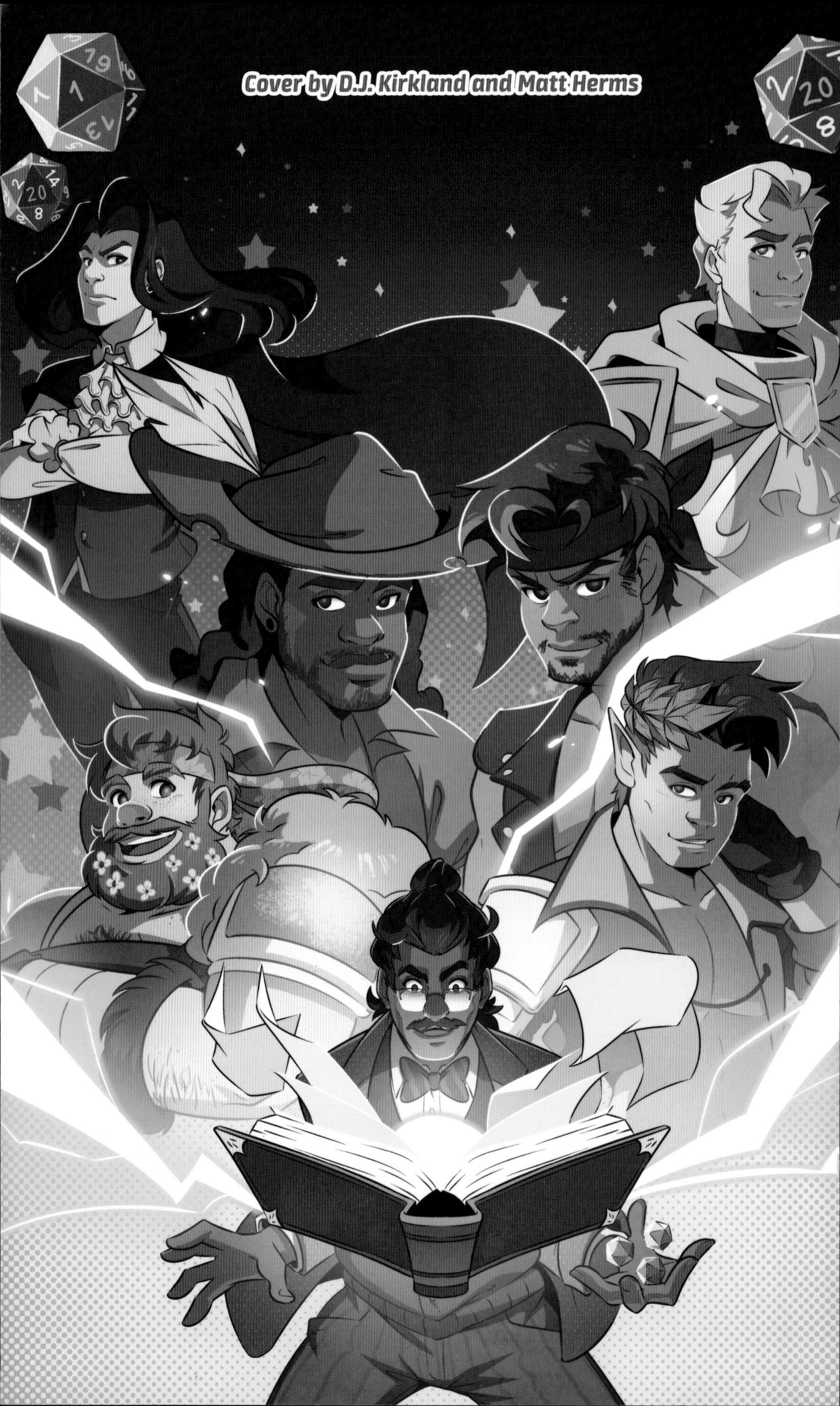

Cover by D.J. Kirkland and Matt Herms

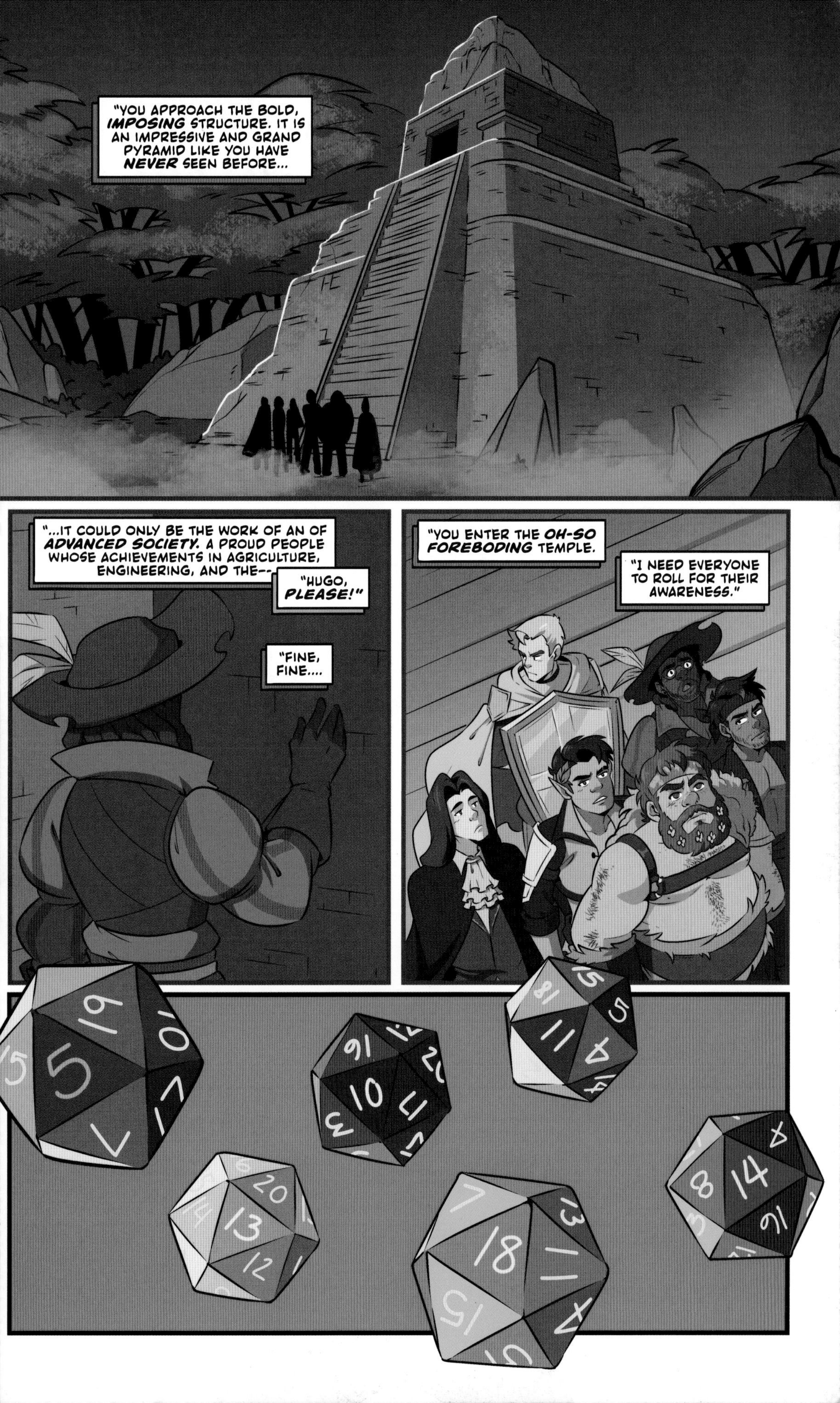
"YOU APPROACH THE BOLD, IMPOSING STRUCTURE. IT IS AN IMPRESSIVE AND GRAND PYRAMID LIKE YOU HAVE NEVER SEEN BEFORE...
"...IT COULD ONLY BE THE WORK OF AN OF ADVANCED SOCIETY. A PROUD PEOPLE WHOSE ACHIEVEMENTS IN AGRICULTURE, ENGINEERING, AND THE--
"HUGO, PLEASE!"
"FINE, FINE....
"YOU ENTER THE OH-SO FOREBODING TEMPLE.
"I NEED EVERYONE TO ROLL FOR THEIR AWARENESS."

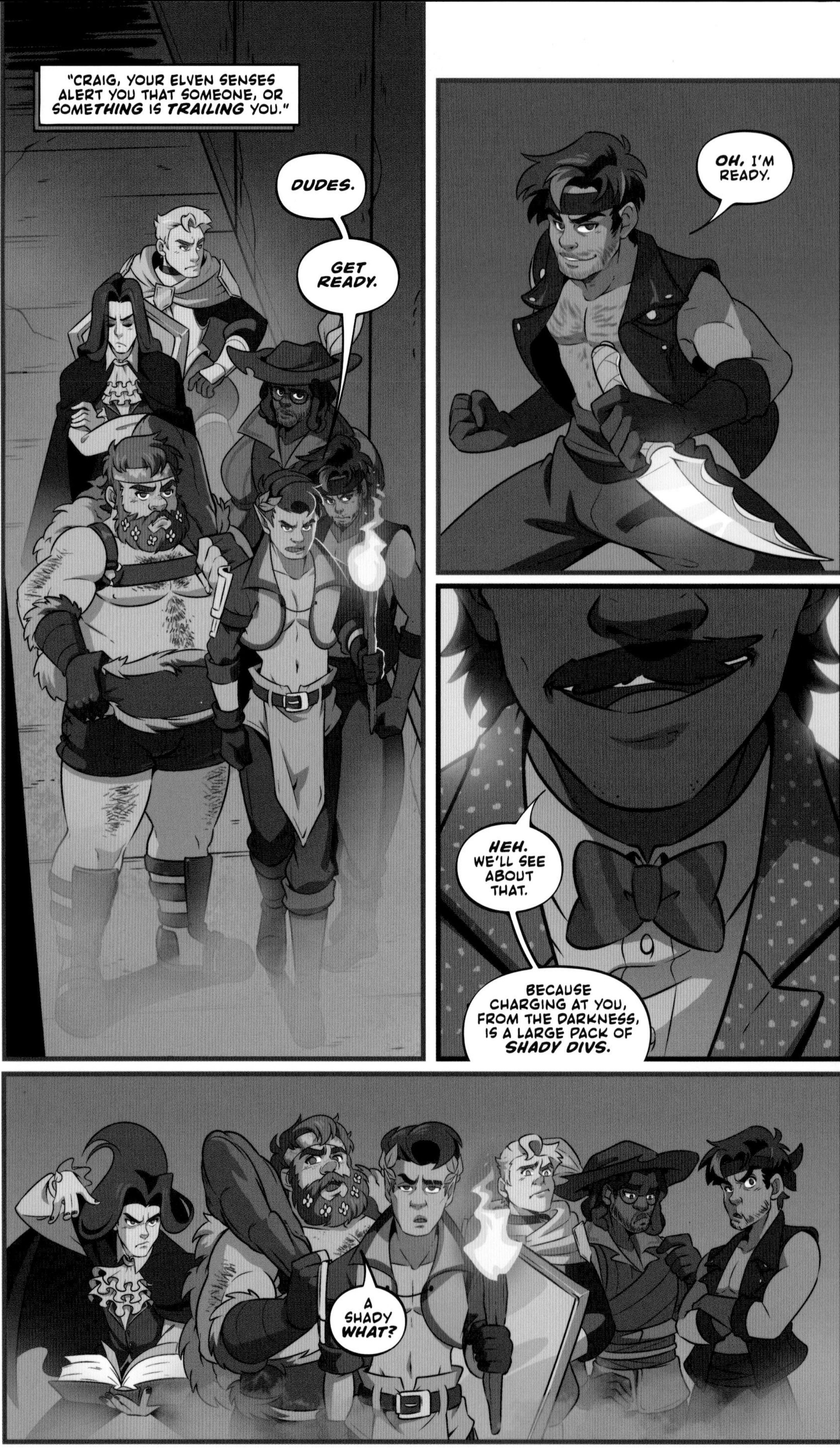
"CRAIG, YOUR ELVEN SENSES ALERT YOU THAT SOMEONE, OR SOMETHING IS TRAILING YOU."
DUDES.
GET READY.
OH, I'M READY.
HEH. WE'LL SEE ABOUT THAT.
BECAUSE CHARGING AT YOU, FROM THE DARKNESS, IS A LARGE PACK OF SHADY DIVS.
A SHADY WHAT?

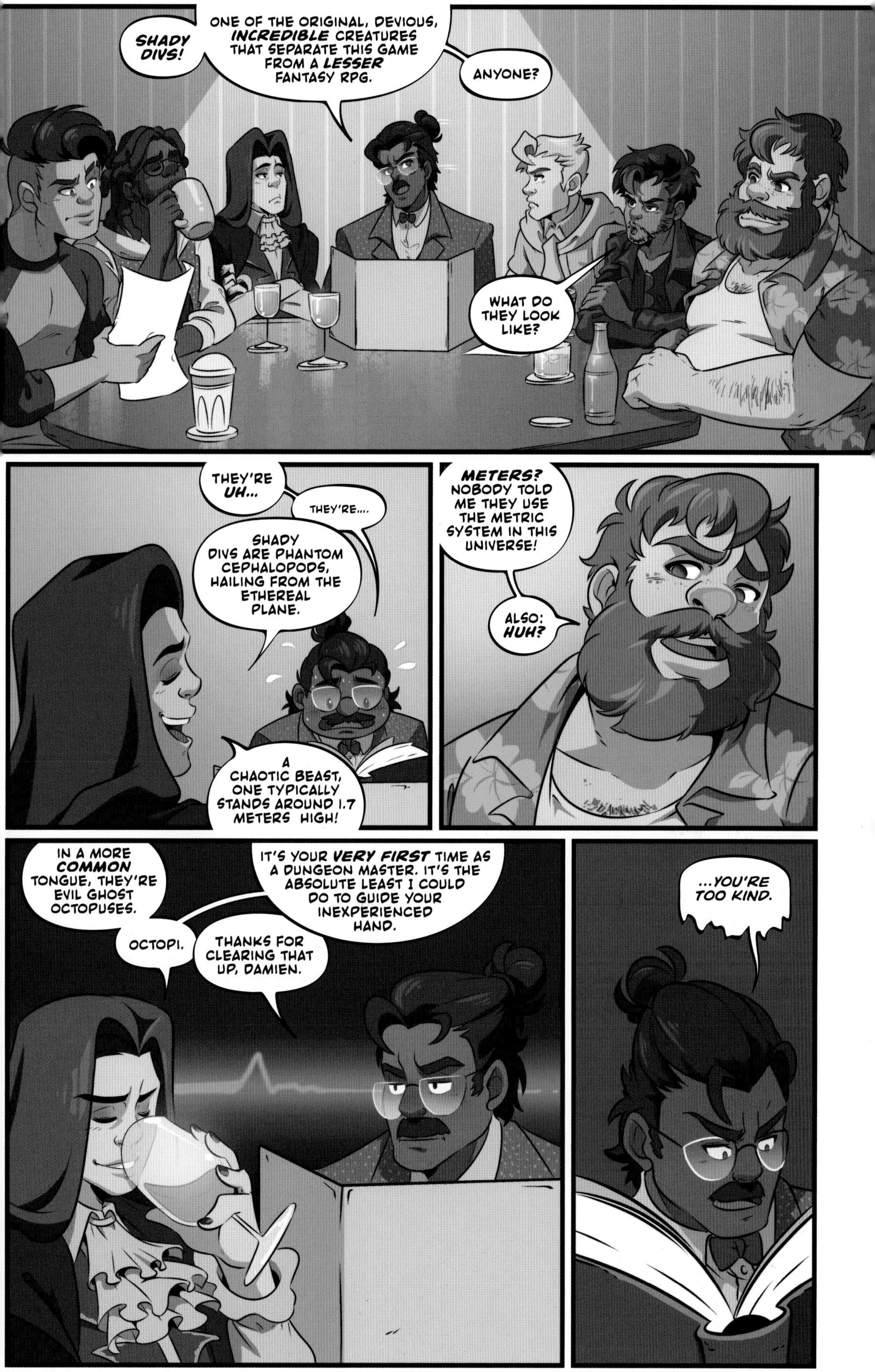
SHADY DIVS!
ONE OF THE ORIGINAL, DEVIOUS, INCREDIBLE CREATURES THAT SEPARATE THIS GAME FROM A LESSER FANTASY RPG.
ANYONE?
WHAT DO THEY LOOK LIKE?
THEY'RE UH...
THEY'RE....
SHADY DIVS ARE PHANTOM CEPHALOPODS, HAILING FROM THE ETHEREAL PLANE.
A CHAOTIC BEAST, ONE TYPICALLY STANDS AROUND 1.7 METERS HIGH!
METERS? NOBODY TOLD ME THEY USE THE METRIC SYSTEM IN THIS UNIVERSE!
ALSO: HUH?
IN A MORE COMMON TONGUE, THEY'RE EVIL GHOST OCTOPUSES.
OCTOPI.
THANKS FOR CLEARING THAT UP, DAMIEN.
IT'S YOUR VERY FIRST TIME AS A DUNGEON MASTER. IT'S THE ABSOLUTE LEAST I COULD DO TO GUIDE YOUR INEXPERIENCED HAND.
...YOU'RE TOO KIND.

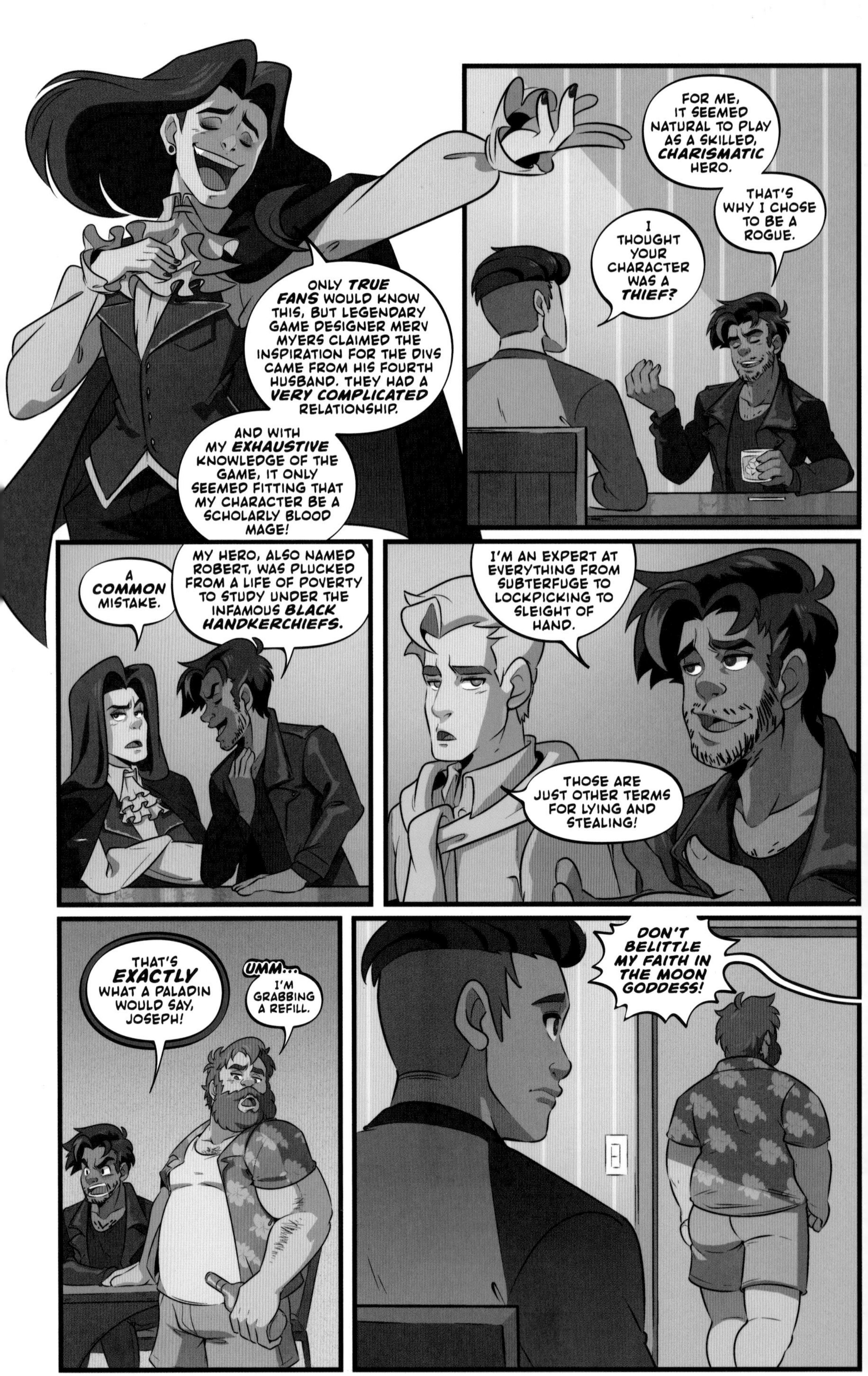
ONLY TRUE FANS WOULD KNOW THIS, BUT LEGENDARY GAME DESIGNER MERV MYERS CLAIMED THE INSPIRATION FOR THE DIVS CAME FROM HIS FOURTH HUSBAND. THEY HAD A VERY COMPLICATED RELATIONSHIP.
AND WITH MY EXHAUSTIVE KNOWLEDGE OF THE GAME, IT ONLY SEEMED FITTING THAT MY CHARACTER BE A SCHOLARLY BLOOD MAGE!
FOR ME, IT SEEMED NATURAL TO PLAY AS A SKILLED, CHARISMATIC HERO.
THAT'S WHY I CHOSE TO BE A ROGUE.
I THOUGHT YOUR CHARACTER WAS A THIEF?
A COMMON MISTAKE.
MY HERO, ALSO NAMED ROBERT, WAS PLUCKED FROM A LIFE OF POVERTY TO STUDY UNDER THE INFAMOUS BLACK HANDKERCHIEFS.
I'M AN EXPERT AT EVERYTHING FROM SUBTERFUGE TO LOCKPICKING TO SLEIGHT OF HAND.
THOSE ARE JUST OTHER TERMS FOR LYING AND STEALING!
THAT'S EXACTLY WHAT A PALADIN WOULD SAY, JOSEPH!
UMM...
I'M GRABBING A REFILL.
DON'T BELITTLE MY FAITH IN THE MOON GODDESS!

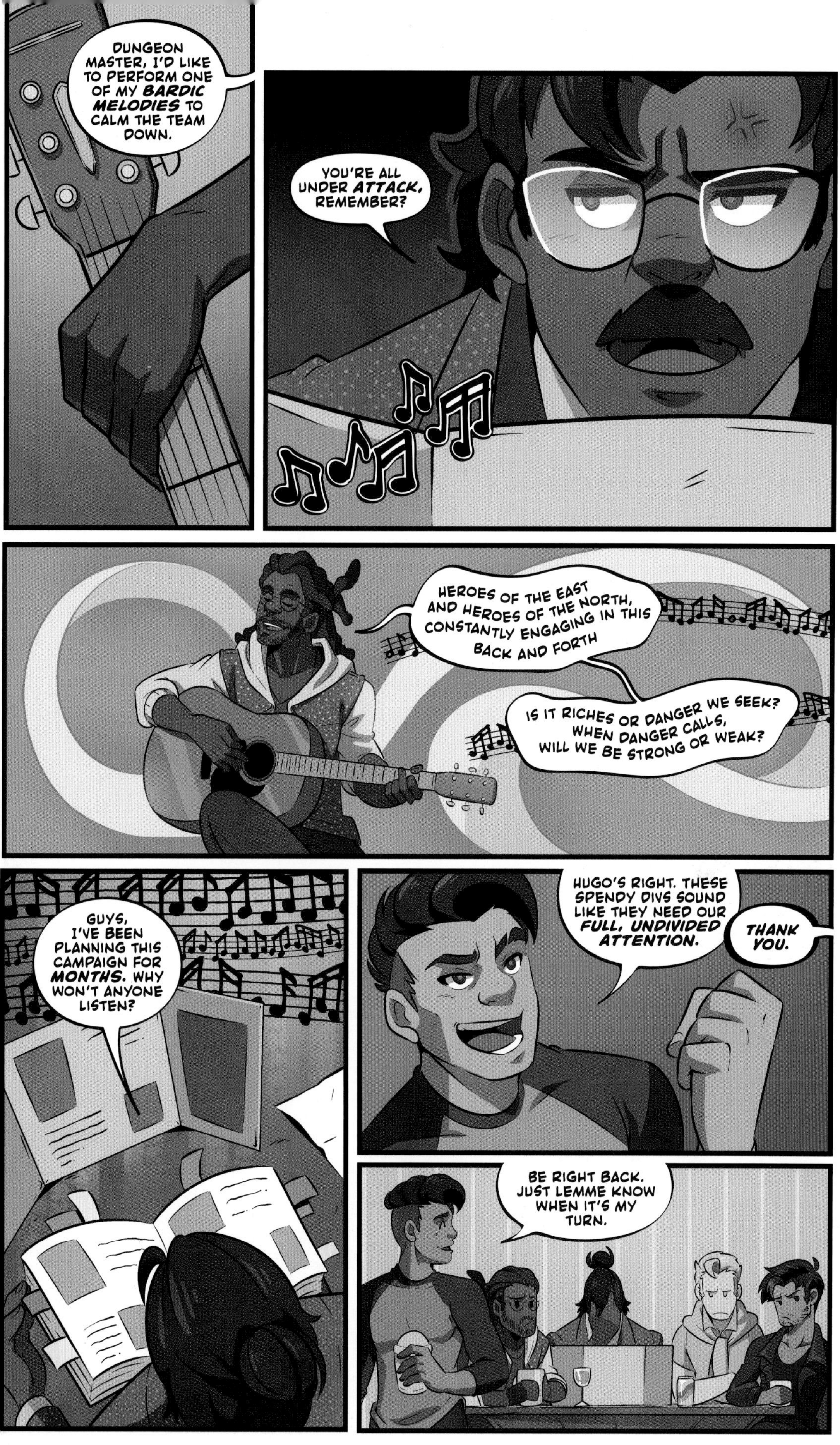

DUNGEON MASTER, I'D LIKE TO PERFORM ONE OF MY BARDIC MELODIES TO CALM THE TEAM DOWN.
YOU'RE ALL UNDER ATTACK, REMEMBER?
HEROES OF THE EAST AND HEROES OF THE NORTH, CONSTANTLY ENGAGING IN THIS BACK AND FORTH
IS IT RICHES OR DANGER WE SEEK? WHEN DANGER CALLS, WILL WE BE STRONG OR WEAK?
GUYS, I'VE BEEN PLANNING THIS CAMPAIGN FOR MONTHS. WHY WON'T ANYONE LISTEN?
HUGO'S RIGHT. THESE SPENDY DIVS SOUND LIKE THEY NEED OUR FULL, UNDIVIDED ATTENTION.
THANK YOU.
BE RIGHT BACK. JUST LEMME KNOW WHEN IT'S MY TURN.

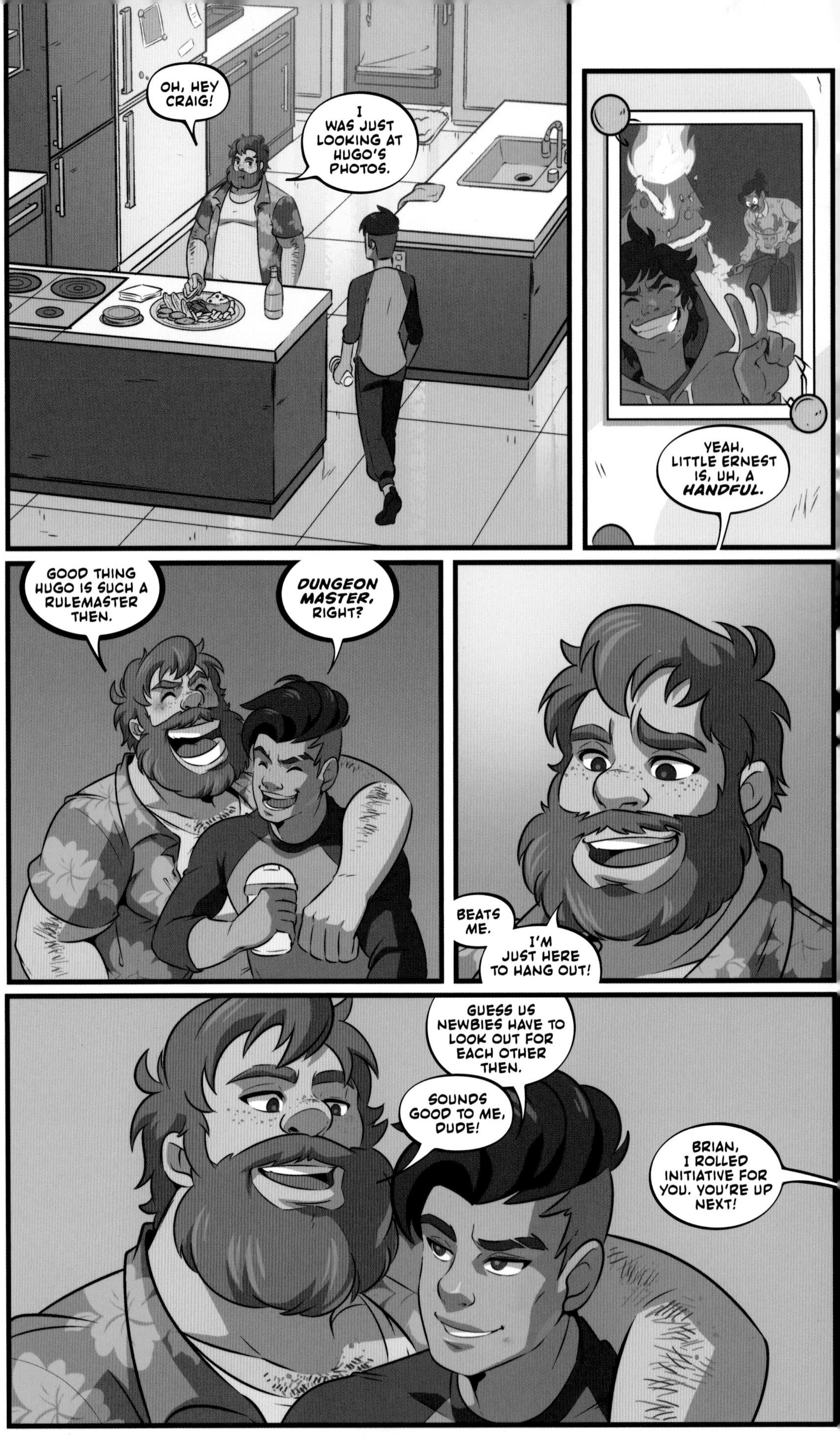
OH, HEY CRAIG!
I WAS JUST LOOKING AT HUGO'S PHOTOS.
YEAH, LITTLE ERNEST IS, UH, A *HANDFUL.*
GOOD THING HUGO IS SUCH A RULEMASTER THEN.
DUNGEON MASTER, RIGHT?
BEATS ME.
I'M JUST HERE TO HANG OUT!
GUESS US NEWBIES HAVE TO LOOK OUT FOR EACH OTHER THEN.
SOUNDS GOOD TO ME, DUDE!
BRIAN, I ROLLED INITIATIVE FOR YOU. YOU'RE UP NEXT!

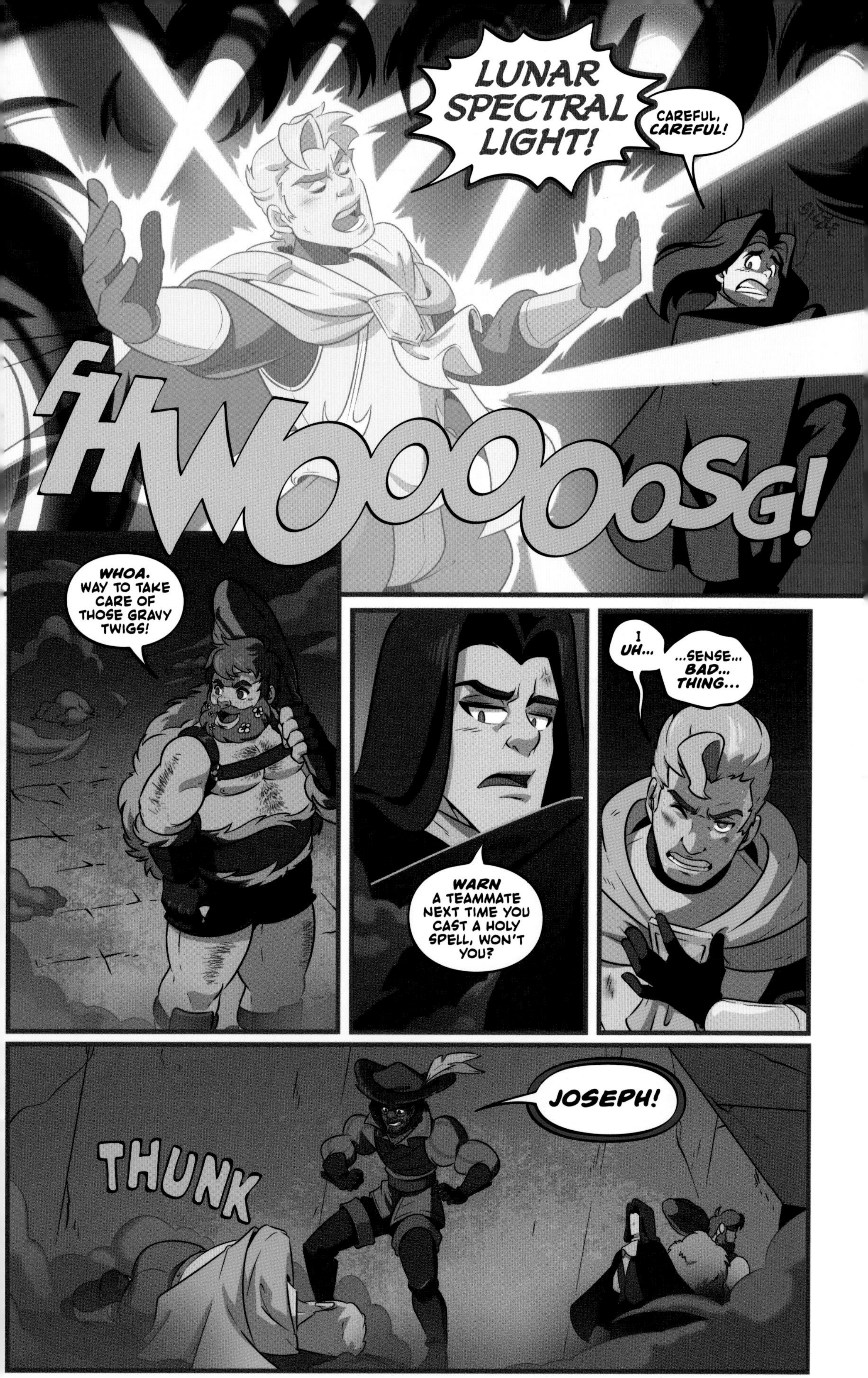
LUNAR SPECTRAL LIGHT!
CAREFUL, CAREFUL!
FHWOOOOOSG!
WHOA. WAY TO TAKE CARE OF THOSE GRAVY TWIGS!
WARN A TEAMMATE NEXT TIME YOU CAST A HOLY SPELL, WON'T YOU?
I UH...
...SENSE... BAD... THING...
JOSEPH!
THUNK

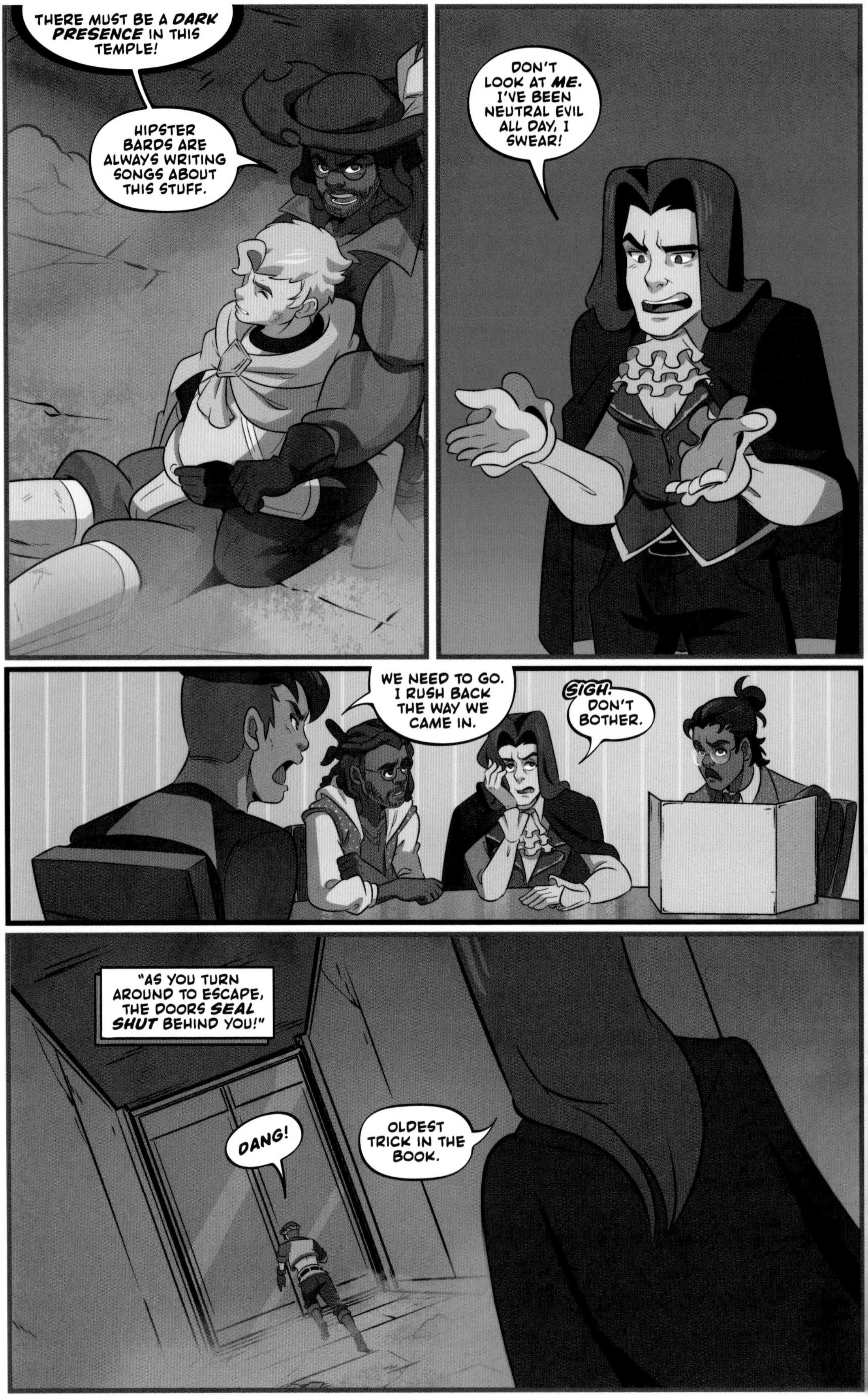
THERE MUST BE A DARK PRESENCE IN THIS TEMPLE!
HIPSTER BARDS ARE ALWAYS WRITING SONGS ABOUT THIS STUFF.
DON'T LOOK AT ME. I'VE BEEN NEUTRAL EVIL ALL DAY, I SWEAR!
WE NEED TO GO. I RUSH BACK THE WAY WE CAME IN.
SIGH. DON'T BOTHER.
"AS YOU TURN AROUND TO ESCAPE, THE DOORS SEAL SHUT BEHIND YOU!"
DANG!
OLDEST TRICK IN THE BOOK.

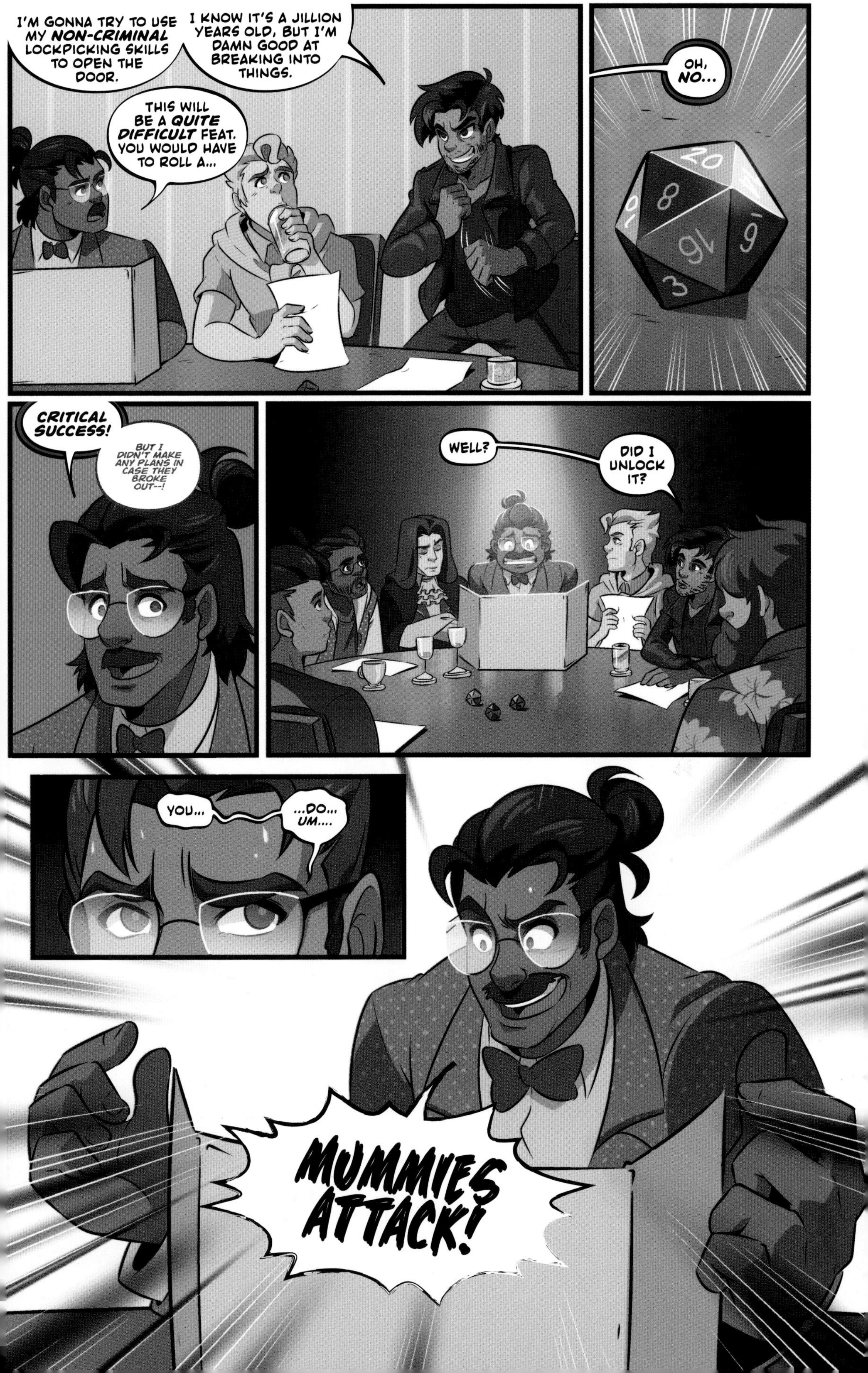
I'M GONNA TRY TO USE MY NON-CRIMINAL LOCKPICKING SKILLS TO OPEN THE DOOR.
I KNOW IT'S A JILLION YEARS OLD, BUT I'M DAMN GOOD AT BREAKING INTO THINGS.
THIS WILL BE A QUITE DIFFICULT FEAT. YOU WOULD HAVE TO ROLL A...
OH, NO...
20
8
10
16
9
3
CRITICAL SUCCESS!
BUT I DIDN'T MAKE ANY PLANS IN CASE THEY BROKE OUT--!
WELL?
DID I UNLOCK IT?
YOU...
...DO... UM....
MUMMIES ATTACK!

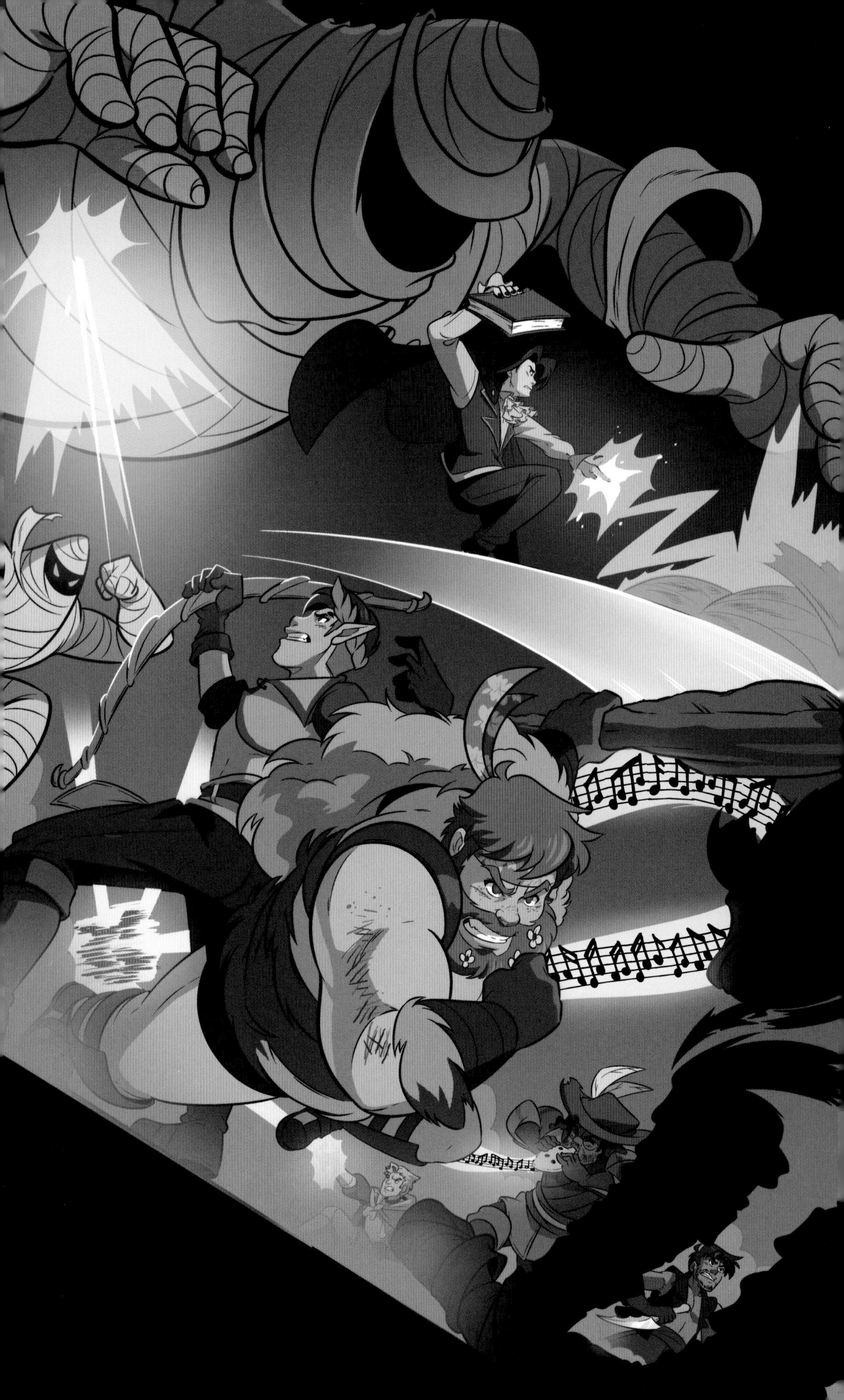

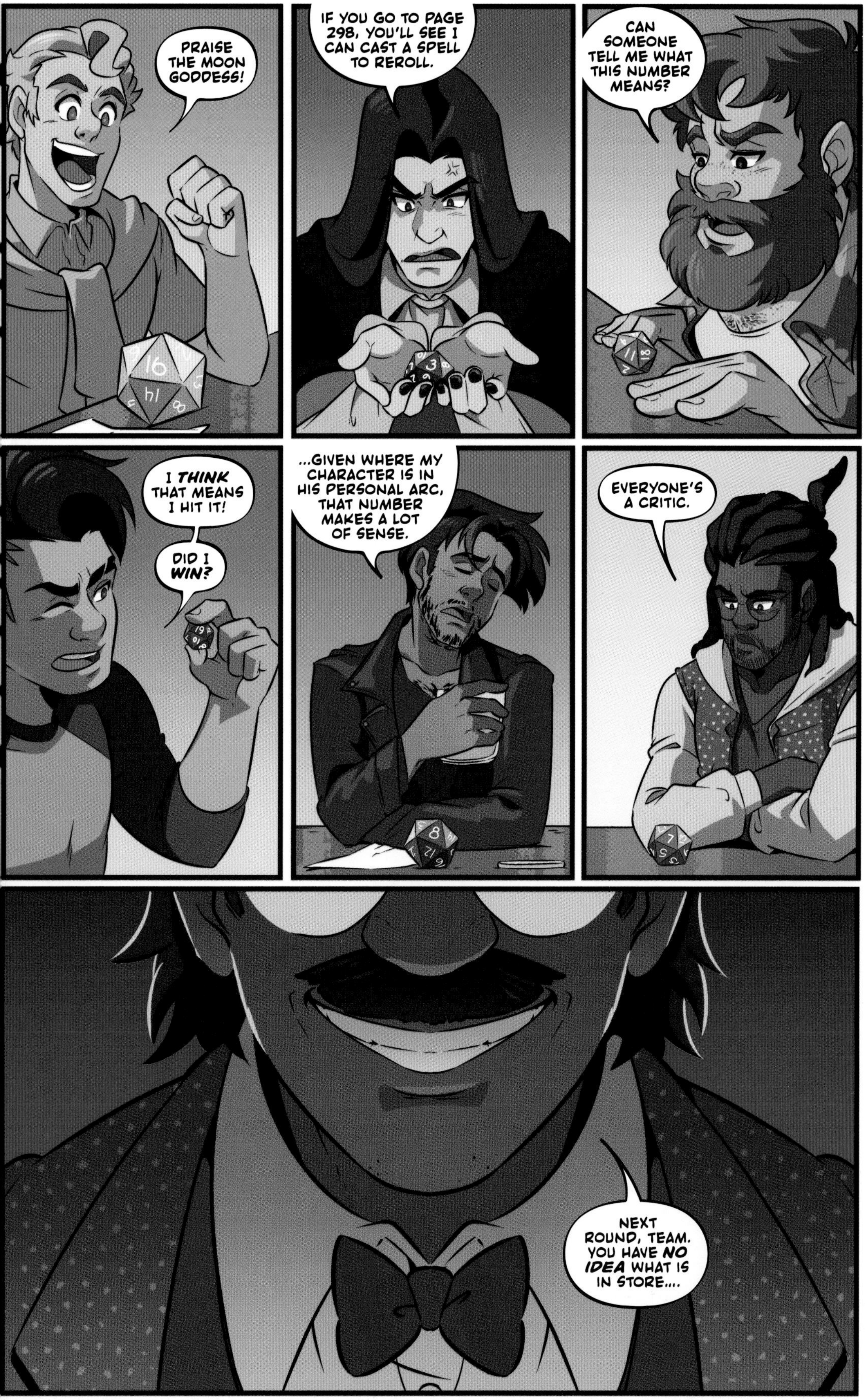
PRAISE THE MOON GODDESS!
IF YOU GO TO PAGE 298, YOU'LL SEE I CAN CAST A SPELL TO REROLL.
CAN SOMEONE TELL ME WHAT THIS NUMBER MEANS?
I *THINK* THAT MEANS I HIT IT!
DID I *WIN?*
...GIVEN WHERE MY CHARACTER IS IN HIS PERSONAL ARC, THAT NUMBER MAKES A LOT OF SENSE.
EVERYONE'S A CRITIC.
NEXT ROUND, TEAM. YOU HAVE *NO IDEA* WHAT IS IN STORE....

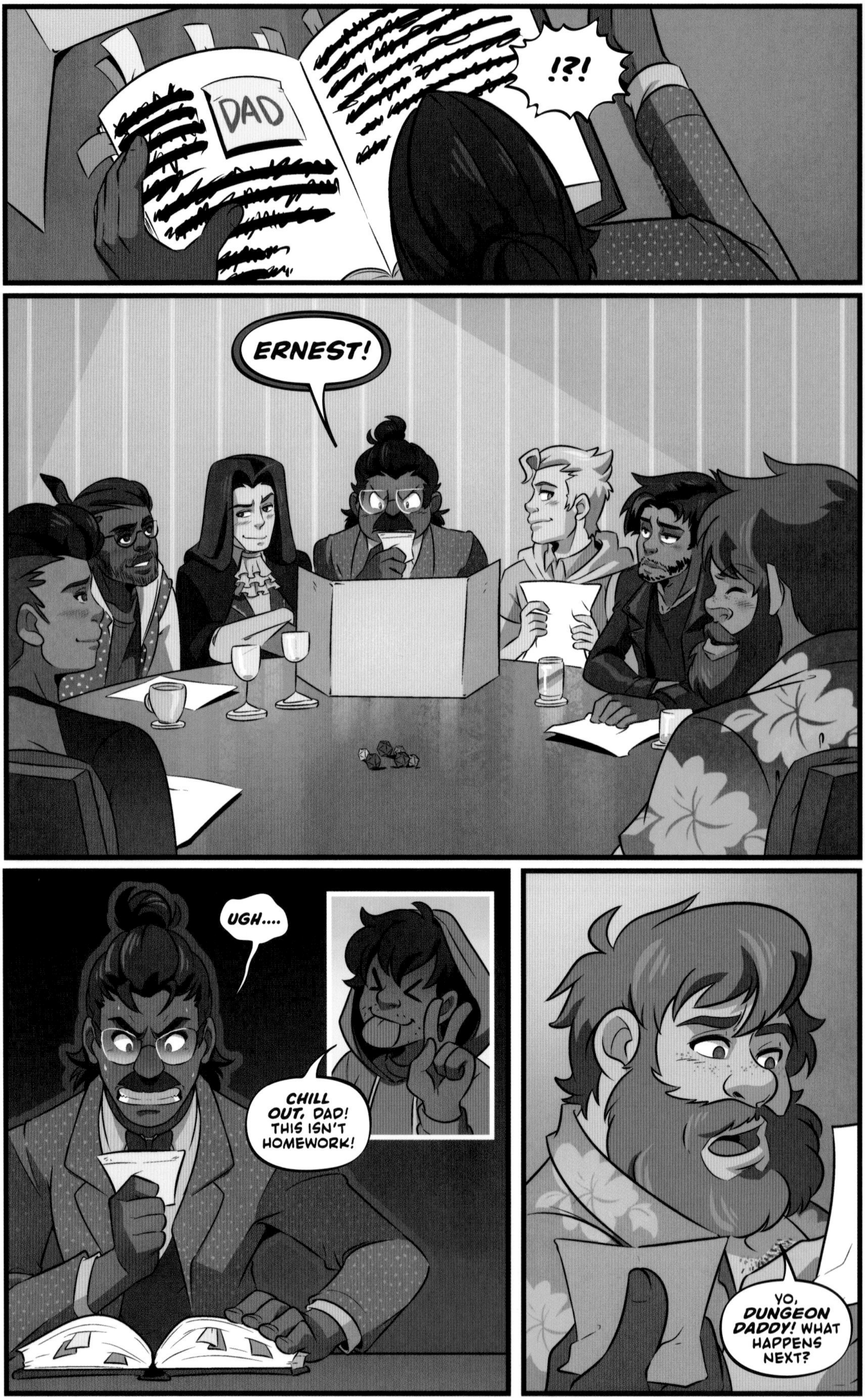
DAD
!?!
ERNEST!
UGH....
CHILL OUT, DAD! THIS ISN'T HOMEWORK!
YO, DUNGEON DADDY! WHAT HAPPENS NEXT?

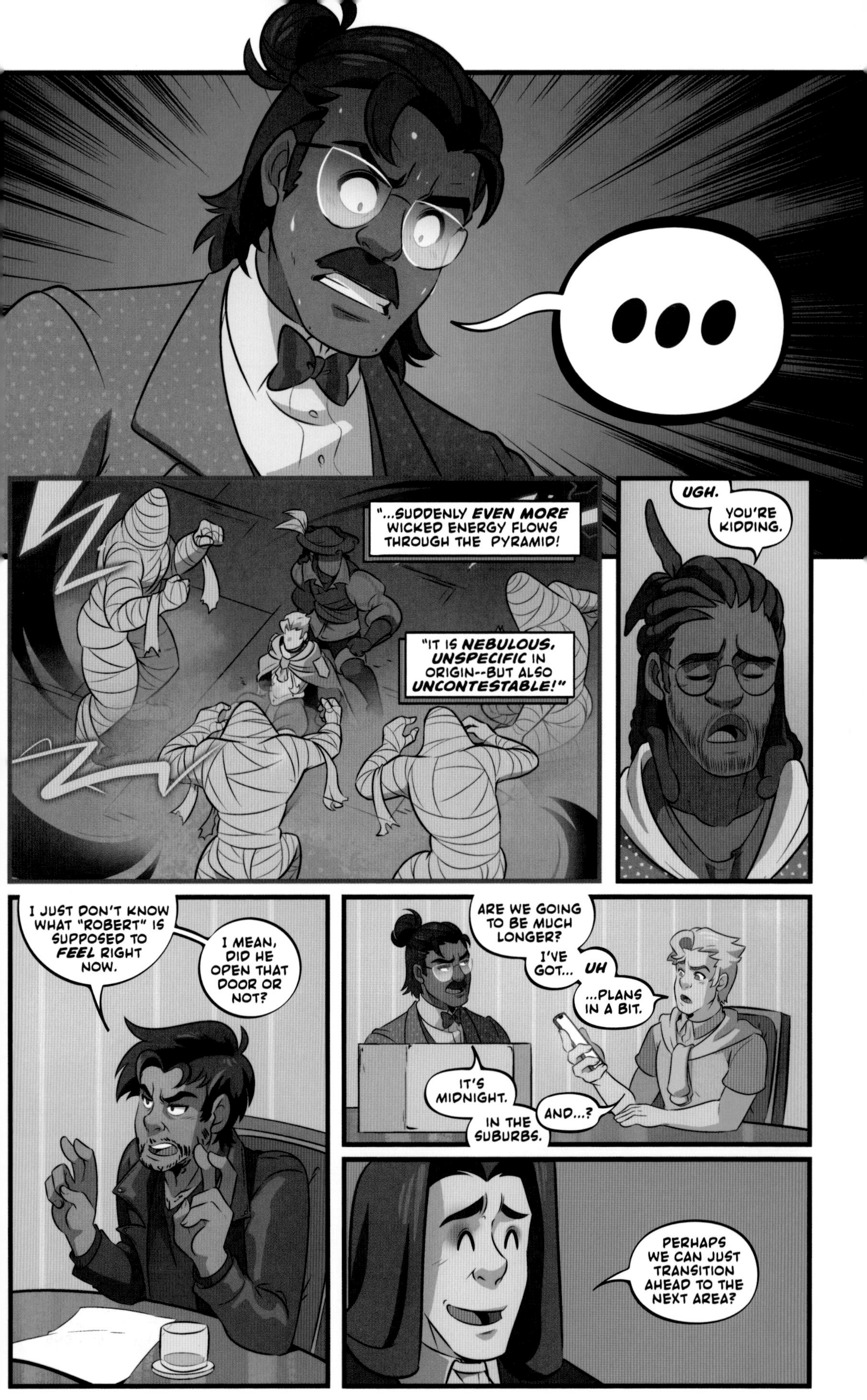

•••
"...SUDDENLY *EVEN MORE* WICKED ENERGY FLOWS THROUGH THE PYRAMID!
"IT IS *NEBULOUS, UNSPECIFIC* IN ORIGIN--BUT ALSO *UNCONTESTABLE!*"
UGH.
YOU'RE KIDDING.
I JUST DON'T KNOW WHAT "ROBERT" IS SUPPOSED TO *FEEL* RIGHT NOW.
I MEAN, DID HE OPEN THAT DOOR OR NOT?
ARE WE GOING TO BE MUCH LONGER?
I'VE GOT... *UH*
...PLANS IN A BIT.
IT'S MIDNIGHT.
IN THE SUBURBS.
AND...?
PERHAPS WE CAN JUST TRANSITION AHEAD TO THE NEXT AREA?

WE PLAY THE ADVENTURE AS PLANNED.

GRAAAAAAAAGH!!!

SORRY, BOYS.

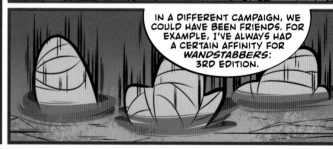

IN A DIFFERENT CAMPAIGN, WE COULD HAVE BEEN FRIENDS. FOR EXAMPLE, I'VE ALWAYS HAD A CERTAIN AFFINITY FOR WANDSTABBERS: 3RD EDITION.

AGH!

ROBERT!

HEAL ME...

HEAL ME, PLEASE?

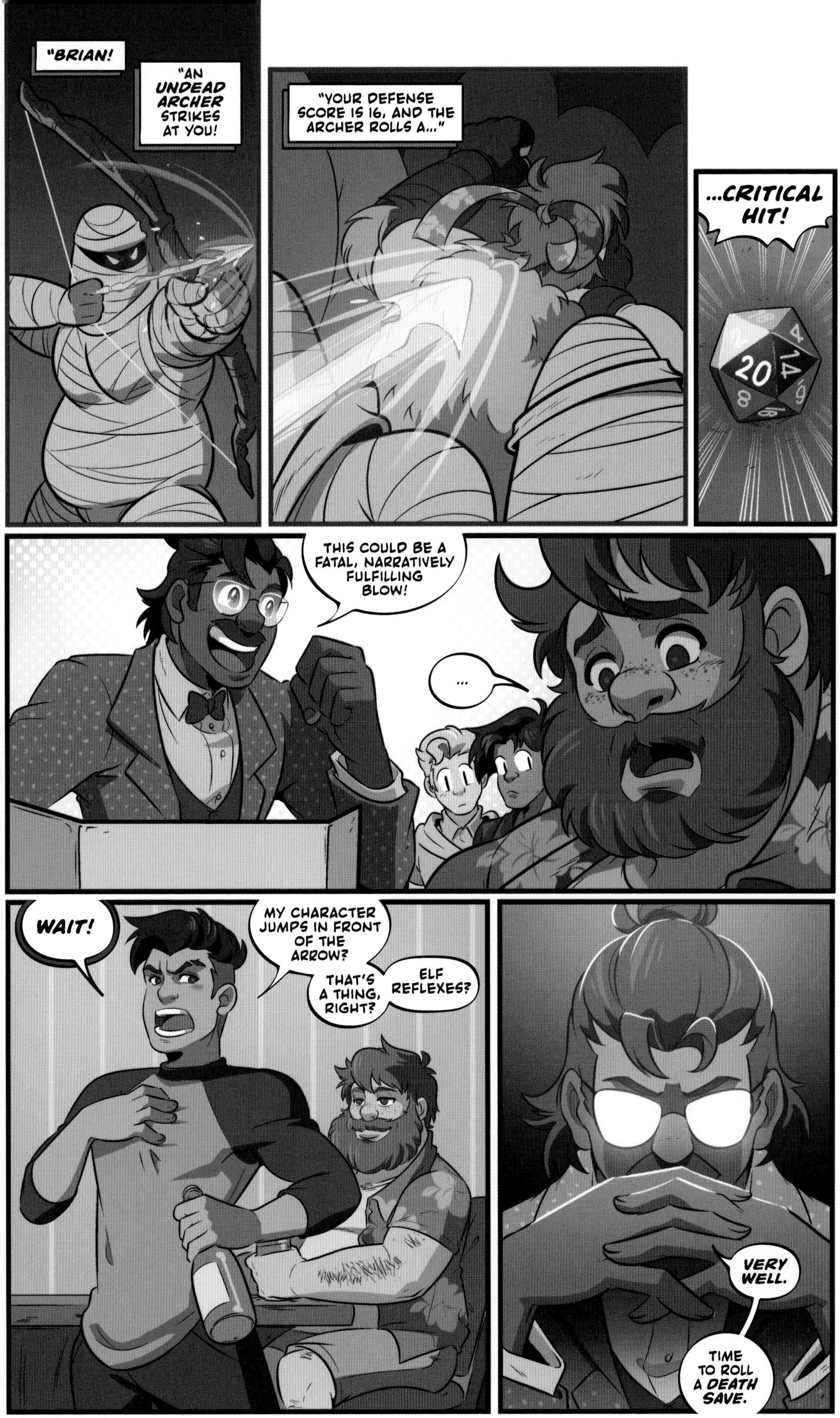
"BRIAN!
"AN UNDEAD ARCHER STRIKES AT YOU!
"YOUR DEFENSE SCORE IS 16, AND THE ARCHER ROLLS A..."
...CRITICAL HIT!
20
THIS COULD BE A FATAL, NARRATIVELY FULFILLING BLOW!
...
WAIT!
MY CHARACTER JUMPS IN FRONT OF THE ARROW?
THAT'S A THING, RIGHT?
ELF REFLEXES?
VERY WELL.
TIME TO ROLL A DEATH SAVE.

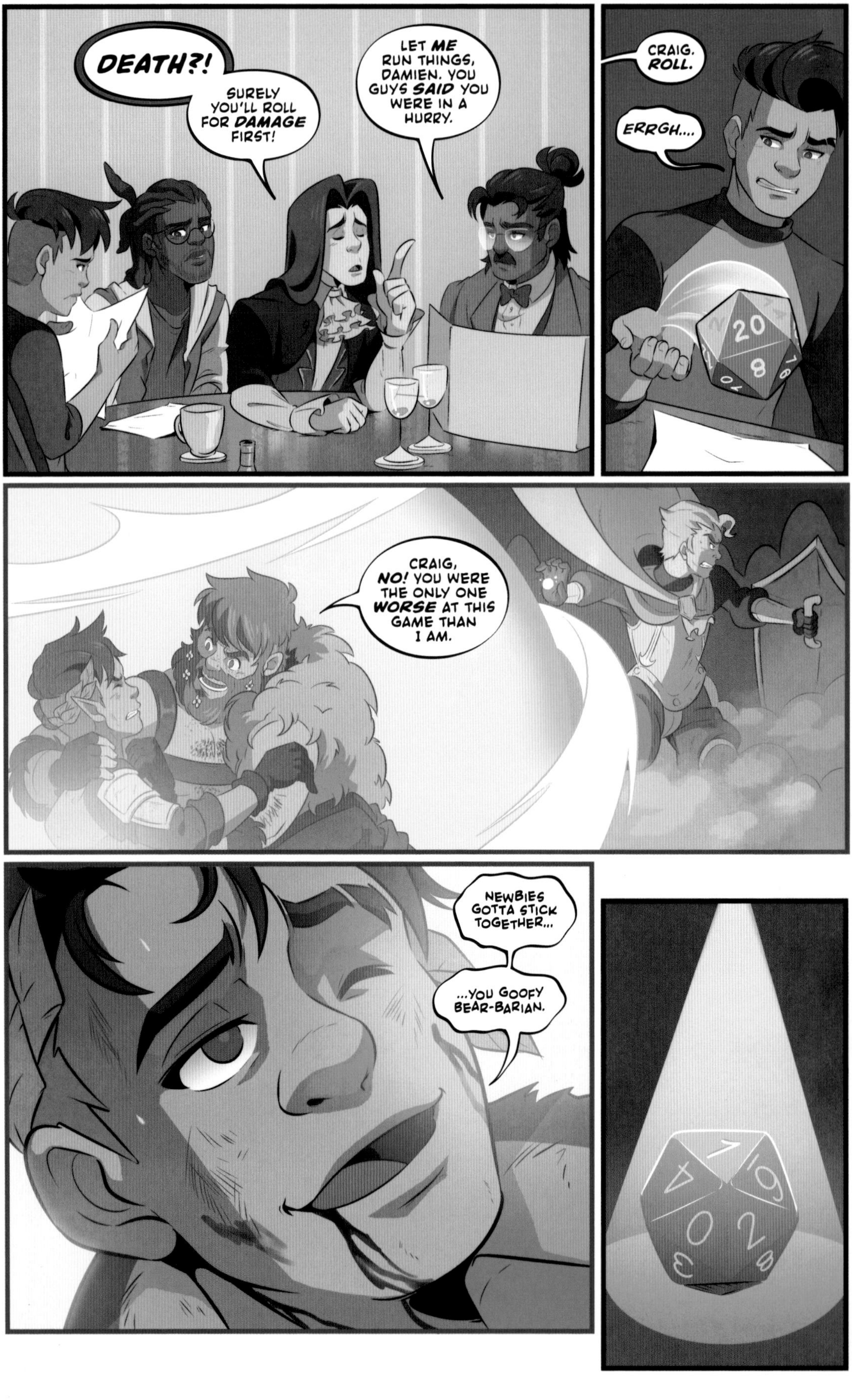
DEATH?!
SURELY YOU'LL ROLL FOR DAMAGE FIRST!
LET ME RUN THINGS, DAMIEN. YOU GUYS SAID YOU WERE IN A HURRY.
CRAIG. ROLL.
ERRGH....
CRAIG, NO! YOU WERE THE ONLY ONE WORSE AT THIS GAME THAN I AM.
NEWBIES GOTTA STICK TOGETHER...
...YOU GOOFY BEAR-BARIAN.

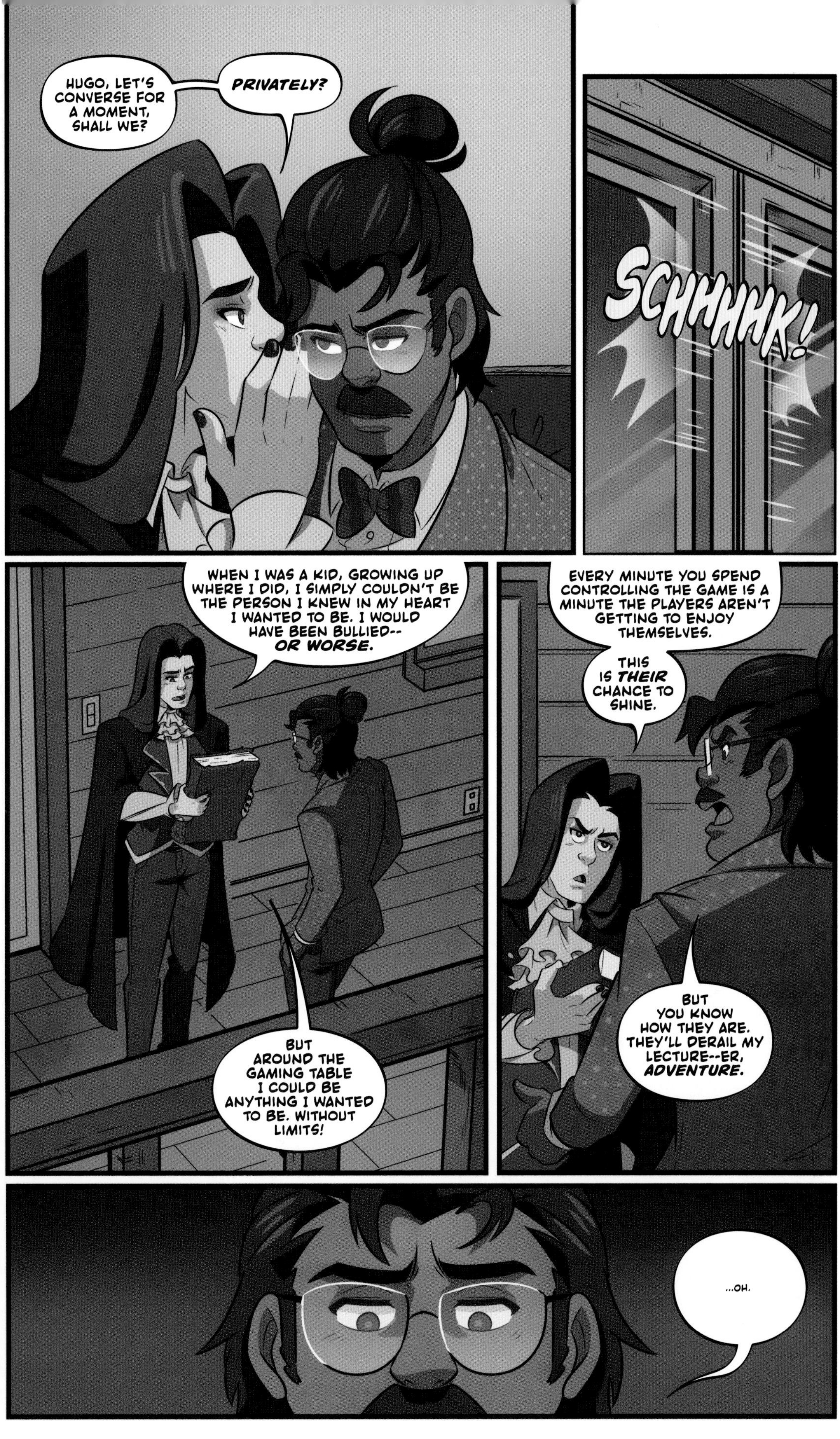
HUGO, LET'S CONVERSE FOR A MOMENT, SHALL WE?
PRIVATELY?
SCHHHHK!
WHEN I WAS A KID, GROWING UP WHERE I DID, I SIMPLY COULDN'T BE THE PERSON I KNEW IN MY HEART I WANTED TO BE. I WOULD HAVE BEEN BULLIED-- OR WORSE.
BUT AROUND THE GAMING TABLE I COULD BE ANYTHING I WANTED TO BE. WITHOUT LIMITS!
EVERY MINUTE YOU SPEND CONTROLLING THE GAME IS A MINUTE THE PLAYERS AREN'T GETTING TO ENJOY THEMSELVES.
THIS IS THEIR CHANCE TO SHINE.
BUT YOU KNOW HOW THEY ARE. THEY'LL DERAIL MY LECTURE--ER, ADVENTURE.
...OH.

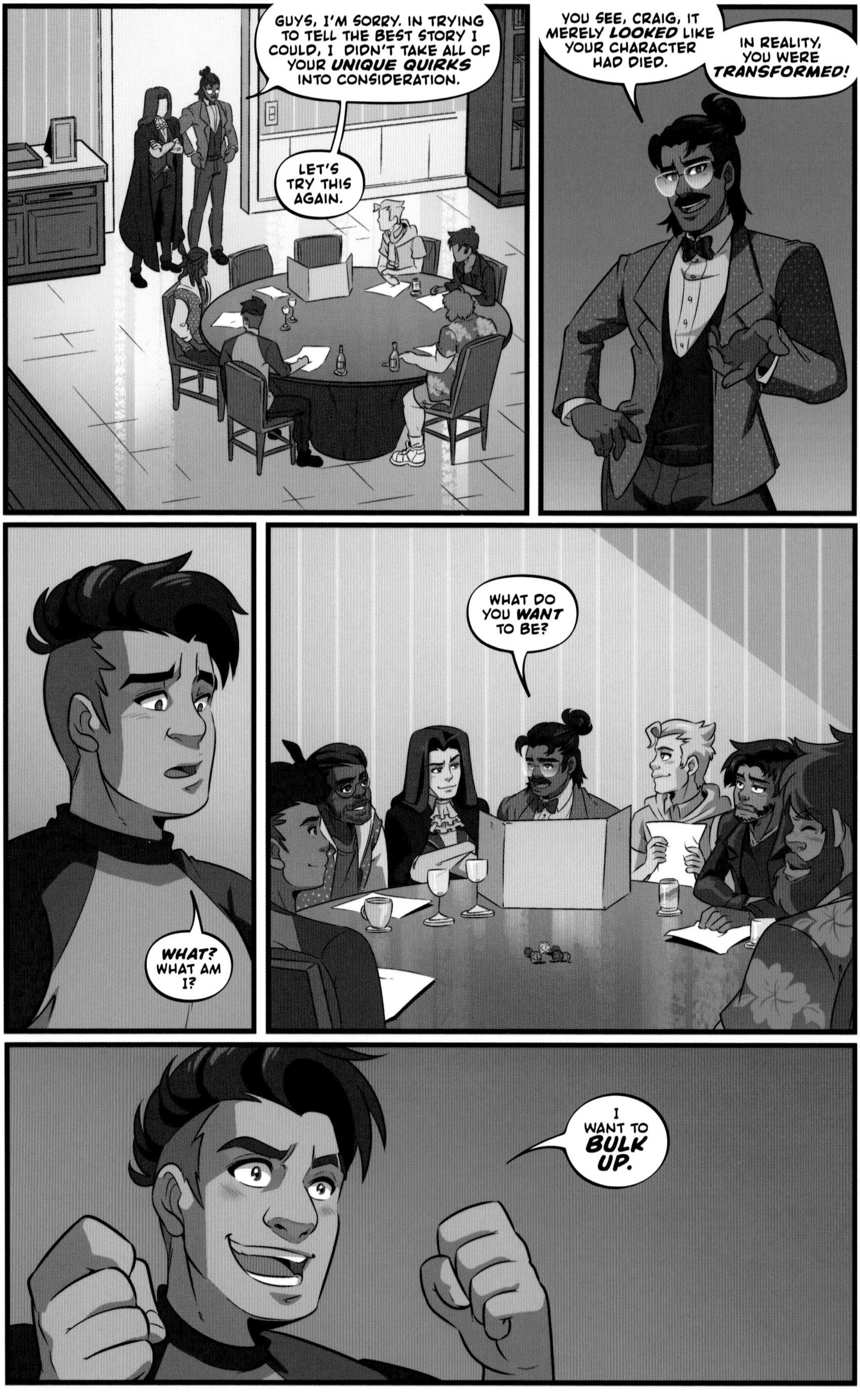
GUYS, I'M SORRY. IN TRYING TO TELL THE BEST STORY I COULD, I DIDN'T TAKE ALL OF YOUR UNIQUE QUIRKS INTO CONSIDERATION.
LET'S TRY THIS AGAIN.
YOU SEE, CRAIG, IT MERELY LOOKED LIKE YOUR CHARACTER HAD DIED.
IN REALITY, YOU WERE TRANSFORMED!
WHAT? WHAT AM I?
WHAT DO YOU WANT TO BE?
I WANT TO BULK UP.

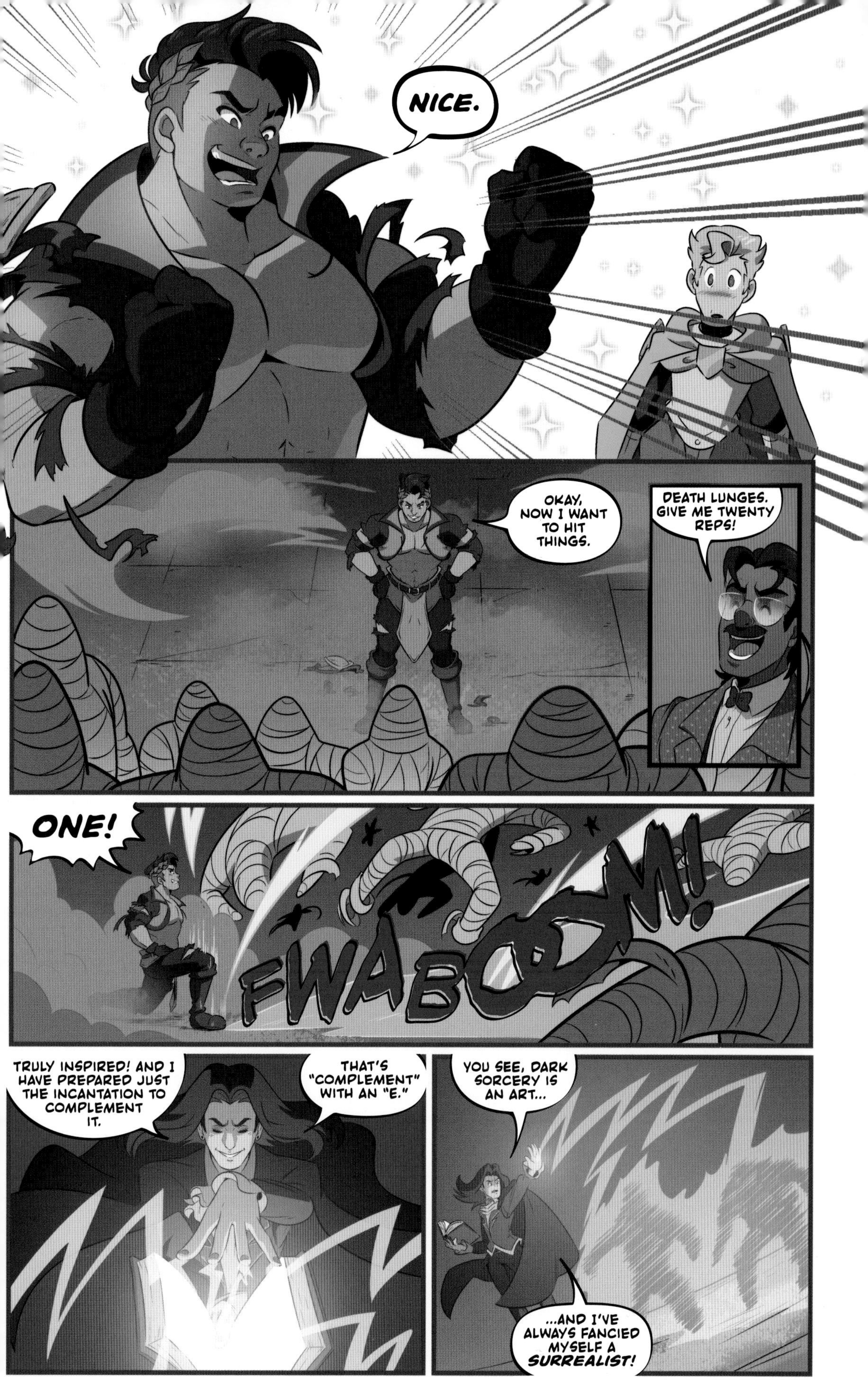
NICE.
OKAY, NOW I WANT TO HIT THINGS.
DEATH LUNGES. GIVE ME TWENTY REPS!
ONE!
FWABOOM!
TRULY INSPIRED! AND I HAVE PREPARED JUST THE INCANTATION TO COMPLEMENT IT.
THAT'S "COMPLEMENT" WITH AN "E."
YOU SEE, DARK SORCERY IS AN ART...
...AND I'VE ALWAYS FANCIED MYSELF A *SURREALIST!*

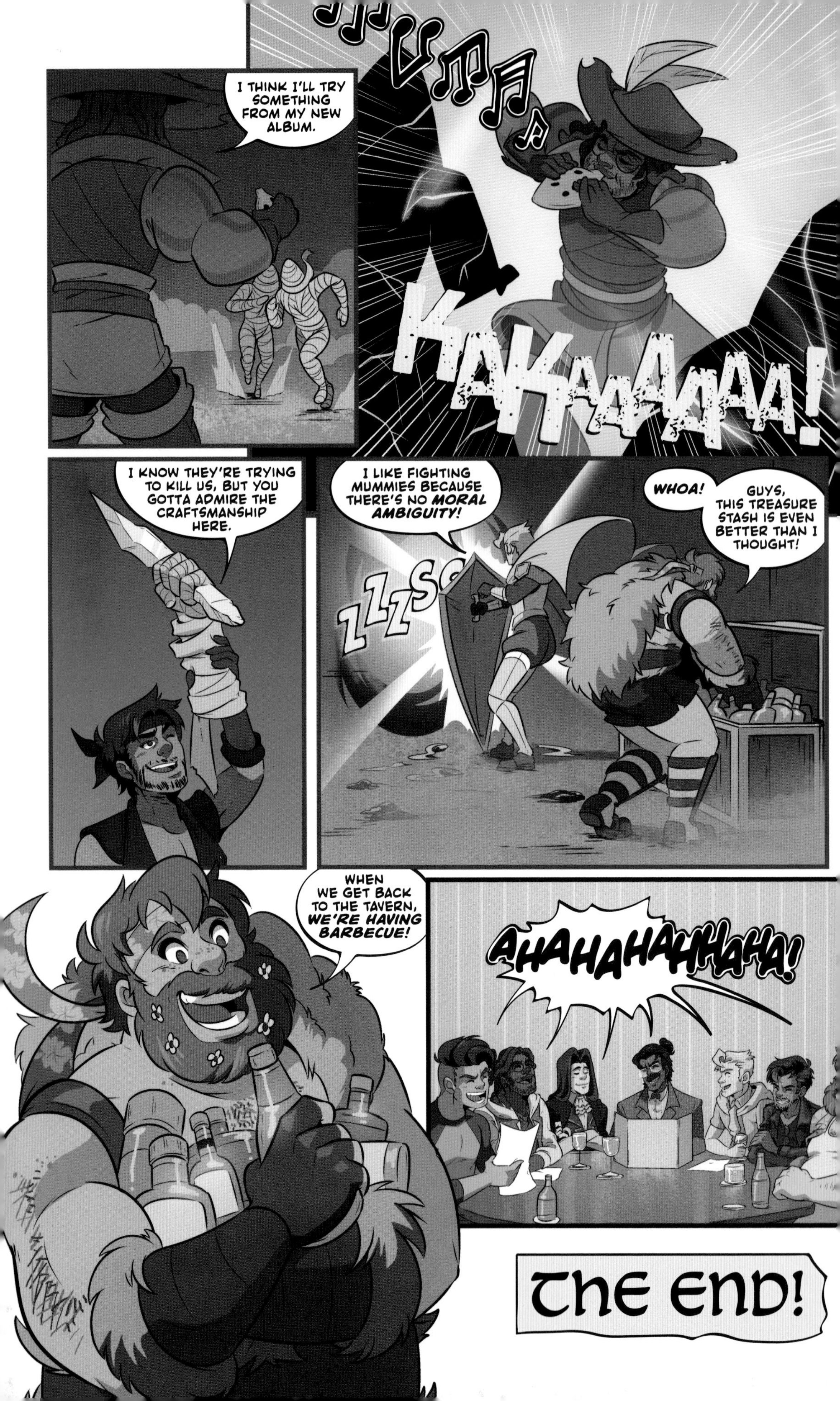
I THINK I'LL TRY SOMETHING FROM MY NEW ALBUM.
KAKAAAAAAA!
I KNOW THEY'RE TRYING TO KILL US, BUT YOU GOTTA ADMIRE THE CRAFTSMANSHIP HERE.
I LIKE FIGHTING MUMMIES BECAUSE THERE'S NO *MORAL AMBIGUITY!*
ZZZSS
WHOA!
GUYS, THIS TREASURE STASH IS EVEN BETTER THAN I THOUGHT!
WHEN WE GET BACK TO THE TAVERN, *WE'RE HAVING BARBECUE!*
AHAHAHAHHAHA!
THE END!

CREATOR COMMENTARY

COVER ART AND LETTERING COMMENTARY

WITH KRIS ANKA AND HASSAN OSTMANE-ELHAOU

KRIS (cover artist): How could I say no to these Daddies? They are such a fun cast of characters that drawing these covers was a no-brainer. The big trick with all of them was finding a way to make sure each of the covers were "sexy" in some way. Issue 1 was probably the easiest for that: Craig (my personal fav Daddy). You can never go wrong with a nice lounging and "oops is half my shirt fallen off oh well" cover. Issue 2 was equally fun—I decided to go with a classic vampire-about-to-bite-the-neck-seductively image. Issue 3, while being one of the more simpler conceptually, was one of the more difficult executions. The "selfie" cover is always a nice go-to but takes a lot of details to really sell it: a fairly realized background, correct perspective, and camera details so it's immediately recognizable. Another hurdle was that a lot of Mat's tattoos didn't have references, so I had to design them myself, which was a fun challenge. Issue 4 took a little while to get an idea for, but we settled on wanting to lean into the competitive nature of the two Dads and really go over the top with the science fair setting in the issue. Issue 5 was a lot of fun! This was the first time I'd drawn all the Dads together, but I also got to draw them in their D&D outfits that D.J. designed. You know I had to get Craig front and center.

The collection covers were a long process, actually. I felt it would be a missed opportunity not to do a shirtless cover, especially given that we wanted a variant of the main cover, and that seemed like the perfect place. I pitched around a lot of different ideas, but once we got the thumbs-up on doing a swimsuit cover, I revisited the drawing board (so to speak) to find a concept that could work in two different settings and outfits while the poses stayed the same. So where we ended is what what you see: a lounging backyard barbecue that could turn into a lounging beachside barbecue.

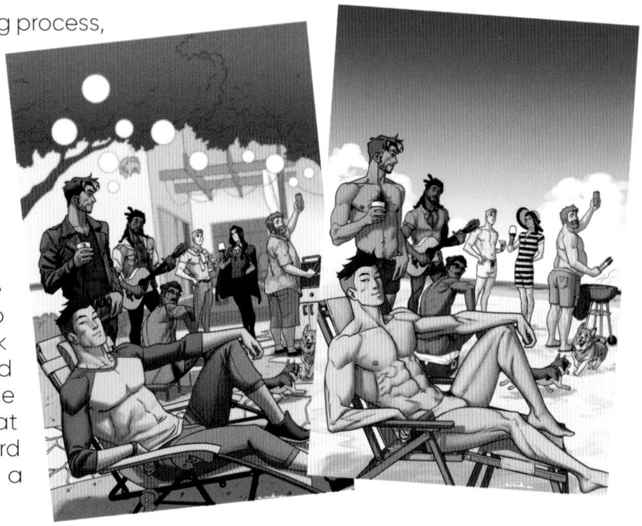

HASSAN (letterer): For me, lettering always starts with matching a style to the artwork, which is especially difficult when you're working on a series that has new creative teams every issue. So I wanted to find something that suited everyone, because I think lettering is a good way to ground a series which is visually changing, so it can anchor the issues. After looking at everyone's art ahead of starting, I settled on a bouncy font that had a bit of fun to it, and mostly big, airy balloons to match. (It's a weird thing, but I like those wide O's on fonts, especially when you open up the balloons to match, as big ovals.) I basically wanted something that was fun and had some energy to it, to match all the stories and Daddies. Hopefully it works, and the connective tissue through them disappears into the background as readers get into it.

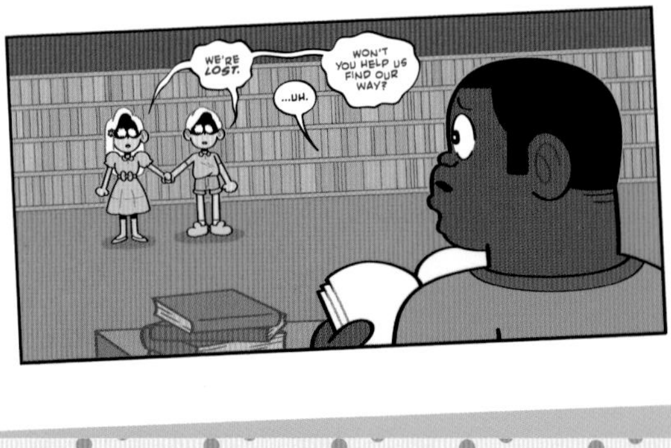
WE'RE LOST.
WON'T YOU HELP US FIND OUR WAY?
...UH.

For my favorite issue, it was a difficult toss-up between 4 and 5! Hugo is definitely my Dream Daddy (a secret wrestling fan? yes please), but Joseph and Brian having a fierce Dad competition over their kids in the library had me cracking up while working on it, and I think is a fun showcase of the different things you can do with the Daddies. So don't make me pick!

ISSUE #1 COMMENTARY

WITH WENDY XU AND RYAN MANIULIT

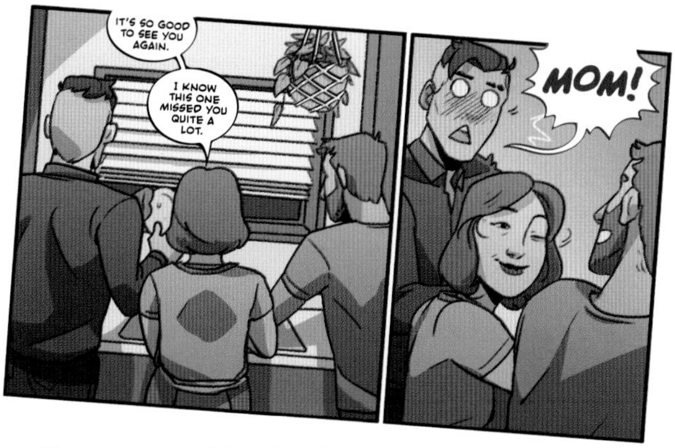
IT'S SO GOOD TO SEE YOU AGAIN.
I KNOW THIS ONE MISSED YOU QUITE A LOT.
MOM!

WENDY (writer): When [editor] Ari approached me to write Craig's issue of *Dream Daddy*, I could not be more excited—I have a not-so-secret fondness for gentle bros, and I was determined to cram as many things as I personally liked (Asian aunties, birds, Craig thirst-traps) in this story. You can say that it was a bit of selfishness on my part, but I also had to do this within the very loose plot guideline I was given: Craig and Player Dad go to their college reunion. But what's the point of a Craig issue without him showing off his ripped bod in some way? So I *had* to write the scene where Player-Dad goes upstairs and he's in a towel. And then there has to be some kind of bird adoration, so I had the guys leave the reunion and get attacked by a seagull (on a personal note, my partner hates seagulls because one stole his grilled cheese at Disney when he was a child. This was also done to troll him, a bit). Finally, I love watching Maangchi's Youtube cooking channel, and I wanted to incorporate some of her spirit into the story. I felt like Craig would have a Maangchi-esque mom. All of those motifs combined to make the story what it is, and I had a blast working on it! Ryan's art style fit everything so perfectly, it was like he read my mind when it came down to drawing all of it, and the art is where the real heavy lifting comes in comics. So mad kudos to Ryan for doing such a beautiful job!

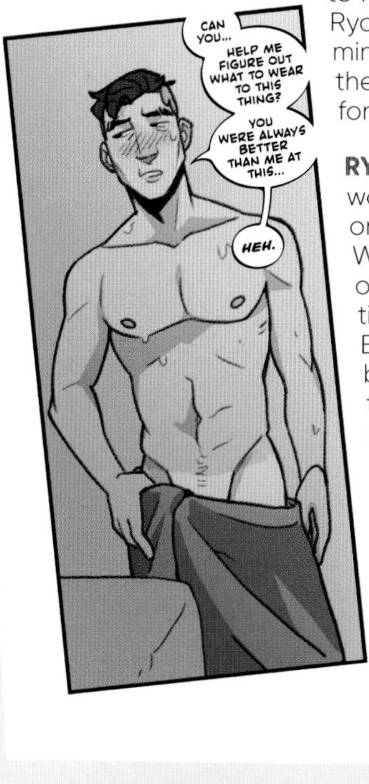
CAN YOU...
HELP ME FIGURE OUT WHAT TO WEAR TO THIS THING?
YOU WERE ALWAYS BETTER THAN ME AT THIS...
HEH.

RYAN (artist/colorist): Being asked to work on *Dream Daddy* was actually such a surprise! I hadn't ever considered working on something from a large IP before, but after learning that Wendy Xu was going to be writing it, I couldn't say no! Not only was it my first contracted work, but it was also my first time working with a writer who cared so much about the topic! Everything went so well and for some reason I thought it would be a good idea to get a puppy mid-production, which slowed things down quite significantly, but everyone was so understanding and I still managed to get everything done in time! My favorite part had to have been seeing the team's reactions as I turned in new works! I also very much loved drawing the hottest dad in the *Dream Daddy* series. *wink* Thanks to Wendy for bringing so much character to these boys! We work well together!

ISSUE #2 COMMENTARY
WITH LEE C.A. AND JACK GROSS

LEE (writer): While writing "Let the Right Dad In," I wanted to maintain *Dream Daddy*'s signature campiness without forgoing its heart and self-awareness. There's always going to be pressure when writing pre-established characters, but when you're a trans man writing a well-loved trans character, there's definitely added weight. That said, it was a blast. The original writers excelled with Damien by highlighting his personhood and not making his struggles as a trans man the central focus, so I mostly spent my time reading up on morbid Victorian era-facts like gelatin how-tos.

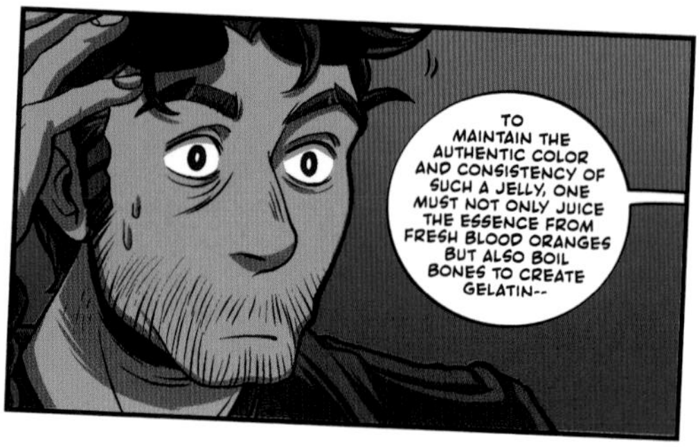
TO MAINTAIN THE AUTHENTIC COLOR AND CONSISTENCY OF SUCH A JELLY, ONE MUST NOT ONLY JUICE THE ESSENCE FROM FRESH BLOOD ORANGES BUT ALSO BOIL BONES TO CREATE GELATIN--

Robert was the real challenge. He's a pretty nuanced guy with inner demons and niche interests. This isn't to say he's inherently bad. Life happens, and it happened to him hard. I kept that in mind while replaying his route and fell in love with him all over again. Mostly, he's kind of lonely, and that loneliness gave him time to sit in his head and conjure up vampire suspicions.

It was important to me to make sure Robert's slayer antics weren't too intense to readers. Hunting someone in any way could be perceived as a lot, but I don't think Robert would hurt a fly, and even the new Daddy, aka Damien, can kinda see that. Damien takes it in stride. Likely, Mary gave him the heads up.

Above all else, I just wanted it to be clear Damien and Robert were on their way to becoming enduring friends with more in common than they thought.

JACK (artist/colorist): Since I was drawing for an IP other than my own, I replayed both Damien and Robert's routes and made sure to take note of their sprites' mannerisms and quirks. I really wanted to nail the faces and body language to stay true to the source material. Also, Lee's script called for specific references, so I spent a lot of time researching the films he mentioned. He always makes this part of the process really painless, and I appreciate that every time we work together. I don't often work in color, so referencing the actual backgrounds was important... though I also learned a lot about how the game's backgrounds are designed best for the characters in each route, so crossing some of them over made for interesting color problems to solve, but that was a really cool part of crossing over from game to comic.

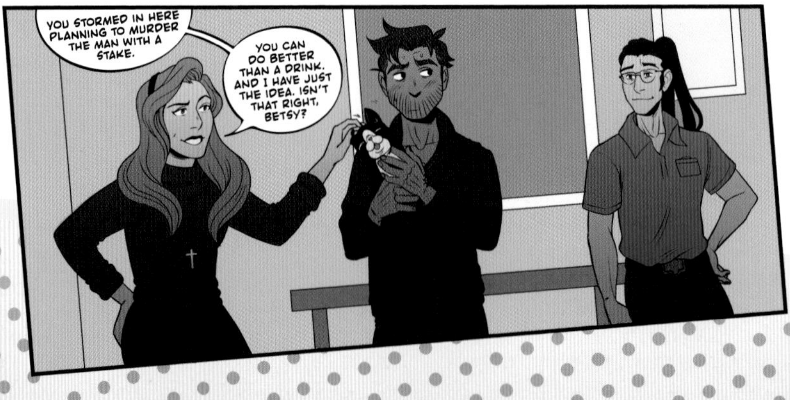
YOU STORMED IN HERE PLANNING TO MURDER THE MAN WITH A STAKE.
YOU CAN DO BETTER THAN A DRINK. AND I HAVE JUST THE IDEA. ISN'T THAT RIGHT, BETSY?

ISSUE #3 COMMENTARY

WITH LEIGHTON GRAY, VERNON SHAW, JARRETT WILLIAMS, AND JEREMY LAWSON

LEIGHTON AND VERNON (writers): We both feel weird about writing things in the singular so instead we're sitting on a couch with a Google Doc open between the two of us while we eat cheese. Anyway, one of us graduated from film school (Vernon, California State University, Northridge, emphasis in cinematography) and the other dropped out of art school (it's me, Leighton! Art school is a scam!) and we wholeheartedly guarantee that we are both as insufferable as that implies. You might have already gathered this from all the ham-handed film and TV references in this issue. Unsure why Oni Press let us do that, but we're grateful that they did! We had a blast writing this issue because it's pretty much just the "Local Ad" episode of *The Office* and we got to rewatch the "Mr. Plow" episode of *The Simpsons* as "research." Doing goofs with cute Dads is pretty much the only thing that alleviates the crushing existential terror that has befallen us due to that wish we made on that monkey's paw to get our game made into a comic.

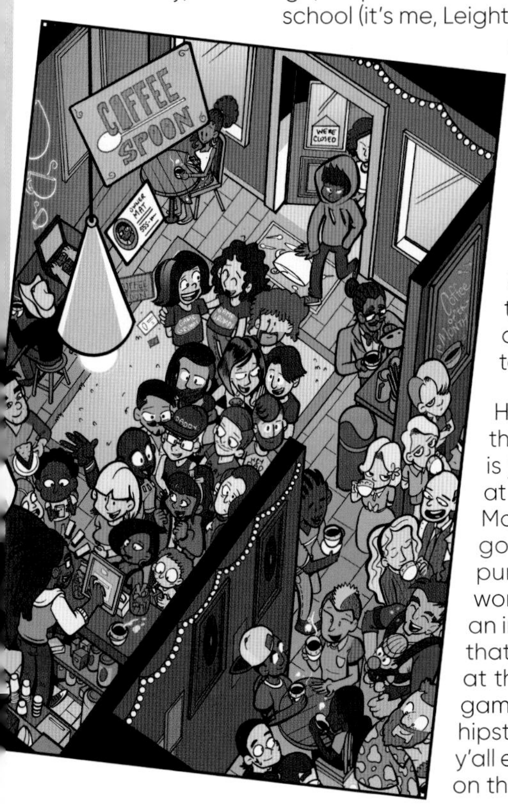
COFFEE SPOON

Have we provided any relevant information about this comic other than bits? No. So here goes: Robert is just repeating things that we've both screamed at each other directly after watching specific movies. Mat not wanting to be on camera and needing to go lie down because things are overwhelming is purely autobiographical. There are people in this world who have dedicated their lives to mastering an instrument that you don't even touch and we feel that is noble and just. Many people in the big panel at the end are our lovely friends who worked on the game, although Vernon is still not sure which bearded hipster with glasses is supposed to be him. We hope y'all enjoy this comic as much as Robert enjoys dunking on the "films" of Nicholas Winding Refn.

JARRETT (artist): The *Dream Daddy* experience was pretty dope! I thought the script was great because it gave me an opportunity to explore my favorite dad, Mat! The film component was equally interesting to me and I loved incorporating film motifs throughout the issue's design.

My fave pages: 1) The Coffee Spoon Creative Session with all the Dads. Jeremy Lawson's colors here are spot on. 2) The sequence of Amanda sitting in her chair getting made up by Mary (I just like the expressions on that page a lot). In fact, Mary got a lot of funny moments in this issue. 3) The final splash page of the packed Coffee Spoon took a lot of work but it was worth it for that shot.

JEREMY (colorist): I fell in love with *Dream Daddy* after watching the Giant Bomb Dating Games episode on it (it was #4, if you want to check that out later), and getting to work on the comic was a personal highlight of 2018. I've colored Jarrett before and had a rough idea of what he'd be doing art-wise, so my focus for colors on "Dream Ad-y" was to blend his exaggerated style with the game palettes (and play with lighting). Since there'd be more camera angles of the different locales than the game, I needed to match everything up and keep the sense of space. Jarrett gave me specific instructions to make the Player Dad look like him, and for Mat and the others it was a matter of simplifying to keep cruising through panels. That dramatic reveal of Robert and everyone's reaction to him is my favorite sequence. It's so anime. I love it. Coloring Robert was fun in general, haha. It's always a bit of a challenge working on a licensed book because you're walking this line of trying to stay true to the source material while making it your own. Hopefully we succeeded!

ISSUE #4 COMMENTARY

WITH C. SPIKE TROTMAN, DREW GREEN, AND REED BLACK

SPIKE (writer): Did you know this is my first work-for-hire job in comics? Yeah. Twenty years after getting started in self-publishing, and then moving into small press publishing! Wild. Glad I did it, though. I don't regret anything I've done in comics, but I'm pretty astonished by how much of my life has been given over to administration in the management of Iron Circus Comics. I don't get a lot of time to be creative, anymore. So, this was a welcome break, and utterly unexpected.

So, a word of advice: tweet relentlessly about the video games you play, everyone. Maybe it'll land you a gig!

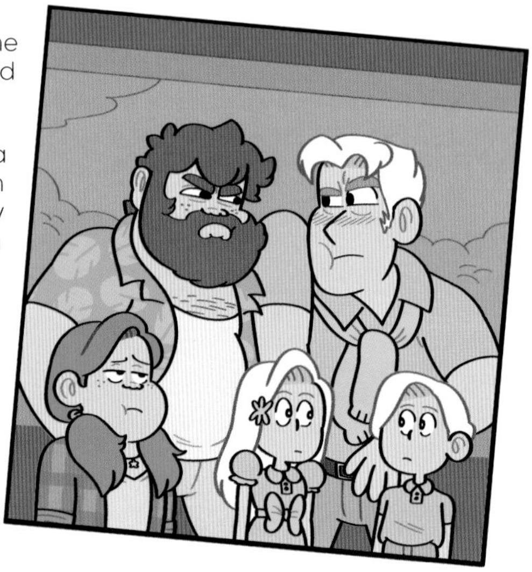

DREW (artist): This project came to me during a short hiatus from my job as a storyboard artist in the animation industry, which was quite lucky! My favorite part about making this comic was having the chance to simplify the character designs from their game counterparts into something more in line what what I'm used to drawing. It's always a fun challenge, picking what elements stand out the most, what to accentuate, what to simplify, what to cut altogether. I had to make up a little along the way, too; it felt right to assume that Brian would be wearing cargo shorts. It's basically part of the Dad uniform! Anyway, I think these characters translated really well into a simpler style, and I hope you think so too. I sure had a ton of fun drawing them!

REED (colorist): This was a really fun project to work on. Getting several different characters and background scenes to all work together is an interesting challenge.

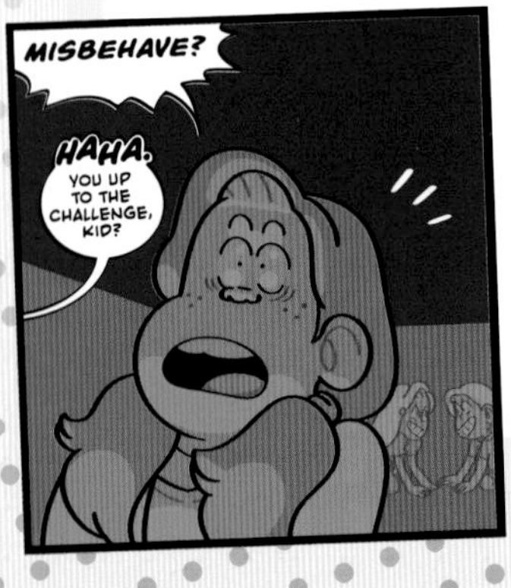
MISBEHAVE?
HAHA. YOU UP TO THE CHALLENGE, KID?

You might notice as you move through the story that the overall key color changes to fit what is happening emotionally in the story. The page thumbnails, to me, look a lot like a rainbow gradient. We go from warm greens, to maroons, reds, oranges and finally turquoise.

Fun fact: I completely colored this comic on the iPad Pro using Clip Studio Paint for iPad. This handy little device enabled me to work on the colors wherever I was, including on a car ride to Disney World.

ISSUE #5 COMMENTARY

WITH JOSH TRUJILLO, D.J. KIRKLAND, AND MATT HERMS

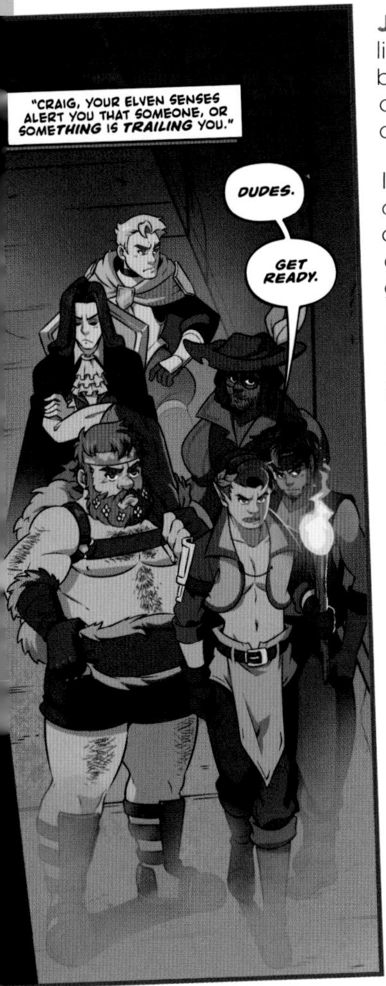
"CRAIG, YOUR ELVEN SENSES ALERT YOU THAT SOMEONE, OR SOME*THING* IS *TRAILING* YOU."
DUDES.
GET READY.

JOSH (writer): I've been playing roleplaying games my entire life, so I pulled from my own experiences. You have to be a little bit of a control freak to run them, and it's tough at first to find a rhythm. The trickiest, but most rewarding part is giving that control to the players. This is Hugo's struggle for the issue.

It took about ten seconds to decide which hero class the different Daddies would be. (Damien is basically a sorcerer already.) D.J. did such an amazing job with the character designs. Brian is maybe my favorite Daddy, so I was very, very grateful for his hero costume when first I saw it!

D.J. (artist): When I was approached to illustrate a *Dream Daddy* comic that was written by Josh, I knew this was going to be a lot of fun! This was a huge exercise in character acting and comedic timing and Josh delivers that in spades. While Craig and Brian were my favorite routes to play in the game, I had the most fun bringing Damien to life and showing off his endless knowledge of tabletop RPGs.

When I was asked to pick a colorist for the issue, Matt was at the top of my list. His understanding of color and how it can convey so many different things really brought the issue to life. I've been eager to collaborate with Matt since starting my career in comics and to no surprise, he knocked it out of the park.

MATT (colorist): I absolutely love D.J.'s artwork, and was so thrilled to have the chance to color for him this issue! For coloring, it was important to clearly define the two stories taking place: the dark, dusty dungeon-crawl and the Daddies playing the game. All the dungeon scenes are trimmed in a rustic red border, the panels filled with dust kicking up at the heroes' feet in a dreary blue-green atmosphere.

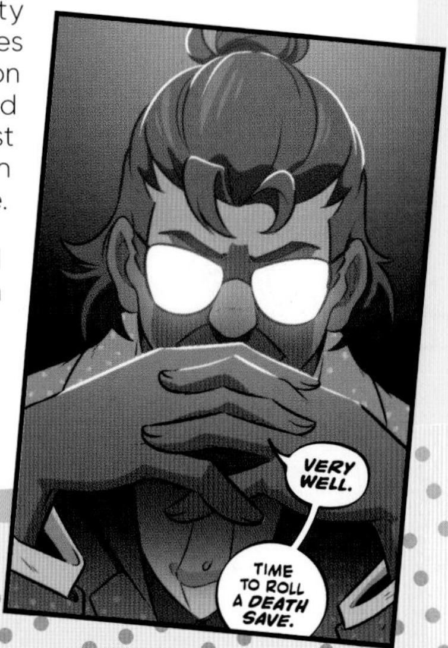
VERY WELL.
TIME TO ROLL A *DEATH SAVE.*

My favorite scenes are in the much more vibrant, colorful "real world," though! D.J. does so many great expressions—you can see the frustration, panic, determination and ultimately joy play across Hugo's face during the course of the game, and it was so much fun adding to those moments with color. (The final panel on page 15 is my favorite!)

CREATOR BIOS

LEIGHTON GRAY AND VERNON SHAW are the co-creators and co-writers of *Dream Daddy: a Dad Dating Simulator*. Both reside within walking distance from each other in the Echo Park neighborhood of Los Angeles, California. Leighton is currently the art director for the Fullbright Company while Vernon is a creative producer at the Let's Play channel Game Grumps. Both were listed in 2017 Forbes 30 Under 30 for games and enjoy watching French neo-extremist horror movies as much as anyone can "enjoy" watching them.
DREAMDADDY.BIZ / @DREAMDADDYGAME

KRIS ANKA is a Los Angeles-based artist, largely known for his work on books like *Runaways, Star-Lord, Captain Marvel,* and *Uncanny X-Men*. He tries his best at drawing hot people.
KRISTAFERANKA.TUMBLR.COM /@KRISTAFERANKA

HASSAN OTSMANE-ELHAOU letters comics while his dog stares at him wondering if that's really a job. He's also the editor of the Eisner-nominated *PanelxPanel*, and the voice behind the *Strip Panel Naked* series.
HASSANOE.CO.UK / @HASSANOE

WENDY XU is a Brooklyn-based illustrator and comics artist. She is co-creator of *Mooncakes*, a graphic novel out in 2019 from Lion Forge Comics. Her short comics and illustrations have been featured on Catapult, the Barnes & Noble Sci-fi/Fantasy Blog, and Tor.com, among other places. She currently works as an assistant editor curating young adult and children's books.
ARTOFWENDYXU.COM / @ANGRYGIRLCOMICS

RYAN MANIULIT (ROAN) is a 23-year-old Seattle-based artist who centers his work primarily around sci-fi and fantasy narratives. He is an avid believer in diversity and inclusiveness in all media and hopes his work reflects that. He's created several erotic comic works funded through Kickstarter and is known for his obnoxious presence on twitter dot com. He currently has 9 non-fish pets. The rest are fish.
ARTROAN.COM / @ARTROAN_

LEE C. A. is a heartpunk from south central Kentucky. When he's not writing comics and prose about cool people crying, he can be found rewatching *The Dark Crystal*, scrolling through the weird side of *Listverse*, and collecting rolls of tape. "Let the Right Dad In" is Lee's first major publication.
LEECAFFIELD.COM / @LEECAWRITES

JACK GROSS lives in Minneapolis where he works full time as an illustrator during the day and draws his webcomic, *Thistlewine*, at night. His mom didn't let him wear skulls when he was in high school. He wears a lot of skulls now. (Sorry, Mom.)
PATREON.COM/JACKLEIGHGROSS / @__JACKARY

JARRETT WILLIAMS was born in New Orleans, LA and graduated from the Savannah College of Art & Design (MFA). He has contributed comics to *Invader Zim* and *Rick and Morty*™, and created three volumes of his pro-wrestling/adventure series *Super Pro K.O.!* for Oni Press. He also completed *Hyper Force Neo* for Z2 Comics. He is currently working on a bunch of original comics but still finds time for video games.
SUPERPROKO.SQUARESPACE.COM / @JARRETTWILLIAMS

JEREMY LAWSON is a cartoonist and comic book colorist from Texas. He spends his time drinking way too much coffee and making comics for kids. Check out his queer all-ages adventure comic *Imp King* and other fun stuff at impkingcomics.com.
IMPKINGCOMICS.COM / @IMPKINGCOMICS

C. SPIKE TROTMAN is a writer, cartoonist and publisher living in Chicago, Illinois. She is the founder of Iron Circus Comics, the curator of the famed *Smut Peddler* series of sexy comic anthologies, and a Kickstarter Thought Leader, having raised over 1.25 million on the platform to date in the name of strange and amazing comics.
IRONCIRCUS.COM / @IRON_SPIKE

DREW GREEN is a cartoonist based out of Burbank, CA. He has mostly been involved in the animation industry, storyboarding for such shows as *Mighty Magiswords, Craig of the Creek,* and more. When he isn't drawing cartoons, Drew is probably attempting to cook perfect Brussels sprouts. He's almost got it.
DREW-GREEN.TUMBLR.COM / @KINGOFSAFARI

REED BLACK is a comic artist with a degree in illustration from Ringling College of Art + Design. Reed lives in Atlanta in a house that makes weird noises when he runs the water.
REEDBLACKCOMICS.COM / @REEDICULE

JOSH TRUJILLO is a writer based in California. He is the creator of *Dodge City, Love Machines,* and the table gaming anthology *Death Saves.* He has also written for cool comics like *Rick and Morty*™ and *Adventure Time.* He loves his dog, his country, and is of good moral fiber.
JOSHTRUJILLO.COM / @LOSTHISKEYSMAN

D.J. KIRKLAND is a comic book artist from Charlotte, NC. He graduated from the Savannah College of Art and Design (SCAD) in 2009 with a BFA in Sequential Art, which is just a fancy word for comic books. When he's not drawing comics, D.J. spends his time doing MORE drawing, playing fighting games, watching anime and talking about all of those things on a podcast with one of his best friends called *Magical Boys.*
DJKIRKLAND.COM / @OHHEYDJ

MATT HERMS has been a comic book colorist and illustrator since 2007, working on everything from all-ages books based on blue video game icons, to superhero teams in every color spandex, to horror books reimagining classic comic teenagers. Matt currently lives with his wife and foster dogs just outside of Washington, DC.
MATTHERMS.COM / @MATTHERMS

READ MORE FROM ONI PRESS!

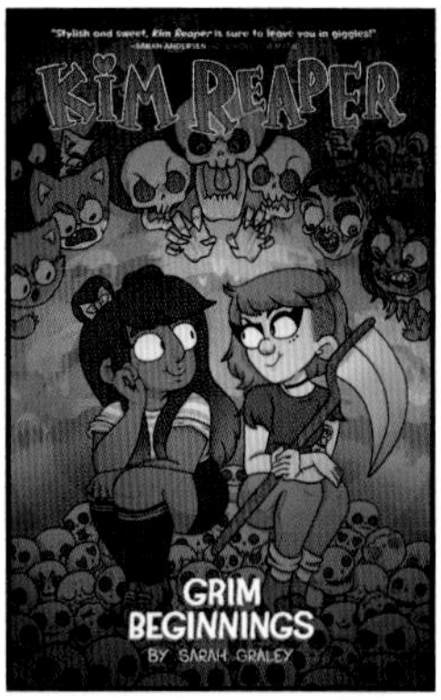
KIM REAPER
GRIM BEGINNINGS
BY SARAH GRALEY

KIM REAPER, VOL. 1: GRIM BEGINNINGS
BY SARAH GRALEY

"In Sarah Graley's delightful new series, Death is not only a beautiful goth undergrad, she's also the object of her classmate Becka's massive crush. Becka's infatuation, captured so wonderfully by Graley's expressive cartooning style, takes the two on a chaotic journey, ranging from university romantic travails to hellish underworld portals." —*Entertainment Weekly*

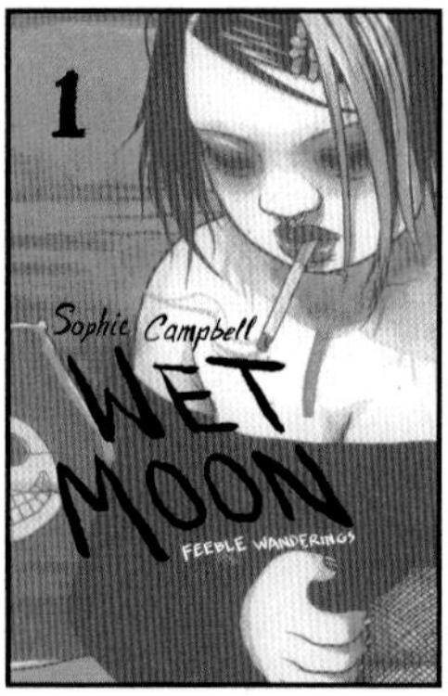
1
Sophie Campbell
WET MOON
FEEBLE WANDERINGS

WET MOON, VOL. 1: FEEBLE WANDERINGS
BY SOPHIE CAMPBELL

"Putting queerness front and center from the very first moments, Sophie Campbell has crafted a slightly horror take on the coming of age/coming out story that you don't want to miss out on."—*Comicosity*

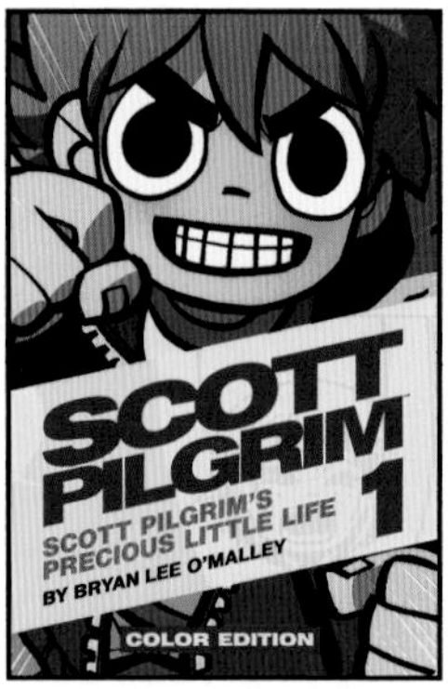
SCOTT PILGRIM
SCOTT PILGRIM'S PRECIOUS LITTLE LIFE
1
BY BRYAN LEE O'MALLEY
COLOR EDITION

SCOTT PILGRIM COLOR COLLECTION, VOL. 1
BY BRYAN LEE O'MALLEY AND NATHAN FAIRBAIRN

"It's part relationship drama, part comedy, part martial-arts parody, and even part video game, with large doses of rock 'n' roll, science fiction, anime references, and fourth-wall breaking."—*Library Journal*

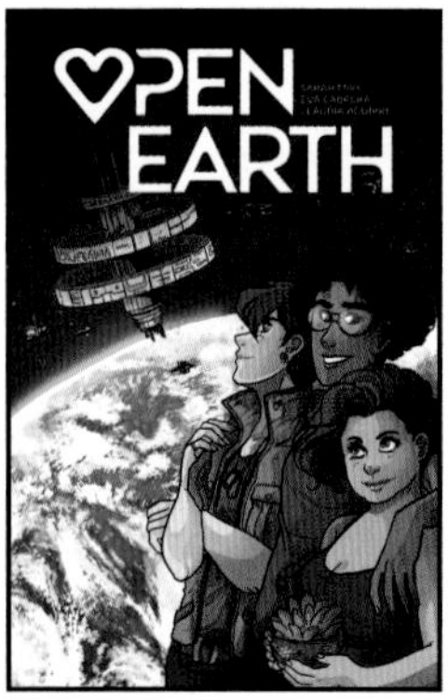
OPEN EARTH

OPEN EARTH
BY SARAH MIRK, EVA CABRERA, AND CLAUDIA AGUIRRE

"For comics fans who dream optimistically about the future, the diverse cast and sex-positive, cooperative storyline combine into a utopian vision."—*Publishers Weekly*

For more information on these and other fine Oni Press comic books and graphic novels, visit www.onipress.com. To find a comic specialty store in your area, visit www.comicshops.us.